City on the Sand

Ocean City, Maryland, and the People Who Built It

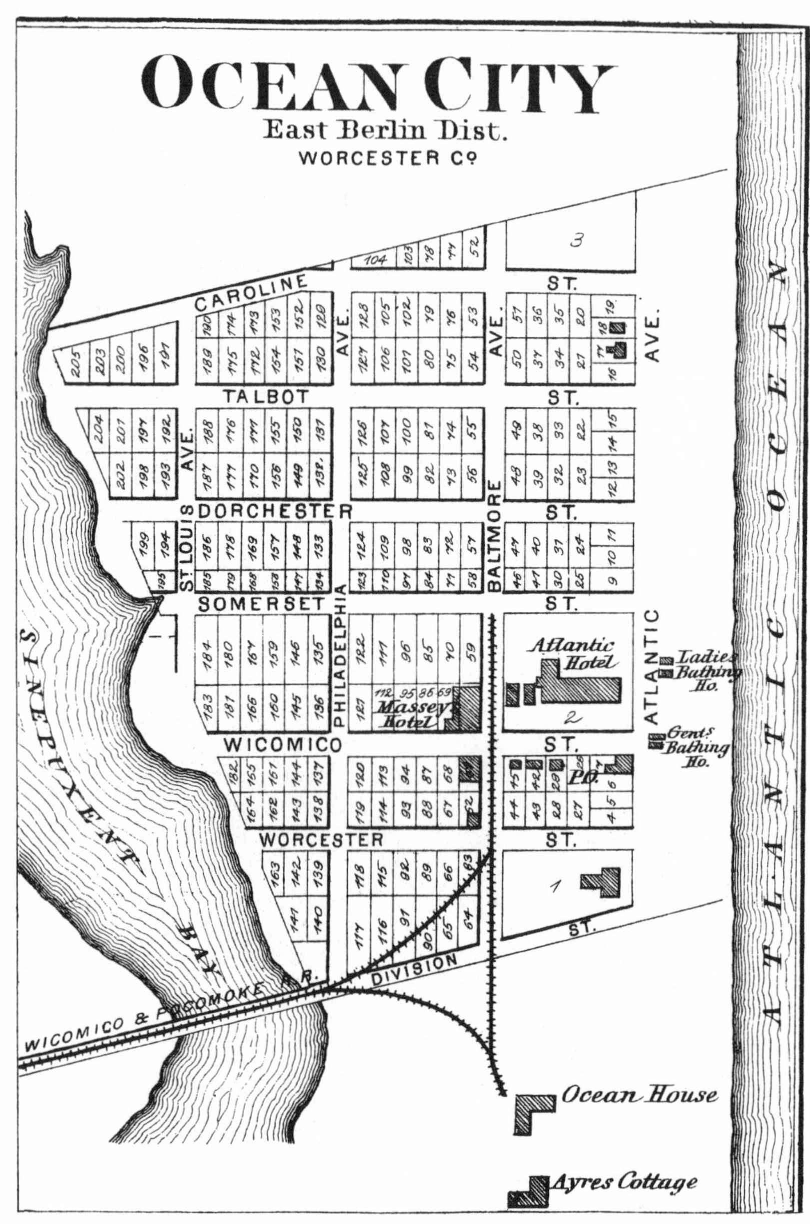

Very early plat of Ocean City. (Courtesy Snow Hill Library.)

City on the Sand

Ocean City, Maryland, and the People Who Built It

by Mary Corddry

Illustrated by Ellen Corddry

Tidewater Publishers
Centreville, Maryland

Chapters 8 and 9 of this work are based upon articles by the author previously published in *The Sun,* and are used by permission.

Library of Congress Cataloging-in-Publication Data

Corddry, Mary
City on the sand : Ocean City, Maryland, and the people who built it / Mary Corddry ; illustrated by Ellen Corddry. — 1st ed.
p. cm.
Includes bibliographical references and index.
ISBN 0-87033-420-4 (hardbound) :
1. Ocean City (Md.) — History. 2. Resorts — Maryland — Ocean City — History. I. Title.
F189.02C66 1991
975.2 ′ 21 — dc20 91-50178
CIP

ISBN 0-87033-551-0 (paperback)

Manufactured in the United States of America
First edition, 1991; third printing, 2003

To my children,

Cecile, Henry, Ellen, David and James, who know well the beaches of Ocean City, and to my grandchildren, Lea and Glenn, who soon will

Contents

City on the Sand

Ocean City, Maryland, and the People Who Built It

. . . like a wise man who built his house upon the rock; and the rain fell, and the floods came, and winds blew and beat upon that house, but it did not fall, because it had been founded on the rock . . . .

. . . like the foolish man who built his house upon the sand; and the rain fell, and the floods came, and the wind blew and beat upon that house, and it fell, and great was the fall of it.

—Matthew 7:24–27

Safe upon the solid rock the ugly houses stand:
Come and see my shining palace built upon the sand.

—"Figs From Thistles," Edna St. Vincent Millay

Introduction

From the air, Ocean City seems to rise directly from the sea, its two bridges like moorings lashing it to the mainland.

On this particular occasion the writer's view is from a light, two-seater plane towing a long banner that bears a message in letters 5 feet high.

The young pilot, and others like him, see more of this elongated and crowded city than anyone else during the high time of the year, from May to mid-September.

From below, the familiar summertime spectacle of an advertising slogan being towed up the beach by a small plane is as much a symbol of Ocean City as the row of stark high-rises at the north end or the landmark pier at the south. "Tio Gringos—Come Taste the Flavor of Mexico," or "Great Kid's Menu, Free Cruise—B.J.'s," read the messages. There are also a lot of "Happy Birthdays" and occasional declarations of love and proposals of marriage.

About six planes and pilots are in action each summer. They average about 50 flights a day and fly as many as 150 flights on some days. Advertisers know that when they fly their messages up the ten-mile stretch of Ocean City beach in vacation season, thousands of people idling on the sand will look up and read them almost by reflex.

For the passenger looking down from the plane, the separation of beach and sea seems to be marked only by the slender white line of breaking surf and the sudden massing of people strung out along it.

For most of its length, this city on the sand is only about four-and-a-half blocks wide. It widens in places where marshes extend like small peninsulas into the coastal bays. The bays that separate the barrier island from the mainland are actually one, but the names change, moving from south to north, from Sinepuxent to Isle of Wight to Assawoman. The narrowest points on the island are where artificial lagoons lined with houses and small-boat moorings slice from the bayside to within only a block or two of the ocean surf.

From above, ones sees a lot more water than land. The bays are two or three times wider than the city except at the south end, where the U.S. Route 50 bridge crosses Sinepuxent Bay to the old part of town. To the north, the more recent Route 90 bridge across Assawoman Bay makes a longer and more graceful crossing, alighting briefly on the Isle of Wight before its long, low arch to 62nd Street and the resort's sleek, new north end.

On midsummer weekends, more than 300,000 people are said to cross these two bridges into Ocean City. Most of them have driven about 150 miles, from Washington or Baltimore or the suburbs that encase both cities. Crossing the Chesapeake Bay, the summer traffic forms an almost solid line threading through the Eastern Shore's fields of soybeans and corn and wide expanses of marsh, sometimes backing up for miles behind drawbridges and small-town red lights. New interchanges and lofty new multilane bridges across Kent Narrows, the Choptank River, and the Nanticoke River exist largely because of ocean beach traffic.

For three months Ocean City becomes Maryland's second-biggest city. Only Baltimore has more people, and it sometimes seems that a good portion of them are at Ocean City. In the wintertime the fifteen-and twenty-story high-rises are almost empty. In the words of one lonely woman who spent a winter in one of them, "It is a spooky place."

Ocean City, with its congested summertime traffic and concentrated development, is only a small segment of the barrier-island chain extending down the coast of the Delmarva Peninsula.

Along the Delaware seashore to the north, beachfront structures seem to be pulled toward towns such as Bethany Beach, Dewey Beach, and Rehoboth Beach like filings toward a magnet, with thinner development and open space between.

To the south, along the Maryland and Virginia Eastern Shore coastline is Assateague Island—part state park, part National Seashore, and part the Chincoteague National Wildlife Refuge. There are campgrounds and public beaches at each end of the island and a string of mobile fishermen between, but the rest is the largely unspoiled domain of waterfowl, shorebirds, and wild ponies.

South of that, thirteen islands, forming a barrier chain four times the length of Ocean City, have been bought by the Nature Conservancy, a national, nonprofit organization that acquires important natural areas to assure their preservation against the pressures of politics and economic progress. The Virginia barriers are wild and open except for occasional remnants of earlier settlements abandoned as the ever-changing sands eroded and shifted around them. In the words of one Conservancy staff member, "We believe it can be shown that the highest and best use [of barrier islands] is to leave them alone and let nature do its thing."

Ocean City is on the farthest end of the scale from nature doing its thing. On this narrow strip of sand rising almost imperceptibly from the sea, there are over 500 rental apartment buildings, ranging from high-rises to cottages; 38 hotels; 81 motels; and a mobile home park with 1,800 lots. There are 158 restaurants, hundreds of home maintenance and supply businesses, 33 banks, and 70 real estate and rental agencies. In the boom decade of the 1970s, 575 single-family dwellings went up and an incredible 10,583 units in multifamily buildings. There are several hundred grocery, candy, clothing, gift, jewelry, and specialty shops, and 66 amusement parks, miniature-golf courses, arcades, and waterslides.

About the only things that most normal communities have, and Ocean City does not, are an undertaker, a graveyard, and an automobile dealership. The reasons for their absence are obvious: both graves and new automobiles require more space and less exposure to the elements than are possible on a narrow barrier island.

Flying over the beach scene a dozen or more times a day, a banner pilot can be gloriously aloof and at the same time very much a part of it. For him, Ocean City combines a commercial venture and a personal adventure that come together in few other places.

Bob Bunting, owner of the banner-plane business, operates it from a runway on his father's Worcester County farm west of the beach. It is an informal setting. A pet goose roams about. The pilots, wearing jeans or shorts and T-shirts, push the Citabria or Scout planes into position for takeoff as casually as if they were skateboards.

A banner with its message is stretched out on the field and the lead rope is suspended between two posts. A pilot flies toward the posts, dips sharply, and reaches from the cockpit to toss out a grappling hook attached by rope to the tail of the plane. The plane pulls up with full power for about 200 feet as the hook grabs the banner rope. There is a sharp and shuddering wrench as the message flutters out behind it.

The pilot doesn't land between banners; he drops one and dips like a runaway elevator for the next. His daring and skill seem out of all proportion to the import of the messages he tows.

The young flyers, like many among the resort's summertime workforce, are in their twenties. Most of them are accumulating the hours they will need to try for a job on a commercial airline. They are a reminder of the barnstorming aviators of another era, as well as a reminder that Ocean City's story is, beyond all else, a story about people.

It is a collection of stories as personal as the one told by a banner pilot's mother who thought it terribly romantic when her son flew low over the family's Eastern Shore farm and dropped a package in the field. When she ran out and picked it up, she discovered that, like many another mother of many another son or daughter with a summer job in Ocean City, she had gotten his dirty laundry.

ONE

The Beginning

A PLACE ACROSS

When Ocean City began it was only a name, a hotel, some lots marked off in the sand, and a group of investors who saw big possibilities in a barren, windswept wasteland. The year was 1875.

If anyone came to this desolate barrier island then, it was by rowboat to hunt or fish. In those years it was one long island extending sixty miles from the Indian River Inlet in Delaware to Toms Cove, Virginia. The island was called Assateague to the south and Fenwick to the north. (The inlet that separates Ocean City from Assateague Island today was not to come until 1933.)

Maps of the ocean floor show that this slender strip of islands is not a separate body of land but rather part of a continuous slope forming the coastal plain of the mainland and the submerged continental shelf. The entire shelf was exposed during the time of the great glaciers. The Delmarva coastline was then many miles east of today's. As rivers cut canyons across the exposed plain they formed what we identify on charts of the ocean floor as Washington and Baltimore canyons.

As the glaciers melted, the sea level rose so that the edge of the continent is now the shelf lying under the Atlantic Ocean. It extends about fifty miles offshore before dropping sharply toward the depths of the sea.

Today's naturalists and geologists are learning more all the time about the fringe of constantly changing barrier islands that outlines like a delicate border the eastern coastline of the United States.

School children on science class field trips walk along these once wild and isolated shores and see visible evidence of the shifts and changes where land meets sea, not only through eons, but daily, as wind and wave wash sand along the beach, pile it into dunes, and carry it across the island to be dropped into the bays on the other side. At low tide on Assateague Island visitors can see old rooted tree stumps a third of a mile offshore and marine fossils have been found well inland on the coastal plain.

Assateague was formed by a combination of forces, we are told by geologists. It was gradually built up southeastward from a peninsula in Delaware as sand washed in from the continental shelf and was carried along the shore by littoral currents. In the pattern of other barriers along the coast, such as Cape Cod, the island forms into a hook at the southern end at Toms Cove, Virginia, where it continues to lengthen visibly every year.

Time and again through recorded history surging tides have washed over the island carving out inlets through its weaker spots between the ocean and the bays behind, creating separate islands and sometimes navigable waterways. Some of the inlets lasted for years and some barely overnight.

To be on the ocean beach, whether the waves are rolling in with a gentle rhythm or crashing against the shore with awesome force, is to sense the sweep of geologic time. The trivial pressures of personal life dissolve into the natural forces that continue to shape the earth.

The Indians who first stood on these shores seem to have been only occasional visitors from their villages on the mainland. Historians differ on whether the Assateagues were a subtribe of the Nanticokes or the Powhatans. In either case, they were Algonquian in origin. They appear to have been friendly, but by the early 1700s had been pressured north into Delaware and then dispersed into Pennsylvania, New York, and Canada.

What they left behind is more Indian place names in the lower Eastern Shore counties than anywhere else in Maryland. In addition to

Assateague (translated "across" or "place across"), the coastal bays that separate it from the mainland are named, from south to north, Chincoteague, Sinepuxent, and Assawoman. Off Assateague's southern end is the Virginia county of Accomack, with mainland villages such as Wachapreague, Nassawadox, and Pungoteague.

It is believed that the first European explorer to come ashore on Assateague Island or the mainland beyond it was the Italian, Giovanni da Verrazano, who sailed along this coast in 1524 under the flag of France. His documentation of the journey is believed by some historians to indicate that he entered what we know as Chincoteague Bay and explored inland as far as the Pocomoke Swamp, calling the area "Arcadia" because of its forests of cedar and pine.

This identity of Verrazano's "Arcadia" is not accepted by all historians. The late and eminent Samuel Eliot Morison wrote in Volume I of *The European Discovery of America* that, after flying the East Coast and studying the terrain, "I have no hesitation in locating Verrazano's Arcadia at Kitty Hawk, North Carolina." In any case, in 1976 an energetic group of Worcester County women headed by the late Agnes Johnson (Mrs. Thomas F.) succeeded in getting approval from the state of Maryland to name the bridge connecting Assateague Island with the Worcester County mainland, the Giovanni da Verrazano Bridge, in honor of the Italian explorer. The bridge was twelve years old then and had opened Assateague to more visitors than had come to the island in its entire history.

The festive ceremony naming the bridge was held on October 2, 1976. It was followed by a reenactment of Verrazano's possible landing on the Sinepuxent Bay shores, a landing perhaps even more perilous than the original because the whole colorful event took place in pouring rain, and the rowboat with its costumed occupants became bogged down in mud before reaching solid land. Since Verrazano sailed along the coast in March, he may have encountered much the same weather four and a half centuries before.

Over a hundred years after Verrazano's landing, in 1650, an English voyager, Colonel Henry Norwood, left the first written account of a visit to Assateague. It was not a pleasant visit: Colonel Norwood and a party of nineteen, including some women, left their ship, the *Virginia Merchant,* on January 3 after it had been battered by a storm. They were on their way from England to the Virginia colony. They hoped to find fresh water, food, and a harbor for repairs. For a reason unknown, they were unable to get back to their ship, which sailed on, leaving them to get to the colony the best way they could. They suffered intense hardship before reaching their destination with the help of friendly Indians.

The difficulties this party endured—finding food and water and weathering freezing winds and a harsh winter storm—could be a clue to why early settlements on Assateague did not last. Inhabitants seem to have come and gone like the shifting sands that shape the island itself.

It was not until the early 1700s that Captain William Whittington obtained a patent from Lord Baltimore for 1,000 acres of land in the Green Run area of Assateague, about fifteen miles south of today's Ocean City Inlet. He became the first Marylander to own land on the barrier island. By 1771, Whittington (then a Colonel) had patented nearly all the land from the Virginia line northward to the future site of Ocean City.

He became the first of many to subdivide Assateague. His parcels ranged from 110 to 500 acres and were intended for grazing and subsistence farming. Fresh water was scarce and the tillable soil poor, and the tracts eventually became "vacant," non-tax-producing land open to public grazing. In the spring, Worcester County farmers would take young stock, both horses and cows, over to Assateague on flat-topped scows and let the animals graze until late November. This required no fences and no fees and was a practice that continued into the 1930s.

There were about ten families living in the village of Green Run in 1887, according to *The Historical Atlas of Worcester County.* Most of them were there because of the Life-Saving Station, which was established in 1875. Four years before, the U.S. Government had created the Life-Saving Service to aid ships and seamen in distress along the coast. The stations were manned by "surfmen" whose exploits will be another part of this narrative. Others in the Green Run village were employed by a whole new industry glimpsed here for the first time—the tourism industry.

On a bayside site at Green Run, Captain James Scott, farmer, waterman, and landowner, had built, in 1869, a seasonal hotel called Scott's Ocean House, with a capacity of forty guests. Captain Scott had moved up to Green Run from the Virginia portion of Assateague before the Civil War. His Ocean House was the biggest development at Green Run before or since. Visitors came from as far away as Pittsburgh, Philadelphia, Wilmington, Baltimore, and Washington, traveling by stagecoach and later by the new railroad to Snow Hill, the county seat of Worcester

County. They then had to hire liverymen to get to Spence Landing, now called Public Landing, about seven miles farther east. At the landing dock a two-masted sailing sloop named the *Fairfield* took them the rest of the way, across Chincoteague Bay to Green Run. Local historians recount that one of the great adventures of the day was to be included in one of the large and well-chaperoned parties of young people who would go for an outing of several days to Ocean House.

It is said that Captain Scott had tentative plans to build cottages in connection with his hotel, but to the end would not consider expanding from his bayside site to the oceanfront. That, he believed, would be to court disaster.

By 1868 the Wicomico & Pocomoke Railroad had been completed from Salisbury to Berlin, the town closest to the beach area. When rumors spread that the railroad might be extended all the way to Sinepuxent Bay, about ten other subdivisions were surveyed and advertised in what is known as the North Beach area of Assateague. None ever seems to have gotten further than paper. (The railroad was to bring profound and permanent change farther north on this island. That story is to come.)

On July 7, 1875, *The* [Baltimore] *Sun* was still running items related to the "rural sports and sylvan pleasures" in celebration of the Fourth of July. *The Sun* ran great segments of some of the orations delivered in Baltimore, and reported a temperance jubilee. Also featured were social items from Cape May and the Saratoga races and accounts of Methodist camp meetings.

Almost buried amid this copy was the headline "Summer Resorts." Under this heading were two related items; it is doubtful that anyone realized at the time that one foretold the doom of the other. One read: "Scott's Ocean House on Green Run Beach, Worcester County, Md., beautifully located and appreciated for fine surf bathing, fishing, shooting and boating and is now open to visitors. Numerous improvements, under the management of James R. Townsend." The other read: "Atlantic Hotel is new summer resort on Synepuxent Bay and the beach, Md., now open to the reception of visitors. The beach and surf bathing are said to be unsurpassed and the bay affords excellent opportunities for sailing, fishing and rowing. It is accessible by Railroad or steamboat from Baltimore. Address Henry Stokes and Co., Berlin, Md."

The opening of the Atlantic Hotel on July 4, 1875, is regarded as the founding date of Ocean City. Ocean House closed in 1894, unable to compete. The new resort taking root to the north became the only survivor of the developments once planned for the old Assateague.

". . . SUCH A MAROONED PLACE"

In July 1872, Alonza Elzey Waters, then ten years old, had an adventure any young boy, then or now, would remember for a lifetime. With his father, Levin Littleton Waters, he left Baltimore by boat and crossed the Chesapeake Bay to Crisfield, a rough-and-ready seafood port on the lower Eastern Shore. From there they boarded a stagecoach and crossed the Shore to Coffin's Landing, an isolated road's end on Sinepuxent Bay (just south of today's Ocean City Airport). At the landing they took a waiting scow across the coastal bay to a barren strip of sand, dunes, and shrub growth washed by the bay on one side and the ocean surf on the other.

At this unlikely destination they joined a small group of men and women whose journeys had demonstrated similar initiative, and began exploring the windswept expanse around them with an even more unlikely objective—to determine the best site for a new seaside resort and whether they should invest in it.

Fifty-four years later, in July 1929, Mr. Waters, then a Baltimore banker, recalled the experience in a remembrance feature in *The Sun*. According to the piece, the initiators of the project were "five enterprising men of Worcester and Wicomico counties." When they proposed to develop the narrow strip of land that lay between Sinepuxent Bay and the Atlantic Ocean and establish a resort, Mr. Waters recalled, "Many a hearty laugh at their expense was enjoyed by the skeptics of the day who asserted that any building erected there would be blown down by the first nor'wester, and that no one with normal mentality would ever come to visit in such a marooned place."

The concept of creating a resort on the wild, white, sandy beaches off Maryland's coast was an idea not totally out of nowhere. Atlantic City, incorporated in 1854, was already thriving, and *The Sun* ran social items throughout the summer about those who were vacationing that week in Cape May, New Jersey.

At about the same time that Captain Scott opened Ocean House at Green Run farther south, an enterprising man named Isaac Coffin, a Worcester County landowner and farmer, opened a one-story guest cottage and barroom on the barrier island of Assateague, just south of what is now Ocean City. He called it Rhode Island Inn, taking the name, according to local lore, from a ship that had wrecked on the beach. A piece of wreckage with the ship's name on it was nailed above the door. The inn was a place where visitors who came to the island to hunt or fish could spend the night.

In an interview for the *Eastern Shore Times* in 1975, Mamie Coffin of Berlin, a grandniece of Isaac Coffin, said that Ocean City's first hotel owner had built another hotel on the west side of Sinepuxent Bay before building Rhode Island Inn. It was called the Hotel Coffin, she said, and ruins of it were then still standing in an open field near the amusement area called Frontier Town. She recalled that Isaac Coffin ferried early tourists to Ocean City before there was a bridge to the barrier island.

Isaac Coffin's tombstone is among the earliest in the Evergreen Cemetery in Berlin where many of Ocean City's best known personalities are buried. Mr. Coffin's grandson, Captain William B. S. Powell, later became a major landowner on the island and the eighth mayor of Ocean City.

Another guest house was built on the island by James Massey of Berlin in 1872. It was later enlarged and named the Seaside Hotel. Early postcards show it to be a four-story frame structure typical of the early resort with wide roofed porches and white porch railings wrapped around its first two levels. The Seaside was destroyed in a great fire in 1925 which devastated three blocks in the old downtown. It was never rebuilt.

Even before the ventures of Mr. Coffin and Mr. Massey, a Worcester county landowner, Colonel Lemuel Showell, built a small cottage, which he shared with friends, on the site that was to become Ocean City. Colonel Showell, a descendant of one of the earliest Worcester County families, had inherited what was then a fortune, earned by his forebears in farming, timbering, water transport, and other commercial ventures. With visions of future development on this little known part of the coast, Colonel Showell and some of his friends organized The Atlantic Hotel Company Corporation in 1868.

At about the same time, a Long Island businessman, Stephen Taber, obtained a patent from the state of Maryland to a large holding on the barrier island, which had originally belonged to Lord Baltimore, proprietor of Maryland. Mr. Taber also acquired a lot of farmland on the mainland across the bay.

The early history of Ocean City is largely contained in newspaper clippings in which old town residents recall accounts they have heard from friends and family. Little or nothing is included in these accounts about what sort of man Mr. Taber was. The early survey and courthouse records even vary in the spelling of his name which is sometimes "Taber" and sometimes "Tabor."

Records in other Eastern Shore counties indicate that the late-nineteenth century was a period when Northern investors, commonly referred to in that era as "capitalists" or "gentlemen of wealth," were looking for good land buys in the region. With the end of the Civil War and the liberation of the slaves, some of the Shore's big landowners found themselves with more land than they and their families could farm themselves and without the money to hire labor. "It is a well known fact," one New York newspaper informed its readers, "that the prices of land in [the Peninsula] of Maryland have been and are now, far below their real value."

Whatever his motives, Mr. Taber became the first and greatest of the land speculators in and around what was later to become Ocean City. In 1868, the same year he acquired the barrier island property, he and a partner, Hepburn Benson of Washington, purchased about 600 acres on the mainland, including an estate called Carmel formerly owned by absentee owners also of the Washington area. Three years later Mr. Benson died, and by 1875, Mr. Taber owned all the property, buying out his partner's widow in a court settlement. On the wild and deserted barrier island he purchased several large tracts, including a 304-acre parcel called Wild Goose Chase and another of about 1,000 acres farther south on what is now the separate island of Assateague.

In between these two holdings he obtained from the state for less than one dollar an acre the patent to a 280-acre site called, for some unknown reason, "Ladies Resort to the Ocean," a name that would prove to be appropriate later when most of Ocean City's early hotels and boardinghouses were built and run by women. It was this tract that Colonel Showell and his associates had in mind when they arranged a meeting with Mr. Taber.

Because Mr. Taber acquired his property and Colonel Showell and his associates organized The Atlantic Hotel Company within months of each other, it is easy to guess that both had an eye on a third event that occurred the same year: the completion of the twenty-four-mile stretch of the Wicomico & Pocomoke Railroad between Salisbury and Berlin, only six miles from the beach. The railroad tied in at Salisbury with a north–south line thereby linking the Shore with Wilmington, Philadelphia, and points north. Not only was the Taber beach property across the narrowest part of the Sinepuxent Bay, it was directly in line with the new railroad. With this in mind, the organizers of The Atlantic Hotel Company approached Mr. Taber with a proposal.

James H. Mumford, a hardware store owner in early Ocean City generally referred to as "Squire," gave an oral account of the meeting many years later to a good friend, Irma Jester. She wrote down what is, though scant, the best account of the meeting with Mr. Taber found anywhere.

Colonel Showell and his associates, Mr. Mumford told Irma Jester, asked Mr. Taber if he would let them have, and at what price, a piece of land on the beach big enough for a hotel. The men were held off quite a while by Mr. Taber, who said that such a sale would break up his land for gunning, which was why he had bought it.

"If I thought it would amount to anything as a resort, I would not stand in the way," Mr. Mumford quoted him as saying. Taber told them he was leaving a few days later for his home on Long Island, and if the men would meet him at the depot in Berlin, he would give them his answer.

At that meeting he offered the group a ten-acre site of their selection if they could raise the money to build a hotel on it. He also agreed that if the hotel were built, he would expand the grant to fifty acres as a site for a town.

From Mr. Mumford's account it is easy to see that the gift of land was astute and that if Mr. Taber were around today, he would thrive in Ocean City. For, if the initial investors were successful, the value of the more than 1,000 surrounding acres he owned would skyrocket.

After Mr. Taber's proposal, the group of potential investors made the journey to the beach described by Alonza Waters in his *Sun* remembrance piece. They chose a site across the narrowest part of Sinepuxent Bay opposite Point Hammock on the mainland, an area now known as West Ocean City.

The group was described in the local *Salisbury Advertiser* as "a prominent group of Eastern Shore, Baltimore and Philadelphia businessmen." In *The Sun* remembrance piece, one of the members, John E. Husband, is described a "capitalist of Philadelphia." Others in the party with Alonza Waters and his father, were his uncle and aunt, Colonel and Mrs. Levin Woolford of Baltimore; his aunt, Mrs. Emily Jones of Princess Anne; Dr. John T. Hammond of Berlin; Dr. William H. H. Dashiell of Quantico; and Dr. William H. Gale, F. F. Ziegler, and Frank Fowler of Baltimore.

Also along that day were the members of the original group all sources identify as "founders," the "five enterprising men" of *The Sun* article: Colonel Lemuel Showell, B. Jones Taylor, R. Jenkins Henry, and George W. Purnell of Berlin, and Purnell Toadvine of Salisbury.

Hillary R. Pitts, a Berlin physician, was the man later chosen as president of The Atlantic Hotel Company. He was also the first president of the Wicomico & Pocomoke Railroad which had built the recently completed line between Salisbury and Berlin. Dr. Pitts is immortalized by the town of Pittsville, which was on the railway east of Salisbury and was renamed for him from Derrickson's Cross Roads, a name that would certainly have been too long for a station name.

The heaviest investor in the new railroad, and later its president, was Lemuel Showell III, known as Colonel Showell, the man who organized

The Atlantic Hotel Company and whose family would play a leading role in the resort's development for years to come.

Lemuel Showell III was born in 1822 at "Cropton," the family homeplace at St. Martins, a rural community later renamed Showell in honor of its most prominent citizen. From his father, Lemuel II, a man of notable thrift and industry, he inherited several thousand acres of land with the slaves to farm it, and ships engaged in coastal trade, particularly the shipment of cypress shingles. (Shingles were one of the lower Eastern Shore's most lucrative products in that day, produced from a unique resource, the ancient trees in the Pocomoke cypress swamp.)

Lemuel II was the most successful, financially, of all the Showells. Lemuel III, Colonel Showell, seems to have been a different sort. As his prominence grew, his wealth is said to have diminished.

Colonel Showell is described in old family papers as a large, handsome man with piercing black eyes. He was known on the Shore and beyond for his charm, generosity, hospitality, and public spirit. His circle of business associates and friends was wide.

For many years the consuming interests in his life were the building of the Wicomico & Pocomoke Railroad and the creation of Ocean City. The two ventures went hand in hand. The considerable energy, cash, and loans he put into both were undoubtedly a drain on the farming, shipping, and timbering interests he had inherited. He donated much of the land for the railroad, and his wide connections and promotional efforts were credited with attracting capital from Baltimore and Philadelphia to build The Atlantic Hotel.

Like other men of property in his generation in other parts of the Shore, he envisioned an extensive and prosperous railroad system that would connect his isolated, rural region to the rest of the Eastern Seaboard. Most of the pursuers of this dream on the Shore, including Colonel Showell, seem to have lost a lot of money attempting to realize it.

Showell was the true country gentlemen, and especially fond of his horses. According to one account, he more than once raced the train on the new railroad, riding his favorite black mare from Berlin to Salisbury.

Colonel Showell died in 1902 at the age of eighty at what had become his favorite retreat, the Showell Cottage in Ocean City. His wife, Annie Bredell Jacobs, died in 1912. Both are buried in Buckingham Cemetery in the nearby town of Berlin. They were survived by three daughters whose lives took them elsewhere, but other branches of the family have been prominent in the affairs of Ocean City to this day.

The Wicomico & Pocomoke Railroad and the men who built it were central to the start of Ocean City. The short rail line began with a small wood-burning locomotive, one passenger car, and one freight car.

John C. Hayman, a Salisbury railroad buff who expanded a high school research paper into a book, *Rails Along the Chesapeake,* published in 1979, uncovered some interesting details about this line. The first locomotive, for instance, was named, for obvious reasons, the *L. Showell.* It sometimes jumped the track. While the male passengers helped set it right, the women picked flowers or huckleberries along the right of way. Another locomotive, *Seaside,* was added in 1873. These wood-burning locomotives had to stop frequently to “wood up” with pine slabs.

The train ran through the rural villages of Walstons Switch, Parsonsburg, Pittsville, Whaleysville, and southeast through St. Martins to Berlin. The prospering railroad soon had a roster of two locomotives, five passenger cars, a baggage car, a mail car, and twenty-two freight cars. The most significant freight became lumber from the mills around Salisbury for the early hotels of Ocean City.

At about the same time the Atlantic Hotel was started, some of the same investors were extending the railroad six miles from Berlin to the west side of Sinepuxent Bay. From there passengers could be ferried directly across the bay to the new resort. Mr. Mumford, in his early, oral account of the resort's birth, said that people were ferried across the bay in "a big monitor [a heavy boat], operated by a big line from shore to shore. A colored man, at each end, pulled the line thus keeping the monitor straight."

For the Atlantic Hotel and the construction soon to follow, building materials had to be transported over the same route as people. The lumber milled in Salisbury was brought by railroad to the end of the line, unloaded onto a barge to cross the Sinepuxent, and then carried by wagon to the building site.

To finance the hotel, the company sold 4,000 shares of stock at $25 a share, raising $100,000 for the project.

When the Atlantic Hotel opened on the Fourth of July in 1875, a reporter for the *Salisbury Advertiser* wrote of taking the train from Salisbury in company with several hundred others. On arrival, they found gathered for the event "a large number of sailing yachts, a steamship, and three other trains, one from Lewes [Delaware], one from Snow Hill and another from Salisbury, which altogether brought to Ocean City about 800 persons. The hotel," wrote the reporter, "is a marvel in architectural beauty and excellence rivaling the finest hotel on the Atlantic Coast."

The name "Ocean City" mentioned in this account, had resulted from a stockholders' meeting in Salisbury when several names, including "Sinepuxent City" and "Beach City," and even "Ladies Resort to the Ocean," were considered and rejected. Ocean City was the popular choice for the resort-to-be.

Early pictures of the Atlantic Hotel show a four-story Victorian-style frame building which extends back from the beach for a full block and has wide, columned porches across the front and down the sides. As if anticipating the flood insurance requirements of the next century, it was built so high off the sand that, according to early accounts, a team of horses could be driven under its porches. It advertised 400 rooms.

The Atlantic Hotel Company had the rest of its 50-acre Taber property surveyed and subdivided into 205 building lots, with north–south avenues and east–west streets. The streets are the same in the old downtown today. They begin with South Division Street at the lower end and continue north with streets named for Eastern Shore counties—Worcester, Wicomico, Somerset, Dorchester, Talbot, and Caroline. The north–south avenues begin at the beach with Atlantic, better known as the Boardwalk, and then Baltimore, Philadelphia, and St. Louis.

The original plat is dated August 31, 1875, a few weeks after the Atlantic Hotel's grand opening. It shows that 104 investors had, on that date, agreed to purchase the first lots in the new resort. The distribution had apparently been made by a drawing. Some of the names on the list—Dashiell, Harrison, Hastings, Lynch, Massey, Purnell, Showell, Whaley—were to figure heavily in Ocean City's future history.

A year later, on July 28, 1876, Stephen Taber deeded to the company, as agreed, the fifty-acre portion of the tract known as "Ladies Resort to the Ocean." The deed refers to the site as Ocean City. It reserves, however, the right of way also granted by deed to the Wicomico & Pocomoke Railroad Company "for the construction, maintenance and operation of a rail road through and along Baltimore Avenue its outer length."

The deed is made out in handwriting on the back to The Atlantic Hotel Company of Berlin. It names as trustees, Hillary R. Pitts, Benjamin Jones Taylor, and George W. Purnell, all of Worcester County.

Mr. Taber stipulated in the deed that any lots remaining after the initial distribution could be sold or conveyed by the trustees "to such persons as they think proper and appropriate the proceeds thereof in such manner as they shall deem most advantageous to the interests of said Ocean City."

The new resort was thus officially established. It was an event strangely absent from the published volumes of Maryland history.

A feature in *The Sun* which ran in July 1925 on Ocean City's fiftieth anniversary, recalled (in a far more florid style than reporters indulge in today) that, "before 1875 Ocean City was only wasteland with wide stretches of white sand lapped by the ceaseless roll of the ocean and the canopy of blue sky above it." Then, the article continued, "Over the sandy roads and through the marshes came the first patron of the Atlantic Hotel."

A FOOTHOLD IN THE SAND

"Ocean City is a history of investments," says John Dale Showell, a resort hotel owner whose family roots go back to the beginning. His assessment is certainly accurate, for scarcely had the first lots been platted beside the new Atlantic Hotel before the first real estate and development venturers began coming in. Today there are seventy real estate agencies with offices in Ocean City.

In John Dos Passos's book, *The 42nd Parallel,* part of his "U.S.A." trilogy published in 1930, the young and ambitious John W. Moorehouse hopes to make his fortune in Ocean City, Maryland. "They say Ocean City has a great future . . . I mean in a kind of real estate way," young Moorehouse tells a young lady he meets on the way. "Why, what have they got at Atlantic City or Cape May that we haven't got here?" declares Colonel Wedgewood, Moorehouse's contact at the fictitious Ocean City Improvement and Realty Company.

As the story progresses, Moorehouse finds marriage to a wealthy young woman a quicker way to the top, the realty company goes bankrupt and his new father-in-law cannot unload the "sandlots" in which he has invested heavily.

Money has been made and lost in large quantities in Ocean City in real life as well as in fiction. But the steady drift of fortune, like the littoral currents of the sea, has been in one direction—upward.

In 1892 The Sinepuxent Beach Company of Baltimore, Maryland, distributed a prospectus. The company had been organized two years before and had offices at the southeast corner of Calvert and Baltimore Streets and at 808 17th Street in Washington. Its president at the time was R. G. Keene of Baltimore; its vice president was Harvey L. Page of Washington.

The new company had purchased the Atlantic Hotel fifteen years after its grand opening. It had also acquired 1,600 acres of land on both sides of the original boundaries of Ocean City, and, on the mainland across the bay, another 800 acres which (according to the prospectus) consisted of "valuable farms adapted to the growth of vegetables and fruits, which are utilized for furnishing supplies to the inhabitants of the Beach property." This was the mainland and beach property earlier acquired by Stephen Taber of Long Island, the first and biggest property owner in what was to be Ocean City. The properties had been conveyed to The Sinepuxent Beach Company by the executors of Mr. Taber's last will in Queens County, New York. (His son, Thomas, in giving up the property, either lacked the speculative instincts of his father or had realized what may have seemed at the time to be a big profit on the initial investment.)

In its 1892 brochure, the Sinepuxent company boasted that it had already sold a large number of lots "to prominent people, including many officers of the army and navy." Lots had been laid out the width of the island, a distance "not more than 400 yards wide, thereby giving a commanding view of both ocean and bay from each lot." The subdivision extended down Assateague Island to South 10th Street, about two miles to the south of South Division Street, which bounded the original city.

At the northern edge of the original town, the company laid out a new street, North Division, and platted numbered east–west streets. This plat extends as far north as 33rd Street. Early plats in the land survey records of Worcester County show Chicago Avenue running north–south along the bayside wetlands parallel to St. Louis Avenue. Only remnants of this street remain between 2nd and 4th streets and 14th and 15th streets.

Mr. Dos Passos's fictitious young promoter, J. Ward Moorehouse, promised in his company's advertising brochure, "the lifegiving surges of the broad Atlantic beating on the crystalline beaches of Ocean City." In even greater hyperbole, the Sinepuxent company promised, in its prospectus, a beach "entirely unlike many places along the Atlantic Coast, in which we find the beach as changeable as the seasons. . . . But here it is firm and unchangeable. The highest tides and severest storms have so far only demonstrated the absolute security of property erected upon it."

Forty-one years later, the great storm of August 1933 washed the Ocean City Inlet through the island and created the fishing and boating harbor that is one of the town's biggest attractions. At the same time, the owners of the lots where the inlet washed through lost their property. The rest of the subdivision platted by The Sinepuxent Beach Company to the south was separated from Ocean City and is now part of Assateague National Seashore. At the southern tip of the resort, South 1st and South 2nd streets are all that is left of the south section of the "unchangeable" beach.

The 1892 prospectus of The Sinepuxent Beach Company did not exaggerate in the statement, "What makes this property especially valuable . . . is the railroad."

The stockholders in the Wicomico & Pocomoke Railroad moved ahead in 1876 with the climax of their venture, a wooden trestle bridge across Sinepuxent Bay to bring trains right into the heart of Ocean City. A rare picture of the long-vanished bridge shows a train with four passenger cars, a baggage car, a coal car, and an old steam locomotive crossing it on a low, narrow roadbed between two wooden rail fences protecting it on both sides. According to James H. Mumford, one of Ocean City's oral historians, the pilings were driven with a pile driver operated by man power, "which was very tedious."

The bridge had a pivotal section in the center which was cranked open by a tender for boat traffic. Wooden planks were put over the ties so that horse-drawn vehicles, and later cars, could use the bridge as well as the trains. It was also used by pedestrians. Users paid a toll, Mr. Mumford said. It cost 5 cents for a person to walk across and 5 cents a wheel for vehicles.

"The train tracks were on there and they had these switches so the train could turn. And if you weren't very careful, you'd get your buggy wheel in there and break your wheel down," Raymond Davis, a Worcester County native, recalled in another transcribed segment of the county's oral history.

In another narrative, Clinton Hudson recounted an adventure that probably occurred frequently. "You went across the railroad bridge, and the cars and the team and all [were] on this same bridge. I remember my dad was in this car one time, this Model T, going over there, and the train was coming off just as we were starting to go on. There wasn't room when the train came to pass. It was just wide enough without the train for two-way traffic. So we had to back up. The train waited for us to back up maybe 20–30 yards."

Sometimes cars were backed up on both sides of the Sinepuxent waiting to cross, a scene to be repeated on summer weekends in the next century when ocean-bound traffic backed up for miles at the Chesapeake Bay Bridge. It was not until 1916 that the state built the first automobile bridge into Ocean City, entering the old downtown at Worcester Street.

The railroad depot was initially on Baltimore Avenue, and the trains took passengers right up to the doorstep of the Atlantic Hotel. The depot was later moved back to Philadelphia Avenue between Wicomico and Somerset streets. The bricks of the old platform are still there today providing a tie to the past that is somehow satisfying amid the glossy new structures replacing familiar landmarks in the old downtown.

The early wood-burning locomotives were replaced by coal engines in 1893, but visitors still arrived in Ocean City sprinkled with soot from the train ride.

The Eastern Shore's railroad system went through a confusion of sales and resales during the period from 1888 to 1894. The Wicomico & Pocomoke Railroad, which brought the first guests to the Atlantic Hotel in 1875, extended westward only as far as the mid-shore town of Salisbury where it connected with the Eastern Shore Railroad, which ran north–south down the Delmarva Peninsula.

Postcard, circa 1910, showing the train crossing Sinepuxent Bay. (Courtesy Ocean City Life-Saving Station Museum.)

There was then no rail line from Salisbury westward, across the Shore to the Chesapeake Bay. To get to Ocean City from Baltimore meant either a journey by steamboat across the Bay and up the Wicomico River to Salisbury, or by steamboat to Crisfield and from there to Salisbury by rail. From Salisbury, travelers connected with a train on the Wicomico & Pocomoke line for the rest of the journey across the Shore to the beach. However the trip was made, it was a strenuous undertaking.

In almost any personal memoir of the early days of Ocean City and the trains that were so much a apart of it, the stationmasters, conductors, and baggage handlers are mentioned by name. Conductors were said to stop the train for such emergencies as a lady's or gentleman's hat blowing out the window.

The investors in the old Wicomico & Pocomoke sold it thirteen years after its completion, to the Baltimore & Eastern Shore Railroad, a company organized by a group of venturesome Eastern Shore business leaders who set out to build an east–west line across the Shore from the Chesapeake Bay. The line was completed in 1890, the year The Sinepuxent Beach Company was organized. The railroad company, however, could not raise the money it needed to retain control of its line, and, in 1894, it was bought at a mortgage foreclosure procedure at a heavy loss to local investors by a group allied with the Pennsylvania Railroad. The railroad then became the Baltimore, Chesapeake & Atlantic Railway, quickly dubbed and fixed in the memory of those who rode it as the "Black Cinders and Ashes."

In the heyday of both the railroad and the early Ocean City fishing camps for the pound netters (the subject of a chapter to come), as many as twenty freight cars would leave the beach packed with fresh fish for Baltimore markets.

But most vivid memories of this railroad are from passengers on excursions to Ocean City. The line ran a steamer from Baltimore to a ferry terminal at Claiborne on Eastern Bay. Passengers then boarded the train for the beach. There would be as many as seventeen cars on one train in the peak years of the Baltimore, Chesapeake & Atlantic Railway. The whole trip, including Bay crossing, took about six hours. The trains rolled along at what was described as a slow pace then but was about twice as fast as freight-only trains can travel on Shore railroads today.

On excursion days, passengers arrived at the beach about 1:00 P.M. and departed at 4:00 P.M., traveling most of the day for just a few hours by the ocean. The round-trip ticket from Baltimore cost $4.50. For either excursionists or vacationers at the early hotels and cottages, the steamboat and train ride seem to be bound inseparably with the memories of the beach and the Boardwalk.

For nontravelers along the tracks as they crossed the Shore, "the trains were the embodiment of all that was romantic and exciting," Kenneth Patrick Falks remembered from boyhood. He lived then in the rural, mid-Shore town of Preston and regularly watched by the railroad tracks as the Ocean City Flyer rushed by "in a shower of cinders," he wrote in a feature published in a local paper in 1952.

In another remembrance piece, Millard C. Fairbank of St. Michaels describes a photograph of what appears to be much of the population of that upper-Shore fishing village dressed in their Sunday best and crowded onto the platform of the train station. The picture was taken in 1907 or 1908. The occasion, Mr. Fairbank explains, was a weekly event in the town—watching the Ocean City Flyer go by.

To understand what an event this was, he explains, one has to understand "how very quiet things used to be in small Eastern Shore towns on Sundays . . . So the arrival of the Ocean City Flyer became a very important thing. It gave Sunday afternoon a purpose, a sense of direction." The whole family would dress up for the stroll to the station. The train they awaited would be making the return trip to Baltimore, passing at about five o'clock in the afternoon. The wait for the train would be a time to visit with neighbors and for children to "scoot around this way and that" with each other.

"Eventually the Flyer would sweep into sight, belching smoke and steam; behind it the maroon-and-gold coaches . . . . We got only glimpses of those magic people on the train . . . . How hot and tired and wilted and uncomfortable the excursionists must have been, having ridden that cinder-laden train across the Eastern Shore in the summer heat. But to me they always were the most enviable people in the world, sitting calmly there in luxury while the train carried them through the day and night."

Mrs. Edward R. Willcox of Baltimore, who grew up spending summers with her grandmother, owner of the Plimhimmon Hotel, was one of the "enviable people" of Mr. Fairbank's memories. She recalls a journey which began at Pier 8 on Pratt Street at 6:30 A.M. With her family, she boarded a steamer and crossed the Chesapeake Bay to Claiborne. Next was the train ride, the most unforgettable part being the old wooden trestle shimmying and swaying under the train when it crossed the Nanticoke River.

"The twice-daily arrival of a train at the railroad station was the event of the day at the old resort," she remembers. "You were greeted by signs advertising the various hotels [that were then going up on the beach]. Porters stood beneath the signs of their hotels so you knew to whom to give your baggage. Then you walked from the station to your hotel. The baggage came over in a horse cart."

In another memory piece written many years ago for a local publication called *Eastern Shore Magazine,* Emma D. Price recalled steaming across the Bay from Baltimore to Claiborne and then making the "hot and dirty trip" across the Shore by train. On arrival, "the grown-ups would be completely worn down," she wrote. "But we youngsters, wildly excited, would be only hot, sticky, and dirty. The minute we set foot on that Boardwalk, stretching out before us, and not more than 50 feet from the ocean, the magical scene would make us forget everything else. We forgot the hot train ride, we forgot that we lived in a big city which we would have to return to. We just kept feeling a quickening of the pulse—a consciousness of glamorous adventure awaiting us."

The trains came into town until 1933, when the storm that created the Ocean City Inlet destroyed the old trestle bridge. By that time, cars had replaced the train as the favored transportation to the beach, though perhaps not as the source of the same vivid childhood memories.

The railroad bridge was not rebuild. All that remains are some pilings and planks on the West Ocean City shore.

The Sinepuxent Beach Company was not the only real estate group to promote Ocean City. In a turn-of-the-century real estate advertisement, the Interstate Realty Co., Inc., Boardwalk, Ocean City, offered, "Ocean and Bay Front lots 25 × 142 feet each, for $25 and upward, $5 down, $1 per week." It was generally considered to be a foolhardy investment. For those who dared, the investment in one lot would today be worth $100,000 to $200,000.

Even up to fairly recent years, investment in undeveloped Ocean City land was not for the fainthearted. In a remembrance piece in *The Sun Magazine*, Frank Fairbank of Baltimore recalled a 1936 estate auction of 280 lots in north Ocean City that had been acquired by a venturesome local landowner in 1915: "A few of the lots were south of 14th Street, where the boardwalk ended then. Most were between 24th and 33rd streets and marked off as full city blocks of twelve lots each. Looking north from 14th Street, you saw only a sweep of ocean, skimpy beach, sand dunes, scattered growths of scrub greenery, and wheeling, squawking gulls."

Half of the onlookers were curious vacationers, he recalled. "The others were local residents. Most of them were sun-and-wind-tanned men in overalls. As it turned out, most of the buying was done by this group.

"What kind of wild intuition gave these men the faith they had in their little wooden town, which they had built on not much more than a big sandbar?" Mr. Fairbank asked. He was then teaching at City College in Baltimore and earning about $1,500 a year, he wrote. He congratulated himself on being smart enough not to lay down hard cash "for a worthless stretch of sand and scrub."

Some of the lots that day sold for as little as $60. The total for all 280 lots was $33,111.50. Within the next fifty years, they were to be worth millions. Mr. Fairbank pointed out that the original owner of this land was Stephen Taber who, in 1868, had obtained it in a patent from the state of Maryland for less than $1 an acre.

Whatever the fortunes of the early investors in Ocean City and the railroads that fed it, one of the claims of the early promoters in The Sinepuxent Beach Company was well established almost from the start: "Despite the fact of the former inaccessibility of Ocean City, and its lack of modern improvements and conveniences, comparatively speaking, a large number of the nicest people from the North, South and West have been in the habit of spending their summers here," the 1892 brochure stated, "and their enthusiasm regarding the natural beauties and advantages of the place have kept it alive."

TWO

The Formative Years

ON THE BOARDS

For the families who established themselves in Ocean City in its early years, there is a strong and special sense of place. The old families in this resort town have shared a community life rooted in the warmth and familiarity neighbors feel for each other in an isolated, rural setting. For generations, these families have married into each other, established churches, admired their children at birthday parties and school plays, and sorrowed together at funerals. At the same time, they have shared the drama of the ocean washing over the town in storms of historic proportion, and have weathered cycles of growth and change in which venturers in wider variety than most small towns experience have come and gone and stayed.

And always a part of their daily life is the unreal world of vacationers who come here to shed routine activity, dress, and sometimes good behavior. It is the beach, of course, that is the reason for the town's existence, and almost from the beginning it has been the Boardwalk that has set it apart as a vacation town.

An eighty-year-old Worcester County native remembers vividly how, as a child, his heart would beat with excitement when crossing the bridge to Ocean City and first glimpsing the Ferris wheel that was its dominant feature against the skyline.

Crossing the U.S. Route 50 bridge to downtown Ocean City today, a two-year-old boy points excitedly at the framework of the blood-chilling amusement rides against the sky and cries, "Bowa, Bowa [Boardwalk]." Whatever else has changed in the years between, the response remains the same when the first whiff of sea air combines with anticipation of the Boardwalk and the beach.

As early as 1897, a map of the infant resort shows an elevated boardwalk in front of a scattering of small hotels along the oceanfront, with inclined boardwalks leading to it from ground level. The visitor then, and through the early years of this century, would have looked down on the beach from a boardwalk elevated 10 or 12 feet above it.

The Boardwalk began as a walkway laid in sections in the sand by early business and hotel owners and stored on porches at night and when the tide was high. The beach in the old downtown was very narrow then, and so the permanent Boardwalk had to be built high enough for high tides to wash under it. Bathers sat under the Boardwalk to get out of the sun. Day visitors sat under it to eat picnic lunches. Strollers sat on it with their legs dangling over the side and watched the bathers.

In the lingo of the day, the bathers were called "fanny dunkers," because that is just about what swimming in the surf amounted to. Hotels provided ropes extending from the Boardwalk and anchored in the surf for cautious bathers to cling to.

Ladies shielded themselves from the sun with bonnets and parasols and from the eyes of speculative watchers with bathing garb that covered them from head to toe. The bathing suits "were heavy as lead when they got wet," one early swimmer remembers.

At the turn of the century, women were just beginning to progress from "bathing" to swimming. Dr. Reginald V. Truitt, a Worcester County native well versed in these matters, has pointed out that Goucher College in Baltimore had a pool as early as 1888 and students were actually taught to swim. But for most women on the Ocean City beach during that era, swimming was far too daring to try.

In a piece in *The Sun* in 1953, Nellie Fox of Baltimore, then age seventy-three, recalled scenes from her fifty years as a hotel maid in Ocean City. The women at her hotel, the Plimhimmon, waited until

11:00 A.M. to bathe en masse. "They assembled in the hotel lobby each morning, and they sewed while someone played the piano. At about eleven o'clock the women put on corsets, stockings, bathing shoes, and skirts, and then went off to the water together."

For day visitors on excursions, there were several public bathhouses where bathing attire could be rented.

In oral history tapes on file in the public library in Snow Hill, the turn-of-the-century beach scene in Ocean City becomes a very personal memory.

Out in the ocean there were ropes for swimmers, Mary White remembers. "If they didn't have the ropes, I'd never have gone in the water because as it was, holding on to the ropes, the waves turned me upside down. People didn't go and swim through the breakers like they do now."

It was not just the women who were intimidated by ocean bathing. "I never put my feet in the salt water in that ocean but once in my life," Owen Pilchard, another oral historian, asserted. "One day I was out wading in the ocean. Cold, that water was cold as I don't know what. Never had any desire to wade in the ocean since. That cured me right there."

One of the earliest reports from Ocean City in *The Sun* on July 26, 1875, reflects not only a different approach to ocean bathing in that era, but a different approach to reporting. The item mentioned the drowning of a sixty-year-old man who was swimming in the surf in front of his boardinghouse toward the Atlantic Hotel 100 yards up the beach. He called for help. "A number of gentlemen started out to save him and, with the assistance afforded by holding on to a long rope, they succeeded in seizing him, not, however, before life was extinct. His death," the item continued (somewhat callously, to say the least), "was a forfeit to his rashness in going so far out in the water and in attempting to swim such a distance." Having disposed of that unpleasant incident, the article continued with a listing of recent arrivals to the Atlantic Hotel from Baltimore.

The social items in the newspaper preserve the tone of that era even more vividly than old photographs. The vacationers at Ocean City's early Boardwalk hotels are described with such marvelous phrases as "people of refinement," "the gentlefolk," or "the financially elite."

In those days, morning was the time to be on the beach. It was not the custom to be out in the midday sun. For one thing, the hotels served a big midday meal, and the food they served was one of Ocean City's main

The original Atlantic Hotel about 1910. (Courtesy Ocean City Life-Saving Station Museum.)

attractions. At hotels such as the Plimhimmon and the Atlantic, an orchestra played during the noon meal. During the heat of the afternoon, vacationers napped or rocked in wooden oak chairs on the wide hotel porches. In the evening, they dressed for dinner and to promenade the Boardwalk afterwards. The really "financially elite" might pay 50 cents an hour to be rolled down the Boardwalk in one of the three-wheeled, wicker rolling chairs, then as much a part of the beach scene as the Boardwalk trains are today.

"You had to get dressed up, I mean the best you had, in the evening to go dancing or even to go on the Boardwalk. Nobody'd be caught dead on the Boardwalk sloppy and in clothes like they wear now," Annie Bunting, a treasure trove of early memories, has recalled. The late Harriet Bald, who grew up in the town, once recounted her experience, as a young girl, peering in the windows of the Plimhimmon in the evening at "those beautiful dances and the beautiful ladies in their formal dresses." Bill Shreve, whose grandmother built and ran the Plimhimmon and who spent his boyhood summers there, remembers, "I could never go into the dining room without a coat and tie."

Photographs of the Boardwalk, from the early years of this century into the 1940s, show a scene remarkably like that of today. For one thing, it was just about as crowded then as now. There are the same familiar porches of the old wooden hotels. There is the sign "Dolle's Saltwater Taffy," the amusement rides of Windsor Resort, and the Pier, which, though changed through the years, remains a downtown landmark. But the women of earlier days were wearing dresses, and the men white flannels, jackets, and straw hats. "Looking good," has acquired a whole new meaning since then.

THE PIER

For years, a postcard from the beach could be immediately identified as Ocean City if it had the Fishing Pier in the background. During the 1950s and the 1960s, *The Sun* would run a picture of the crowded beach by the Pier just about every Fourth of July. "I can't remember when the Fishing Pier was not there." said Bill Shreve, who spent his boyhood summers at the ocean in the early part of this century.

The Pier, completed in 1907, was a big achievement for the developing resort. It had been three years in building, the project of the group of local venturers who organized the Ocean City Pier and Improvement Company. The company president was William Taylor, so back then it was sometimes called "Taylor's Ocean Pier."

Since 1907, the Pier has been battered and wrecked by storm, fire, and ice. It has been rebuilt, restored, repaired, and changed even more in character than in structure.

At the end of the original pier by the Boardwalk, the long, white frame Pier building sat on high pilings over the beach. The beach was so narrow then that the building projected partly over the surf. It had a rounded roof and arched windows. Inside were bowling alleys, billiard tables, a silent-movie theater, refreshment booths, and a dance pavilion.

From the main building, the Fishing Pier extended into the ocean. Another building at the ocean end enclosed a roller-skating rink. Day visitors who did not have the time or money to charter a boat, or the equipment for surf fishing, could rent hand lines and fish at no charge from the Pier. With just an hour or two to fish, it was possible to land a good catch of kingfish, spot, hardhead, or trout. At one time, marksmen from far and near would come to Ocean City in the early summer for a week-long trapshooting competition on the Pier. The clay target pigeons would be released and shot down over the ocean.

In December 1925, a horrendous fire destroyed the Pier and Pier building, along with three blocks of the old downtown. The fire started about 7:30 A.M. at the plant of the Eastern Shore Gas & Electric Company at

Somerset Street and Baltimore Avenue. It was driven by a northwest wind.

Everything went wrong. It was so cold that the fire hydrants were frozen. Then the fire engine broke down. To get water, the firemen, all volunteers, had to cut holes in the ice and pump it from Sinepuxent Bay. Women of the town sat on the hoses to keep them from twisting. Volunteer firemen, with their now-antique pumpers, converged on the resort from Berlin, Snow Hill, Pocomoke, and Salisbury. The smoke could be seen ten miles away. By the end of the day, the heavy losses included, besides the Pier, the resort's two early hotels, the Atlantic and the Seaside, two blocks of the Boardwalk, Dolle's Candyland, the Casino Theater, a cluster of amusements, and the C. W. Purnell Cottage.

Irma Jester, whose late husband, Lloyd, had a small lunchroom and souvenir stand on the Pier, said that they were not able to save anything except a bag of green peanuts her husband had for roasting at local fairs. Then, even the peanuts were stolen. They had no insurance because it was too expensive.

After the fire, the Atlantic Hotel was rebuilt, but the old Seaside was not.

Rudolph Dolle, a candy maker from New York, had come to Ocean City with his family in 1905 when the Pier was built. The family had lived over the store, building the business and pulling the famed saltwater taffy by hand. In an account of the fire, *The Sun* estimated the loss of Candyland at $7,000, a big sum for a seasonal business in that day. Dolle's was rebuilt, with new machines added; these are still used today to pull and wrap the taffy. Candyland has been owned and operated by generations of the same family until today, but has been housed in a new building since 1978.

In June 1929, the Sinepuxent Pier and Improvement Company was organized with Clarence W. Whealton, a Salisbury lawyer and state political figure who summered in Ocean City, as president. The company obtained a new franchise from the town and completed a new 700-foot-long ocean Fishing Pier on the site of the old one.

Among the not-so-young who have grown up living or vacationing in Ocean City, some of the clearest memories of youth are of the big band dances in the ballroom of the Pier. The same building is there today, though barely recognizable. It was here that the now older generation danced to "In the Mood" and "Tuxedo Junction" by Glen Miller's band, heard Helen O'Connell sing "Green Eyes" with Jimmy Dorsey's band, or filled the ballroom to capacity to hear Benny Goodman or Harry James. "The ballroom was the 'in' place to spend an evening," in the words of Irma Jester, a resort resident since 1918.

Mrs. Jester is a remarkable lady who reached the age of ninety in 1990. She was a native of Salisbury and at the age of twenty married Lloyd Jester, a widower who had food and amusement concessions on the Ocean City Boardwalk. As his wife her life paralleled the history of downtown Ocean City and as a lifelong school teacher it paralleled the development of public education in Worcester County.

After the great fire of 1925, the Jesters rented space on the Boardwalk across from the Pier where the old Casino Theater had stood. They rented the same Boardwalk site from absentee owners for over sixty years. On it they built a funhouse before which stood "Laughing Sal," a mechanical figure in a tacky print dress who, with her recorded, amplified, incessant, and irresistible laughter, was immortalized by John Barth in his book *Lost in the Funhouse*. "Laughing Sal" is now a display in the Ocean City Life-Saving Station Museum at the south end of the Boardwalk. She has been replaced in her original domain by a video arcade and, beside it, a jewelry shop.

When Lloyd Jester died, his son Eddie took over the business. Then, in 1987, the owner of the Boardwalk site, to whom the Jesters had paid ground rent since 1925, died, and a nephew who inherited it put it up for sale for $3 million. After pacing the floor for several nights, Eddie Jester found two partners and bought the property.

In the summer of 1990, Irma Jester was living in an apartment above the arcade adjoining two other apartments occupied by her son and grandson and reached by a boardwalk across the roof of the arcade. Beyond the potted plants that line the railing in front, Irma Jester looks out over the Pier building and the brightly colored signs hanging from it advertising Photon (a giant laser game), and food, T-shirt, and carnival-type concessions. Beyond, toward the ocean, is a towering water slide and a Haunted House.

The glitter of the Pier building today is a different glitter from that of couples in elegant evening dress who once strolled from the ballroom.

In the 1950s, tastes in music and style were changing. The old Pier had passed its heyday and was in sharp decline. The city used the ballroom for a time as a convention hall and a teen center.

In 1959, a new pier company, which had taken over the franchise from the old one, attempted to build amusement concessions across the beach. The plan, however, was voted down in a special voters' referendum after months of controversy. Opponents had argued that the proposed "honky-tonk" amusements would intrude on the resort's greatest asset, its fine, white, sandy beaches.

Within the next fifteen years, the amusements were built on the beach with council approval. Then in 1975, Charles (Buddy) Jenkins, an Ocean City native and successful investor in many resort ventures, opened the redone Pier building with its souvenir shops and concessions. He said that the project had cost him over $1.5 million. Three years later he got a renewed lease to the Pier from the city which will carry him into the next century.

In February 1979, uncommonly cold temperatures froze the ocean surface into surrealistic ice sculpture and caused chunks to form on the ocean's surface thick enough to crush and destroy about 140 feet from the seaward end of the Pier. Mr. Jenkins contended that to rebuild it to its original length would be of little benefit to fishermen then or in the foreseeable future. He argued also that the long stone jetty, which was built at the Inlet after the storm of 1933, had widened the south end of the beach and changed the flow of the ocean current in that location to such an extent that fishing would not be improved by a Pier extension. The Ocean City Mayor and Council eventually settled for the shortened length.

The Pier remains a downtown landmark, although its main function is no longer fishing and the ballroom is no longer for balls. The fishermen who might once have used the pier now line the long stone jetty at the Inlet.

"I used to just love to sit on the Boardwalk and watch the strollers in the evening," Irma Jester reflected a few years ago. "Everyone was dressed impeccably and it was very romantic."

These days the crowd is all but impenetrable around the Pier on summer weekends and cars circle the big parking lot on the beach beside it. But "romantic" it is not.

THE TRIMPERS AND THE LONGEST-RUNNING RIDE

It was 1892. The Atlantic Hotel was established. The Seaside Hotel and Congress Hall had been built nearby. The federal government had located a Life-Saving Station on Caroline Street at the northern edge of the tentatively growing settlement. Baltimore and Washington investors had begun to take note of the infant resort and had just organized The

Sinepuxent Beach Company, which would expand and promote it in the years ahead.

It was at this point that Daniel B. Trimper of Baltimore made what must have been a very daring decision. He bought two blocks in a town that was still laid out mostly on paper.

Mr. Trimper and his wife, Margaret, were both German immigrants who had met and married in Baltimore. The couple had ten children. Mr. Trimper had opened a bar in Baltimore called Dan Trimper's Silver Dollar Bar, which featured silver dollars embedded in the floor. Why he chose to relocate is unknown; his grandson, Daniel Trimper III, does not know why his grandfather decided to take a chance on Ocean City.

It was an all-or-nothing investment. With a brother he formed a business enterprise called Windsor Resort, which was to include the Windsor and Eastern Shore hotels and an amusement center called Luna Park, with its own boardwalk and a small cluster of rides. A wooden arch over the Boardwalk at the south end with "Windsor Resort D. Trimper Propr." written on it is as much a landmark on old Ocean City postcards as the Pier and Pier pavilion.

The origin of the name "Windsor" is unknown, unless it related to the castlelike turrets on the roof of the early hotel. Part of the hotel remains today, but is unrecognizable behind the facade of the Haunted House in the Boardwalk pavilion. The Trimper home was behind the hotel, and Mr. Trimper was still building it when his family arrived.

The family had never seen Ocean City when, in the dead of winter, they boarded the steamer *Cambridge* in Baltimore and crossed the Chesapeake Bay to Claiborne. Recalling the family story, Daniel Trimper III said that the Bay was so frozen the boat could not reach the dock, and the family had to walk across the ice to shore while crew members tested the footing before them. The railroad had just been completed across the Eastern Shore and the Trimpers, with their trunks, boarded the train for their new and unknown home.

Daniel III's grandfather, the late Daniel Trimper, Jr., who was then a six-year-old carrying a puppy aboard the train in a box, reflected some years ago on the move. "None of us could see what Father saw in Ocean City at that time," he said. "There weren't more than forty permanent residents here. We had no street lighting. You had to carry a lantern to walk out at night. It was spooky in winter when the wind howled around the few houses. In those days, it was a tough and long, drawn-out process even to get the doctor over here from Berlin."

The original Trimper (Daniel B.) kept adding buildings and ventures. At one time, there was a movie theater with vaudeville acts, and an early merry-go-round run by hefty workers turning cranks. There was no electricity in those days. At one point Mr. Trimper created his own, using generators hooked up to two big steam engines. With this rig he operated two rides, a merry-go-round and the Whip, running each one alternately while riders boarded the other. It was the first electricity in the resort, Daniel Trimper III said, and a lot of people came to the amusement park just to see the lights. The Trimper amusements were a venture that would progress from simple crank-turned rides to today's towering chillers known to several generations as Trimper's Rides.

Part of the original Luna Park was washed away in the storm of 1933. The Trimpers lost the building that housed the Whip and a roller-skating rink. Mr. Trimper salvaged most of the rink's fine maple flooring, and Daniel Trimper III has it today in the floor of his home.

The overall effect of the storm was to greatly enhance the Trimper property. Before the storm, the beach was so narrow and the ocean so close that it washed around the pilings that supported the Trimper boardwalk and amusement buildings, and was so high on some nights that the area had to be closed. When the long, stone north jetty was built to stabilize the new Inlet, the sand trapped behind it built up the beach to many times its former width. It became so wide that Daniel Trimper II gave to Ocean City the right of way for two rows of parking. That was the start of the big municipal parking lot at the south end of the Boardwalk.

Some of the Trimpers' valuable Boardwalk property dates back to the time when Stephen Taber owned that whole stretch of the beach and granted the earliest investors the tract to establish Ocean City. The Trimpers had some makeshift buildings on the beach east of the Boardwalk beside their property. They rebuilt them every year as winds and tides took their toll. As the beach built up behind the jetty, the value of the beach property rose even faster, and they built permanent structures on it. When the city claimed the property a few years ago, the Trimpers were able to show in the Maryland Court of Appeals that Stephen Taber had once offered it to the city along with all the beach area from South 2nd Street to Dorchester Street. The city had failed to accept the dedication. The court upheld the right of the Trimpers to the unclaimed property on which they had had buildings for over eighty years. The buildings there today house a Burger King and a gift shop.

One of the Trimper's Boardwalk pavilions, home to the Dodg'ems and some kiddy rides, also houses the oldest continuously operated merry-go-round in the United States. It has wonderful animals—lions, tigers, ostriches, a pig, frogs, a dragon, and mythical-looking prancing horses. Each of the fifty-two animals is today a museum piece.

The exact date of the carousel's arrival is hard to pin down, but sometime around the turn of this century the first Dan Trimper bought it from the Herschell-Spillman Company of North Tonawanda, New York. "It took just about everything he had," his son once said. The new carousel was ornately decorated and steam driven; it was shortly converted to electricity.

The carousel still turns today, original oil paintings and beveled mirrors flashing as it picks up speed, and loud, tinny, rousing music sending forth the sound of continuous festival. A hundred thousand wide-eyed children and nostalgic adults ride it every year. Granville Trimper, one of the fourth generation of the Ocean City Trimpers, runs the rides today. He has had the animals, one by one, refurbished and restored by two local artists to match their original colors as closely as possible. A first-time visitor to Ocean City might miss this treasure entirely, surrounded as it is by the pressing crowds on the Boardwalk, the din of video games, and the perpetually long line of people waiting for Thrashers fried potatoes.

The Trimpers, like their carousel, give continuity to the history of the Boardwalk and of Ocean City.

The first Daniel Trimper died in 1929, and his son took over the amusement center. Like other of the town's established civic leaders, Daniel Jr.'s working life was not confined to one occupation. Besides being president of the family business, Windsor Resort Inc., he was involved with the railroad, marine construction, pile driving, and real estate investments.

He is remembered as a quiet and modest man, but one with an outspoken loyalty to Ocean City that made him unbeatable in local elections. He was elected mayor of the town in 1944 and held the office for fifteen years. When he left that office, it was to accept an appointment as county commissioner for Worcester County. In 1959, the year he resigned as mayor, he was given a Distinguished Citizen of Maryland award by J. Millard Tawes, then governor, for his contributions to the growth and development of "Maryland's only seashore resort."

When he died in 1965 at the age of seventy-nine, tributes in the local papers referred to him with affection as "Old Man Dan." This was partly to distinguish him from Daniel Trimper III and Daniel Trimper IV, who were by then becoming equally active in Ocean City's business and civic affairs.

Both Daniel Trimper IV and his cousin, Granville, have served as president of the Ocean City Council. Daniel Trimper III has avoided politics, but has been successful in a number of businesses, including a pile driving enterprise and a boatyard, as well as the family's original Windsor Resort on the Boardwalk. Like others in his family, he is attuned to the pleasures as well as the profits to be had in Ocean City. He enjoys his boat, the fishing, and the company of family and friends whose lives have been rooted in the community through five or six generations.

"I consider it ruined now," he said of his native town.

Just about any long-established person here has his or her own idea of the big turning point for Ocean City. For Daniel Trimper III, "It was Bobby Baker's Carousel," and that is a subject to come.

THE SHOWELL BLOCK

In 1896, John Dale Showell and his wife, the former Elizabeth West of Accomack County, Virginia, moved to Ocean City from Berlin, a small town on the mainland a few miles away.

Ocean City was then taking root in the sand like an exotic garden and had an allure beyond the farming and timbering interests Mr. Showell had inherited from one of the biggest landowning families in Worcester County. The new resort was already a family adventure. John Dale's uncle and guardian was Colonel Lemuel Showell, the man who had invested much of his fortune in the young Ocean City and in the Wicomico & Pocomoke Railroad that was the key to its existence. Colonel Showell had a homestead in Showell, the nearby community named for him, but was then spending much of his time at a cottage he had built at the beach.

John Dale and Elizabeth Showell began by operating a boardinghouse later known as the Essex Hotel at the Boardwalk and 1st Street. Then they operated the Mt. Vernon Hotel on Talbot Street, a homelike structure that had been built by Lemuel Showell. (It was recently restored as a restaurant in a revitalization effort on that downtown block.) They moved on to a series of ventures that play a significant part in many memories of the old Ocean City.

In the block between North Division Street and Caroline Street, next to the old Coast Guard Station, they built the Oceanic Hotel, a tearoom called the Blue Lattice, Showell's Bathhouse, and Showell's Theater. Most remarkably, they built the resort's first swimming pool at the Oceanic.

The pool was a great curiosity. Old postcards show swarms of people around it, the men wearing coats and ties and their stiff straw boaters, the women well covered in dresses and hats, all watching the young boys who picked up spending money diving into the pool for coins. It was a saltwater pool filled from a pipe across the beach to the ocean.

There was always a concentration of people on the beach at the Showell Block, because that is where excursion people and day visitors could rent bathing suits and change clothes.

Ocean City did not have a beach patrol until 1930. Before that, the U.S. Coast Guard crew stationed at the Caroline Street station was the main source of help for foundering bathers as well as boats.

John Dale Showell was a star baseball player in his high school and college days and also a strong swimmer. He was said to have gone to the rescue of dozens of swimmers in his day. In the few photographs remaining from this era, he seems a low-key, grandfatherly, and gentle person quietly smoking his pipe. A granddaughter, the late Harriet Bald, remembered him as knowing all about the weather, the constantly changing interaction of ocean and beach, and how to fix almost anything needing fixing in his various enterprises.

Of all the characteristics of his grandfather, John Dale Showell III said he was most impressed as a boy, and still is today, not by his grandfather's successful business ventures, but by his baseball prowess. According to a family story, he hit a home run but was told on reaching home plate that he hadn't touched second base. He then ran all the bases again and reached home plate the second time before the catcher had the ball.

When Mr. Showell died in March 1947 at the age of eighty-two, all resort businesses closed for several hours on the afternoon of the funeral. His wife, Elizabeth, had died ten years before. She was the operator of the Blue Lattice Tearoom in the Showell Block. John Dale III remembers his grandmother as always working. "She could handle anything," he said. "She could handle Grandfather. She always seemed to know instinctively whether something would work or would not, and she let him know it."

The second generation of the Ocean City Showells were a son and daughter, John Dale Showell, Jr., and Elizabeth Showell Strohecker. They grew up as involved in the family enterprises as their parents. John Dale, Jr., had been six years old and Elizabeth age one when their parents moved to the resort.

As a young adult, the son built the family a sturdy house on the southeast corner of North Division Street and Baltimore Avenue. He paid $600 for the building materials. The house is still there today, immediately visible to motorists as they enter the downtown from the U.S. Route 50 bridge. A surfing shop called Sundancer on the lower level is operated by a fourth-generation Showell.

John Dale, Jr., married Sarah Hickling, a woman with strong family and social ties to Washington. His life was divided between Washington, Ocean City, and Florida, where he also had business interests. Their two children, John Dale III and Harriet, went to school in Washington, but their summers in Ocean City overshadow all else in their reminiscences of growing up.

For John Dale III, boyhood summers centered around the Showell pool at the Oceanic. His father taught him to swim before he could walk by tossing him into the pool with a rope around his waist and pulling him up and down. He taught other well-known personalities in Ocean City to swim as well—Harry Kelley, the future mayor, for one. As a young boy, John Dale III and his summertime cronies dived for coins in the pool, sometimes making it more exciting by climbing up to the roof of the bowling alley of the Oceanic Hotel for a high dive. It cost 25 cents to swim in the pool, but John Dale III often sneaked his friends in without paying. His father used to complain that the boys made more money from the pool than he did.

No chlorine was used in Ocean City's first swimming pool. John Dale III remembers that his father would clean it once a week. He would dive to the bottom with a crowbar and pry open the heavy plug. The water would rush out, cutting a trough across the beach as it returned to the ocean from whence it had come. His father would then clean the green algae off the sides with a power hose before turning on the big pump that would draw in water through a pipe from the ocean, refilling the pool through the night. No one ever got an earache or any other affliction from swimming in the unchlorinated pool, John Dale said, "and I swam in it every single day."

The heavy, woolen black bathing suits, with big white S's on them, could be rented for 25 cents for either the pool or the beach. They were washed every night in a big wooden tub and put in a wooden barrel turned by a hand crank to spin out excess water. They were hung to dry on the roofs of the Showell buildings, which John Dale estimated must have covered about an acre. Nowadays, in a most unexpected place—the private museum of Lawrence W. Burgess, in an old chicken house at a crossroads called Hudsons Corner in rural Somerset County—a visitor will come upon racks of the old woolen bathing suits once rented at Showell's Bathhouse and the wooden tubs in which they were washed. Burgess bought them at a sale years before for his collection.

The man responsible for those suits during most of the years of their use was a lifelong employee of the Showells named John Dale Smack, but known to the family as "Happy Jack." He also polished and waxed the bowling alleys and did whatever other jobs needed doing. (His son and namesake was later to serve for many years as a town councilman in nearby Berlin.)

In the bowling alley, John Dale Showell III picked up summertime spending money as a "pin boy." Bowlers paid 15 cents a game, or a "string," as his father called it, and the pin boys got a 3-cent share of that.

Later, when he was about twelve years old, he got the most coveted job of all. He became a substitute on the Beach Patrol. There were only about nine or ten lifeguards then, and they were paid $17 a week. But there were other benefits. The hotel at the beach where a lifeguard was on duty would send out lunch. And the girls were always impressed.

The lifeguards met every morning at Showell's soda fountain at the bowling alley. They played odd man out to decide who would pay for milkshakes before they walked up the beach to their assigned places. Since they were not paid until the end of the week, Poxie Jarman, who ran the fountain, kept the tab till then.

At the end of the season there would be a big dance at the Pier, and the lifeguards would supplement their seasonal incomes by splitting the profits.

It is of such things that strong attachments are made.

John Dale III had finished Georgetown Prep School and was on the way to Georgetown University when his plans were changed by World War II and enlistment in the U.S. Marine Corps.

After the war, "I went straight to Ocean City," he said. He went to work for the Bank of Ocean City, of which he is still a director. Then he went into real estate and acquired several major properties.

One of them is the West Ocean City house on Wire Creek where he and his wife, Ann Lockhart of Wadesboro, North Carolina, moved in 1947 and where his four children were reared. It is a real "homeplace" kind of property with a rambling house and a swimming pool which is really a cut in the marsh-rimmed creek. In the marsh there are hundreds, maybe thousands, of ducks that are fed tons of corn every winter, and in the yard, an open boat from one of Ocean City's early fishing camps.

John Dale III is 6 feet 6 inches tall and looks every inch the country squire. His twenty-five-acre property was once part of an estate called

Carmel, which was one of the mainland properties bought in 1868 by Stephen Taber, the man from Long Island who had, at about the same time, obtained the patent to the land on which Ocean City was founded.

Mr. Showell also bought in the 1950s a block of oceanfront land at 37th Street in Ocean City on which he and his family built and operated a hotel, Castle in the Sand, and several cottages. He acquired another piece of property by the West Ocean City fishing harbor and had investors lined up first for a major seafood harbor and then a very up-scale vacation development. Both projects were blocked by environmental controls that have developed at both the state and federal level since the early 1970s. He has now sold the property to another developer, James B. Caine, who plans a multimillion-dollar marina.

Like other of Ocean City's long-established property owners, Mr. Showell feels that many of the government's wetlands and other controls are unnecessary and confusing intrusions into private property rights.

In John Dale's line, the family is now into its fifth generation. Of his four children, three are building their lives in Ocean City, and the return of the fourth seem imminent. John Dale V was christened in January 1990.

His father's sister, Elizabeth Showell Strohecker, who shared the running of the original Showell Block on the Boardwalk, was deeply involved in the affairs of the town for her entire lifetime.

At the age of nineteen she became the town's postmistress. The post office was then located in the family-owned Mt. Vernon Inn on Talbot Street. It also functioned as an information center for strangers in town and a news gathering place for townspeople. The young postmistress initiated door-to-door mail delivery in Ocean City, an innovation that was not altogether welcome because residents no longer had the daily opportunity to meet and talk at the post office.

For most of her life, Mrs. Strohecker ran the Showell Theater on North Division Street, operating the projection equipment and lining up the films. That was in addition to managing the other family businesses and her own rental properties, and taking an active role in St. Paul's By-the-Sea Episcopal Church and civic organizations.

She had two daughters, Elizabeth Gordy and Margaret Hall, who inherited their mother's vitality and developed their own Ocean City real estate and business ventures. They have produced a new generation as involved in Ocean City business and civic life as their forebears, and the sixth generation is growing fast.

The Showell property at North Division Street, once such a vital part of the old downtown, has been sold. A new, masonry building with a whole new look occupies the site.

Tastes and styles change fast in Ocean City, and even more changing are the contours of the beach. It is the old families that give the city its continuity. They will keep cropping up in this narrative like the characters in a James Michener novel.

ON THE BACK STREETS

In the resort's earliest days, as on a new frontier, it was the churches that declared the scattering of simple wooden buildings on a barren and windswept strip of sand, to be a settled community. The same 1897 map that showed the first hotels, rooming houses, and Boardwalk also identifies four churches on the back streets—Episcopal, Methodist, Presbyterian, and Catholic. Too small to have full-time pastors, all four depended on visiting clergymen and lay leaders.

St. Paul's By-the-Sea Episcopal Church began about 1880 as a small building near the Congress Hall Hotel where some of the early patrons were particularly interested in having a place for services. By the turn of the century, the old property had been sold to Christopher Ludlam, Ocean City's first commercial fisherman. The proceeds from the sale were used to build a new church on two donated lots at 3rd Street and Baltimore Avenue, where it stands today. The original property now lies beneath the Ocean City Inlet.

St. Paul's By-the-Sea has been supported by the first Trimpers and Showells who moved to Ocean City and by generations of both families. Today both the original church and a sister church are located at 100th Street.

Little is known of the earliest Methodist Church marked on the 1897 map on Dorchester Street. The congregation met in various places in the town's early years. An established church was not built until 1919. The Atlantic United Methodist Church, which stands today at 4th Street and Baltimore Avenue, replaced the earlier building on the same site in 1962.

The Presbyterian Church began about 1890 with Sunday School meetings organized by Ella Dennis, an early hotel owner, in a former saloon building. In 1909 a benefactress, Alice Waggaman, an investor in The Sinepuxent Beach Company, donated a lot on the corner of Baltimore Avenue and North Division Street to the congregation. With fund-raising efforts, such as the sale of flowers and homemade candy on the Boardwalk, a church was built at a cost of $1,000. It then officially became the First Presbyterian Church. Its first elders are members of families that are represented in its active membership today, but the church itself is at a new location farther uptown.

St. Mary's Star of the Sea Catholic Church, built in 1878, was among the first buildings and the first church in the newly established town. According to the Church history, it was built by Bishop Thomas A. Becker of the See of Wilmington, who spent the summer months in Ocean City and had all the priests of the Diocese there once a season for a spiritual retreat.

The only Catholics in the resort then were vacationers. As the year-round population grew, so did the Church. Today there are three Catholic churches, but the initial one is still active on Baltimore Avenue in the old downtown.

In 1898 St. Rose's Summer Home for Orphans was built in Ocean City by the Sisters of Charity of Washington, D.C. Thirteen years later, in 1911, the double-square, brown-shingled building at 14th Street and Baltimore Avenue was bought by the Dominican Fathers of Catholic University as a summer home for students preparing for the priesthood.

To the people of the town it was known simply as "the Home." It figures heavily in the memories of those who grew up in Ocean City or nearby because it was "up the beach" and identified the area where young people congregated on summer evenings around campfires.

In the 1950s "the Home" became two separate hotels, the Broadripple and the LaGrande, set apart in a still sparsely developed, sandy block. One of the buildings remains in the heart of the downtown today behind the Beach Plaza Hotel. It was bought by the Brice Phillips family, owners of the famed Phillips Crab House and other restaurants in Ocean City as well as in Baltimore, Washington, and Norfolk. The building has been restored to house some of the scores of young people who work in the Phillips restaurants in the summer, a young work force that outnumbers the entire population in the early days of "the Home."

Since Ocean City from the start has been a kind of communal business for people who live there and a place of escape for the people who visit, it is easy to overlook the mundane, everyday life it shares with every other small town. Its children, for instance, must go to school.

The men who had the means and the spirit to gamble on the railroad and the first real estate ventures that created Ocean City, had probably received their early education in an academy in Snow Hill or Berlin and then been sent away to college. These early academies were supported by civic-minded and prosperous local trustees, private tuition payments, and state allocations.

The nation was in the midst of the Civil War when Maryland rewrote her constitution, including in it provisions that were to be the foundation of the present system of public education (except for the segregated schools for blacks). Three academies in the county then agreed to transfer their property to the public school board.

The free schools were a great addition to community life. At the turn of the century, Worcester County had about forty-five one-room schools and six high schools.

Dr. Reginald Truitt, a renowned biologist who was reared in the Worcester County village of Box Iron recalls that the typical school of this period had a blazing red wood burner that often smelled from having been blackened by the teacher. Students in the early schools drank from a common dipper at a pump primed by volunteers.

"Teachers were strictly warned against smoking, drinking, visiting pool halls or similar places of low entertainment," Dr. Truitt wrote in his remembrances of this era. Teachers then were paid by term rather than by month. "A teacher was expected to save a portion of each paycheck to provide for the declining years which lay ahead. One who demonstrated a lack of thrift and threatened one day to become a burden to society, lost the respect of the community and perhaps a job." To keep Worcester County teachers abreast of educational change, Teachers' Institutes were held in September, generally at Ocean City's Atlantic Hotel, Dr. Truitt recalled.

The late Elizabeth Gordy, one of the third generation of the Showell family to live in Ocean City, had among the family mementos the 1901 report card of a relative attending the Ocean City School. It is signed by the teacher, Minnie K. Hearne (later to be Minnie Jones), who also ran a summer hotel on the Boardwalk (the Belmont-Hearne, a hotel still run today by her granddaughter, Kate Bunting). The subjects included, along with the expected spelling, history, and geography, offerings such as algebra, Latin, and word analysis. The student was graded according to a percentage scale signifying "perfect," "good," "tolerable," and "nothing."

The facilities do not appear to have been as advanced as the course offerings. The first public school available to children of the early resort was a wooden, shedlike building on the mainland in West Ocean City. Children had to walk across the railroad bridge to get there. The same building today is used as a corn crib on a nearby farm.

Sometime around the turn of the century, a public elementary school was built on the island. An early photograph shows it to be a building very like countless rural farmhouses of the period—wooden frame, two-story, with a roofed porch across the front and a sharp-pitched gable centered above it. The school had no indoor plumbing. It was fortunate that the town was then only a few blocks long and even fewer wide, because the children had to go home to use the necessary facilities. Drinking water came from an outdoor pump next door.

Although exposed to winds and storms sweeping across the sandy reef, the building remains today as the Bamboo Apartments at 3rd Street and Philadelphia Avenue.

Irma Jester taught at both the West Ocean City school and the one in the Bamboo building. She remembers how the stairs in the Bamboo shook when the wind was blowing and how parents came to get their children when a storm was coming.

Besides being the teacher, she was also the janitor, nurse, doctor, treater of toothaches, and upholder of cleanliness. She remembers answering an ad once and getting fifty cakes of Lifebuoy soap for the washing of hands at bucket or pump. She was later moved to an older, seventh grade class in the building that is now the Ocean City Hall.

As a teacher Irma Jester has traveled a long road in a single lifetime. She taught school in Worcester County for forty-six years, progressing from the one-room West Ocean City school, to the schools in the Bamboo and City Hall buildings, to Buckingham High School in Berlin and the new consolidated Stephen Decatur High School serving Berlin and Ocean City.

The City Hall building, which housed the town's first high school, began as quite another project. It was built in 1915 by the State Department of Education as a training facility for teachers and a summertime headquarters for the state department. This was ten years before the Maryland State Normal School (now Salisbury State University) was established in Salisbury. The only teacher training available in Maryland then was at Towson State, which was a lot farther away from the Eastern Shore than it seems today.

The State Department's facility in Ocean City did not work out, and after only two years it was sold to Worcester County to house the first Ocean City High School as well as, later on, the elementary grades.

Years later, in 1968 after first consolidation and then integration changed the whole Worcester County school system, the school building, with its distinctive dome, was sold to Ocean City by Worcester County for $90,000. Renovated, added to, and landscaped, it has served the town ever since as the Ocean City Hall.

The building, like most of the town officials who have occupied it, has its roots in the life of a small town, but in recent years has seen issues and controversies of a magnitude equal to those of any big city.

It was 1920 when Ocean City built its first firehouse. "It was a big community project for then. You'd have thought we were building the Waldorf Astoria," Mrs. Levin Bunting, one of the town's premier oral historians, has recalled.

When The Sinepuxent Beach Company of Baltimore and Washington began peddling lots in Ocean City in 1891, it promised, among other services to its development, fire protection in the form of two hand-drawn hose wagons. But there was no organized fire company.

The resort's first volunteer fire company was organized in 1905. Captain William B. S. Powell, the initiator of many a project in the young Ocean City, was president. The company met at various locations and rented space for its equipment before the undertaking of the big building project Mrs. Bunting described.

There were community dances, plays, and suppers to raise money for the company's new headquarters on Dorchester Street. The site of the original firehouse is where the Ocean City Police Department now is.

The company today has five stations and is headquartered at 15th Street. It is one of the biggest and best-equipped volunteer companies in the state. It has to be—not only must it respond to fire, but be prepared for shipwrecks, hurricanes, and floods.

Captain Powell, the fire department's first president, keeps cropping up in memories of the early resort in first one role, then another. His grandfather, mentioned in an earlier chapter, was Isaac Coffin, Worcester County landowner and builder of the Rhode Island Inn, the earliest hostelry to be built on the barren barrier island which became Ocean City. Captain Powell was one of the resort's early mayors, serving for four years, from 1912 to 1916. Before that, from 1902 to 1909, he was keeper of the Green Run Life-Saving Station on Assateague Island. The Green Run Station was one of the first to be established along the coast by the U.S. Life-Saving Service to aid seamen and ships in distress.

The men who manned the stations were forerunners of today's Coast Guardsmen. The keeper, known as the "Captain," was the officer in charge of a crew of "surfmen," who patrolled the beach on foot or on horseback and kept a "watch" in the tower of each station. Rescues made by open dory launched through the surf are the subject of many tales of heroism and stamina during the forty years (1875 to 1915) of the Service's existence. More of this story will be told in a chapter to come.

Captain Powell was also keeper of another station at North Beach on Assateague from 1909 to 1911. In a photograph taken on the porch of the Belmont Hotel sometime early in this century, he stands on the edge of a family group looking as detached and inscrutable as Charles Bronson in his stiff black suit with his big drooping mustache. Captain Powell was a man who seemed to sense a great destiny for Ocean City and invested a lot of energy and money to help push it along. He is remembered as owning more property than he could keep track of, both north of town and to the south on what is now the separate island of Assateague. He grazed beef cattle on Assateague and bred a tough and hardy Brahman bull to withstand the rigors of island survival.

A pictorial history of Ocean City compiled in 1979 by George and Suzanne Hurley contains a double-spread photograph of a beach scene in the days when men wore flat-billed caps and young boys wore knickers and knee socks. The youngsters on the beach are riding ponies that they rented for 10 cents a half hour from Captain William B. S. Powell and Joe Hickmont.

In a series of memory pieces written for a local newspaper, the late Edgar Gaskins, an Ocean City builder who cherished the town's history and heritage, tells of the prize fights that were part of town life in the early 1930s. They were promoted by Captain Powell and held under floodlights in the open-air arena he built at South 1st Street and Baltimore Avenue. The arena was enclosed by a high board fence and had wooden bleachers. Spectators paid a dollar admission fee for the Saturday-evening bouts. It was a popular attraction and the crowds were big.

Most of the young boxers were from the Eastern Shore and Mr. Gaskins recalled such names as Russell Dennis of Salisbury and the Crawford brothers from Cordova near Easton. The boxing came to an end when the storm of 1933 washed over the arena and wiped it out forever.

For some long-time residents of this town, a vivid memory of those prize fights is one of the most ardent fans—the late Harry W. Kelley, who, as a young boy, would climb down into the ring to spar with the boxers. Harry Kelley was later to be equally combative as one of Ocean City's most popular and widely known mayors and is the subject of an entire chapter to come.

WILLIAM PRESTON LAWS AND THE CHAMBER OF COMMERCE

William Preston Laws was ninety-seven years old when he died at Peninsula General Hospital Medical Center in Salisbury on January 4, 1990. His death lighted a flare of reminiscence about the old downtown. For those who knew it well, he was as much a part of it as a familiar landmark.

On several of the most significant occasions of his life he was extolled by the local press as a segment of Ocean City history. One such occasion was in 1971, when he retired from business. For fifty-two years W. P. Laws Meats and Groceries had supplied most of the hotels and rooming houses in the old town. For many of those years, his was the only butcher shop in town. If he had no other distinction at all, and he did, a major one would be that from the time he took over the store in 1919 until his retirement, he was in it regularly every weekday from 6:00 A.M. to late in the evening.

The women who ran their own kitchens in the early hotels bought their meat from Mr. Laws. He cut it to order, trimming off the fat, and supplied home-dressed chickens from local farms along with true Eastern Shore delicacies such as muskrats in season.

In the early days he had a two-wheeled pushcart for deliveries. The paved road went only as far as 3rd Street, and he had to push his cart through the sand to destinations farther up the beach, such as the Dominican Home at 13th Street.

The Laws market was more than a place of business. It was a gathering place for cronies. Local merchants, hotel men, customers, and non-customers passed the time of day around the big, black iron pot-bellied coal stove and planned projects for the town such as the Chamber of Commerce, which was organized in 1950.

The Chamber, which has thrived ever since, was not the first such organization to have emerged from the gatherings in Mr. Laws's store. It was just the first to succeed. Before that at least three groups, variously named, had organized and disbanded. The first was in the early 1920s, back when there were only about eight buildings north of 4th Street.

The presidents of that early group were principal players in the resort's early history: Dr. C. W. Purnell, who bought the Atlantic Hotel in 1923; Captain W. I. Purnell, commander of the U. S. Coast Guard station; and Robert Lee Cropper, who had a hardware business down near the fishing camps. Other participants were Ralph Dennis, principal of the Ocean City High School and a founder of the volunteer fire company, and Frank Truitt, cashier at the Bank of Ocean City which had been formed in 1916.

Mr. Laws once gave a reporter a succinct explanation of the demise of that early group: "They all got mad at one another," he said. The anger was probably the result of a common practice of the early hotels: the proprietors would send porters to meet the trains and compete with each other to take passengers and their baggage to their hotels, whether they had originally planned to stay there or not. This did not produce goodwill among hotel owners. The local businessmen would hash things out around the stove in Mr. Laws's store on winter days when things were slow.

It was around this stove that Ocean City's long-surviving Easter Celebration and Parade was born in the early 1940s. The first sunrise services were on the Boardwalk at Somerset Street in front of Dr. Francis Townsend's drugstore. A bandstand was built on the beach there, and the programs became better every year, largely because of the band organized and directed by Frank Sacca.

Mr. Sacca owned a restaurant on Baltimore Street across from the Bank of Ocean City. His was one of the first Catholic families in Ocean City, and they were active in the development of St. Mary's Star of the Sea Catholic Church. Mr. Sacca was at one time or another a member of the town council and president of the volunteer fire company. But, most memorably, he was a musician. He play the violin, cello, saxophone, and clarinet. He gave music lessons, and the band he organized was an important part of community life, playing in firemen's parades and on summer evenings in the bandstand as well as for the Easter programs.

The bandshell is now gone, but the Easter program is a tradition, and Mr. Laws had the informal local title of "Mr. Easter."

In 1974 he was recognized as one of the town's major resources in assembling its history and planning the big 1975 celebration of its centennial. Mayor Harry W. Kelley appointed him honorary member of the Centennial Commission in charge of arranging a visit by President Ford.

The Ocean City bandstand, circa 1920. (Courtesy Ocean City Life-Saving Station Museum.)

The Ford visit did not work out, but it was widely believed that if anyone could make it happen, Mr. Laws could. This belief was founded on one of the high points in his life, the time he went to the White House and chatted about Ocean City with President Franklin D. Roosevelt.

He and a group of friends had arranged the meeting to present the president with a mounted sailfish caught off the coast from the Ocean City fishing harbor. Included in the group were John B. Lynch, owner of the Commander Hotel; James D. Jarmon, of the Rideau Hotel; Captain Crawford Savage, owner of The Majestic Hotel; Captain Talbot Bunting, and Mr. Laws. These men hoped to draw the eyes of the nation to their developing resort by getting Mr. Roosevelt to come to Ocean City for the fishing. Years later, Mr. Laws could describe the visit in detail, how they entered the president's office feeling like a bunch of country boys, how the others simply shook hands, and how he lingered behind for about ten minutes to talk.

He said that he suggested to the amiable Mr. Roosevelt that he come down for the marlin fishing, but the president said his boat drew 14 feet of water and could not get through the Inlet. Later on, however, Mr. Roosevelt did come to Ocean City to fish in a charter boat off the coast, and caught a white marlin.

Today's thriving Ocean City Chamber of Commerce, which took shape in Mr. Laws's store in 1950, began with a membership of 200 local businessmen. William I. Donohoe, then owner of the Plimhimmon Hotel, was the first president. Mr. Laws later served as president, in 1958 and 1959.

In 1981 Mr. Laws was named Ocean City's Outstanding Citizen of the Year at a big banquet at the Sheraton Fountainebleau. He was cited as a person who was always honest and hardworking, tireless in his efforts to promote Ocean City, and compassionate about less fortunate people. Residents remembered that during the Depression years he had freely extended credit to customers who could not, and sometimes never did, pay.

Besides the Chamber of Commerce and the Easter programs, he had, through the years, been involved in one way or another with projects from the first paving of Baltimore Avenue and the town's first post office, to getting the state to build Ocean City Convention Hall and, more recently establishing the Ocean City Life-Saving Station Museum at the south end of the Boardwalk. He was an elder of the First Presbyterian Church and a member of the Ocean City Council, serving two terms as its president.

Mr. Laws was born in Salisbury, about thirty miles away. As a youth, he learned the butchering trade there in a small shop on Dock Street (now Market Street). When World War I came, he enlisted as a butcher and was sent to France to cut meat for the Allied troops. He worked his trade near the battleground of Cherbourg, so close "you could hear the guns."

Back home, he went to work for John B. Lynch in the meat and grocery store on Baltimore Avenue. He soon bought into the store, and both he and it became an integral part of just about everybody's memories of the old downtown.

The block of buildings where his store flourished was the old town's center of business. It housed the Bank of Ocean City, the gas company, telephone company, power company, a restaurant, and a clothing shop. The building is still there, with its upstairs porches forming an arcade over the sidewalk, but the businesses occupying the space are quite different now.

Through the years, as one of the constants of Ocean City behind the counter of his store, Mr. Laws was backed up by his wife, Catherine Petitt Laws, a native of the nearby town of Snow Hill. Besides filling in behind the counter, she taught for many years in the Ocean City School at 3rd Street in the building which later became, and remains today, the Ocean City Hall.

Comparing the days when much of the resort's business was hashed out around the old stove in the Laws store and today's Chamber of Commerce, Mrs. Laws once told a reporter, "They were more outspoken back in those days. Now, in their meetings, they're more tactful, but they mean the same things."

DOCTOR FOR ALL SEASONS

From 1900 to 1945, Dr. Francis J. Townsend was Ocean City's doctor, dentist (he pulled teeth only), pharmacist, veterinarian (he once sewed up a horse that had been hit by a car), city councilman, interim mayor, and enterprising businessman. A mark of his place in the resort's life was the extraordinary gesture made by the town when he died in the summer of 1945. His funeral was July 4, the absolute heart of the resort season, but all businesses closed that afternoon for three or four hours.

His son, Dr. Francis J. Townsend, Jr., followed his father in profession and place. The lives of the two men are pretty much the history of Ocean City's health care.

The first Dr. Townsend came to Ocean City from Snow Hill on the mainland, a few miles away. He had started out reading law. Then he studied pharmacy and went to medical school in Richmond. After establishing himself in Ocean City, he married Anna Rayne, whose family was as much a part of the old town as Dr. Townsend became. The Rayne family owned the Rayne Hotel, rooming houses, and a soda and sandwich shop.

Dr. Townsend built the Washington Pharmacy at Somerset Street and the Boardwalk, and he and his family lived above it. Francis Townsend, Jr., was born there. A model of the old building is among the exhibits in the Ocean City Life-Saving Station Museum today, but the building itself is gone. The family later had a home on Baltimore Avenue, where most of the town's original families had big, old Victorian houses that are either gone or changed in character today.

Baltimore Avenue was a thoroughfare of sand when Dr. Townsend began his practice. He made better time on house calls by riding his bicycle up the Boardwalk than by driving an automobile on the streets. He sometimes made as many as six house calls between midnight and 8:00 A.M.

Many of his cases involved typhoid fever. Sinepuxent Bay was polluted then by raw sewage that was emptied through open sewers directly into the bay, and the drinking water was questionable. (Whatever today's environmental transgressions may be, at least that era is past.)

The nearest hospital then, as now, was Peninsula General Hospital in Salisbury. The only practical way to get a patient there was by railroad, but for a while the only train left at 6:30 A.M.—a poor schedule for emergency cases.

In 1939, Lloyd U. Watson, the Salisbury benefactor who gave Peninsula General the Watson Memorial Building, gave Dr. Townsend a Pontiac ambulance. Dr. Townsend turned it over to the Ocean City Fire Department, which provided a driver when one was needed for the thirty-mile run to the hospital.

As the town grew, Dr. Townsend built another drugstore and soda shop on the Boardwalk at 6th Street, and one on Baltimore Avenue between Talbot and Caroline streets. The original Washington Pharmacy is the one that figures most vividly in residents' and visitors' memories of the old town.

Francis Townsend, Jr., has an early childhood recollection of the big fire of 1925 that burned the Pier, a section of the Boardwalk, and the Atlantic Hotel. He remembers that Dr. Charles Washington ("Wash") Purnell had just bought the Atlantic when it burned down, and that his father turned over the apartment above the drugstore to the Purnells while it was being rebuilt. Dr. Townsend was instrumental in organizing the Sinepuxent Pier and Improvement Company after the fire to build the new Pier that still exists today.

In the early 1940s, Dr. Townsend built at his own expense the bandstand by the Boardwalk in front of his drugstore where the Easter services were held and where Frank Sacca conducted his band concerts on summer evenings.

Dr. Townsend, Jr., remembers clearly how he helped prepare for the first Easter service, borrowing from churches and hauling to the Boardwalk the chairs, podium, and piano. When the piano was being hauled back to the Presbyterian Church, it keeled over and fell off the truck, exploding into a shower of strings, keys, and kindling.

Building the bandstand was not entirely philanthropic, Dr. Townsend, Jr., recalls. When the crowd dispersed after an event there, a good part of it came into the drugstore's soda fountain.

Another of Dr. Townsend's now-historic and profitable enterprises was ownership of the rolling wicker chairs that were a feature of the early beach scene.

As a boy, the younger Townsend was as enterprising as his father. He sold saltwater taffy on the Boardwalk. He shined shoes. He set up pins in the Pier bowling alley. He sold newspapers for Teddy Lauer, for whom his son was also to sell papers forty years later. He remembers pulling his wagon and yelling out, "*Baltimore Sun*!"

The year he sold fireworks in front of the Washington Pharmacy, he made enough money for his father to encourage his first investment. At the age of twelve he bought a share of AT&T stock. He still has it today, increased into many more shares and still designated as being held "under the guardianship of Frank J. Townsend."

One of his most vivid memories of an Ocean City storm is of one in the 1930s. Dan Trimper, Jr., an uncle of his who owned a pile-driving business as well as Boardwalk amusements, was cutting holes in the floor of the Washington Pharmacy and driving in supportive pilings right in the middle of high winds and rain.

The younger Townsend remembers the first movie he ever saw in the old Casino Theater on the Boardwalk. "There was a lot of dueling in it," he said. And he remembers the whole week's billings at the Capital Theater at the time of the great storm of March 1933. On Monday and Tuesday, the days of the actual storm, the film (with memorable appropriateness), was called *Hell Below.* Wednesday and Thursday, in the immediate aftermath, the new film was *It's Great To Be Alive.* Friday and Saturday, as the town picked up the pieces, the next film was *I Cover the Waterfront.*

Dr. Townsend, Jr., graduated from the University of Maryland School of Medicine and was in the navy in World War II. After a deluge of letters to the navy from the townspeople pleading the need for his services at home, he was discharged in 1946. He returned to take up where his father had left off.

His father, he said, had spent his years in practice getting up at 7:00 A.M. and working till midnight, with house calls often made in the hours between. "I was raised in that tradition and thought that was what you were supposed to do," he said.

Dr. Townsend retired in 1987. Since then he has been deeply involved with a committee of citizens who are trying to raise the local share of the money for a nonprofit $15-million Atlantic General Hospital to be built in the nearby town of Berlin to serve the beach area.

Speaking before local groups for the fund drive, Dr. Townsend can trace with personal memories the history of medical services in Ocean City. There were three full-time doctors in Ocean City at the end of the war. The town has grown a lot faster than its medical services: Today, with a population many times as big, there are only four full-time doctors.

In the 1990s, Ocean City patients are still being taken by ambulance twenty-five or thirty miles to the regional hospital center in Salisbury. Ambulances make the run from Ocean City about 1,200 times a year. They are manned by trained emergency personnel, but for residents and visitors to the resort area they do not represent the security of a hospital close at hand.

Dr. Townsend and his wife Lillian live in a comfortable home in West Ocean City. They have reared four children, two daughters and two sons, one a doctor.

The families of both the doctor and his wife have been entwined with the resort for almost a century and have given stability to the ever-changing scene. The couple remain an island of tradition in a sea of casualness and change. "I still wear a coat and tie when we go out to dinner," Dr. Townsend says, "and I want my wife to look good."

THREE

A Woman's Place

When friends used to tell other friends they were staying at the Plimhimmon, it was said with a certain air. That is the memory one Shore native has of the hotel.

Another native recalls "a spectacular pantomime performance of *Cinderella* staged at the Plimhimmon Casino by the young crowd who spent the summer at the beach. There was always youthful festivity and dancing there."

The Sun ran social items listing guests at the Plimhimmon. An item that appeared in August 1923, for instance, reported that Governor Albert C. Ritchie was spending the weekend there. It continued with a description of a costume ball the same weekend: "with the moon lending luster to the many colored lights and the gorgeous costumes, making a real fairyland scene."

The creator of this memory-making setting was a young woman named Rosalie Tilghman Shreve—just one of a generation of remarkable women in Ocean City. Some of these women were widows and some were the wives of fishermen. It was they who turned the resourcefulness, industry, and organizational abilities required of a wife, mother, and hostess, to the building and management of the resort's first hotels.

ROSALIE SHREVE AND "THE PLIM"

Rosalie Shreve had grown up amid elegance. Her home was Plimhimmon, a Talbot County estate at the edge of Oxford. The name comes from a mountain in Wales, although the spelling was somehow changed from the original "Plinhimmon."

Her father was General Tench Tilghman, grandson of Colonel Tench Tilghman, who had been Washington's aide-de-camp in the Revolutionary War. General Tilghman seems to have spent his life living up to his descent from an American hero. Today he is a central figure in the assiduously preserved heritage of Oxford.

In his youth he went to Dickinson College in Carlisle, Pennsylvania, and to the U.S. Military Academy at West Point, before taking over the management of the family's extensive land holdings on the Eastern Shore. An innovator in agriculture and in business, he spent much of his private fortune on projects for the enhancement of the community, and thereby lost much of it. The biggest and most costly of these projects was a branch from the Delaware Railroad into Talbot County, ending at Oxford.

He was for many years president of the Maryland & Delaware Railroad Company. Ground was broken for the long-dreamed-of branch line in December 1856, but construction was delayed by another event which cost him dearly, the Civil War.

General Tilghman was a Southern sympathizer. His sons fought for the Confederacy. With the loss of the traditional slave labor at Plimhimmon, the family, in the description of a local diarist of the day, was "in possession of large property, large debts, large pride, large wants . . . . The young ladies [Tilghman's daughters]. . . milked the cows while their father the General held the umbrella over them to keep off the rain."

In spite of all his troubles, the determined General Tilghman continued with the building of the Maryland & Delaware Railroad. It was completed in 1869, with a terminus in Oxford, but only after General Tilghman's railroad company was forced into bankruptcy and taken over by another.

Meanwhile, events elsewhere were shaping the nation's destiny, and were about to converge with the personal destiny of Rosalie Tilghman, the general's daughter.

Late in the Civil War, a young student, Thomas Jefferson Shreve, left the University of Virginia to join the Confederate army. He was captured in Leesburg when trying to cut some horses off a Union Army picket line, and was sent to the prison at Fort Delaware on Peapatch Island south of Wilmington.

The fort is now a national park. "I have been there and seen where he was imprisoned below the water line. It was pretty awful," said L. G. (Bill) Shreve, a grandson now living in Baltimore.

The young prisoner became ill, and with the death rate from tuberculosis already high, he was released on his written word that he would not go south of the Potomac River before the end of the war.

He made his way down the Eastern Shore as far as Talbot County and got a job on the Maryland & Delaware Railroad, which General Tilghman was determinedly building. There he met the general's seventeen year-old daughter, Rosalie.

The two were married and moved into a house in Oxford known then and now as the Grapevine House. It was a historic house even then, built in 1780 and named for the large grapevine that had been brought from the Isle of Jersey and planted in the front yard.

The war ended. Thomas and Rosalie had two sons. But their well-being was short-lived. Thomas Jefferson Shreve died in 1867 of an unspecified illness, probably tuberculosis, which had begun in the Union prison.

Rosalie was barely twenty when she became a widow with two sons to rear. Her father died seven years later, a man saddened by the war and failed business ventures.

The young widow moved to Baltimore. Rosalie bought a place on Madison Street immediately behind the old University Club, and ran it as a boardinghouse. "She was very tenacious. She had these kids to raise, so she had to do something," recounts Bill Shreve, her admiring grandson.

Ocean City was just beginning to develop. With an instinct for its possibilities, she went there in the early 1890s, rented the Goldsborough Cottage, and opened a summertime boardinghouse. It was so successful that in 1893 she built the Plimhimmon Hotel.

She must have borrowed the money, Mr. Shreve surmises. From some point in his childhood, he remembers the figure $9,000 as the cost of that first hotel building. When it was first built, the hotel was just a long, narrow, three-story building without any of its later appurtenances, but it did have the distinctive tower that is retained on the Plimhimmon Hotel today.

Bill Shreve is retired from a long career, first as a colonel in the Pacific theater in World War II, then in the CIA. He and his wife, Barbara, have returned to their native Baltimore and live in a town house in Cross Keys.

Their town house is full of beautiful antiques from Plimhimmon, the old family estate at Oxford. The furnishings from Plimhimmon have been divided ten or twelve different ways, he said. The number and quality of the pieces in his share of the division are a vivid reminder of the opulence that surrounded Rosalie Tilghman Shreve in her girlhood.

It was from this background that she created what was described in the social pages of *The Sun* as the "homey elegance" of the Plimhimmon Hotel. The hotel guests came from Washington, Philadelphia, Annapolis, and, most of all, Baltimore. "It was a success immediately," Bill Shreve said. He attributed its success to "one solid reason—the food. The food was always unbelievable."

The story behind the Plimhimmon's legendary food begins with a trip Rosalie Shreve made to the market in Baltimore one morning. She asked a young black boy who was hanging around the market if he would like to make a few cents and carry her grocery bags back to Madison Street, where she lived.

The association that began with that encounter lasted for a lifetime. The name of the young boy was Robert Downs. He went to Ocean City with Mrs. Shreve and served as the chef at the Plimhimmon for over forty years. In the wintertime, when the hotel closed and the Shreve family went back to Baltimore, he became the chef in the cafeteria at the Savings Bank of Baltimore, now called the Bank of Baltimore.

At the depth of the Depression, in 1932, a vacationer could have a single room at the Plimhimmon, with a bathroom at the end of the hall, and three meals a day, for $18 a week.

Bill Shreve remembers the menus with awe. For breakfast a guest was offered a full choice of juices, fresh melons from nearby Eastern Shore farms, any kind of cold or hot cereal, eggs in any form, bacon, kidney stew, sometimes lamb chops, toast, jam, tea or coffee. For dinner there would be a choice of several soups, chicken, fish, lamb or beef, fresh farm vegetables such as squash, string beans, and corn, fresh baked bread, and dessert.

He remembers that the baker's name was Fike, and that in the wintertime he baked at the old Tome School at Port Deposit.

Vendors used to come to the hotel bringing all the chickens, turkeys, guinea hens, and fresh vegetables. His mother never went anywhere to buy anything except to go down to the W. P. Laws market on Baltimore Avenue to pick out her meat.

When she first built the Plimhimmon, the resourceful Rosalie Shreve included a system to generate her own electricity. A steam engine ran the generator, and when it let off steam every morning at about ten o'clock, some neighbors were not very happy. However, the system supplied not only the Plimhimmon's electricity, but generated enough to sell to a neighboring hotel and several cottages.

In 1913 Mrs. Shreve built the Rose Cottage behind the hotel on the west side of Baltimore Avenue, where she stayed with her family and where friends visited. Later she build an Annex to "the Plim" and the Plimhimmon Casino. The Casino was a center for much of the young resort's social life, providing an orchestra for nightly dancing, dance classes, and matinee dancing.

At her death in 1924, Rosalie Shreve left Rose Cottage to the Diocese of Easton as a vacation house for the Episcopal clergy. Her gift of choir stalls to St. Paul's By-the-Sea is still in use.

Rosalie Tilghman Shreve was probably the only early hotel owner who did not actually live in Ocean City. She and her family lived in Baltimore; they opened the hotel about June 10 and closed it the week of Labor Day. Bill Shreve remembers that every window had a custom-made, tongue-in-grove board stored under the dining room. Each board had a number and was put over the matching window for the winter.

Mrs. Shreve is directly responsible for many of the earliest and most pleasant recollections of Ocean City in the memories of family members in her own generation through to her grandchildren's.

After her death, the hotel was run by her family until 1941, when it was sold. It was destroyed by fire in 1962, but was rebuilt to look as much as possible like the original.

Its present owner, the Harrison Group, will be another story belonging to both the old and the new Ocean City.

JOSEPHINE RICHARDSON HASTINGS, PIONEER WOMAN

The remarkable women who built and ran most of Ocean City's hotels in the early years of this century are known today only by shreds of memory from long-gone years. Memories are tricky, shaded as they are by dozens of circumstances. But perhaps the way we seem to others is, in the end, as much a reality as what we do and feel from day to day. In any event, it is our only reality when it comes to people we have never known. The women who have come to be known as Ocean City's "pioneer women" were too busy in their kitchens to be concerned with posterity.

One of these women who is remembered with perhaps the greatest awe is Josephine Richardson Hastings, wife of Kendall C. Hastings, a carpenter of whom little has been passed on, and mother of six children. She is said to have started her highly successful business career by keeping a cow in her backyard and selling milk for 5 cents a quart.

Her home was in the heart of the old downtown on Baltimore Avenue between North Division Street and 1st Street. Recognizing the opportunity offered by that location, then the most desirable in town, she converted it into a boardinghouse. She then acquired the cottages on each side of her house and incorporated them into one building which she called the New Avalon. It was later to be known as, and remains today, the Del-Mar-Va Hotel.

Mrs. Hastings sold the Avalon in 1916 and built a new hotel on the Boardwalk, the Hastings. Like the other hotels of that era, it looked like a rambling Victorian home with porches and railings across two levels and a raised wooden walkway from the downstairs porch to the elevated Boardwalk. (It was torn down in 1975 to make way for shops and downtown parking space.) Behind it she built a comfortable home known as The Hastings Annex.

After running The Hastings for about six years, Mrs. Hastings sold it, and the Annex, to Willye Jones Conner, a recently widowed mother of three. (Shortly after that, Mrs. Conner married one of Ocean City's leading commercial fishermen and became Mrs. Charles Ludlam.)

Mrs. Hastings then built The Shoreham on the Boardwalk at 4th Street and another house behind that on Baltimore Avenue. The Shoreham was similar to The Hastings in style but considerably bigger. It is still in business today. Mrs. Hastings later built two guest houses on Baltimore Avenue.

All of these hotels, in the tradition of the period, operated with the American plan, serving three meals a day to the guests.

In 1926 her final achievement was to build The Mayflower Hotel at 12th Street and the Boardwalk. It was one of the biggest and best hotels in Ocean City, a big brown-shingled, three-story structure in a double-L shape with two sections connected by a small mid-section. Rows of rocking chairs graced its porches. (The Mayflower was torn down in 1988 to make way for new and modern construction.)

At the time of her death a few years after The Mayflower was completed, Mrs. Hastings had become one of the biggest and most successful property owners in the resort.

What is so remarkable about this story is that Josephine Hastings could neither read nor write.

"She was smart," said Hilda Savage, an old friend whose family owned The Majestic, another hotel. "I've seen her sit down with her bean pot and drop one bean in a jar for each ton of coal as it was delivered. She was all business. In the summer she did nothing but work, and she made her children do the same."

"Remarkable, yes," said Kate Bunting, one of Ocean City's present-day hotel-keeping women, of Mrs. Hastings's unlettered business achievements. "But remember, income tax was not so complicated then and there were no social security records to be kept until 1935."

That, of course, is a good point, but the handling of financing, construction, quantity food purchasing, and hotel and restaurant staffs would seem a bit of a challenge to the most highly literate, let alone a woman who signed her name with an "X."

ELLA DENNIS, OLDEST CONTINUOUS HOTEL OWNER

Ella Dennis achieved a kind of immortality with her oft-repeated statement made at the age of eighty-six: "Ocean City is 70 percent built by women and run by women—and the men are all henpecked."

By that time Mrs. Dennis had owned and operated the Dennis Hotel on Baltimore Avenue for fifty-six years. Three years before, she had been honored as Ocean City's oldest continuous hotel owner with a citation presented by Governor Herbert O'Connor, a frequent resort visitor, and Mayor Daniel Trimper, Jr. She continued to operate the Dennis Hotel until her death in 1952 at the age of ninety-one.

She and her husband, Reverly, moved to Ocean City in 1890, presumably because of her poor health. Ocean City was then being promoted by The Sinepuxent Beach Company as a place where proximity to the Gulf Stream assured mild winters beneficial to anyone with a respiratory weakness.

Mrs. Dennis's health did not seem to be a problem in the years that followed. In 1892 she and husband built the downtown hotel, which she ran while he operated a store and soda shop in the same four-story wooden frame building. The establishment faced Baltimore Avenue at the corner of Dorchester Street and had the old resort's characteristic porches and railings across three levels in front.

Besides being one of the first women to build a hotel, Ella Dennis is recognized as one of the founders of the First Presbyterian Church in Ocean City, initiating its early meetings in a former saloon.

The Dennises had six children. A daughter, Savannah Carey, owned and operated the Del-Mar Hotel on North Division Street, until her death in 1955.

The old Dennis Hotel was bought and torn down by the city in the 1960s to make way for downtown parking space.

JOSEPHINE LEWIS MASSEY AND THE HAMILTON

In a booklet published in Ocean City's centennial year, 1975, Florence Massey Black wrote a chapter called "Pioneer Women" in which she divided "these women who built Ocean City" into three categories: "(1) widows with children to support; (2) women with husbands in business, such as commercial fishing, merchants, watermen, etc.; and (3) women with inadequate husbands; drunkards, lazy men, or business failures." She puts her grandfather, the husband of Josephine Lewis Massey, in the too-much-of-a-gentleman-to-work category.

Mrs. Massey came to Ocean City about 1890 with her husband, James, and her son, J. Alan. Their family roots were in the mid-Shore town of Greensboro in Caroline County.

During their first ten years in Ocean City, the Masseys rented and operated boardinghouses in first one and then another of the existing places—The Mt. Vernon, the Gables, and the Tarry-A-While. "The responsibility of these undertakings rested solely upon Mrs. Massey," Mrs. Black wrote. "Her son was too young, and her husband was too much of a 'gentleman,' too highly educated, and too fond of liquid refreshment to work."

In 1901 Mrs. Massey acted on an opportunity to buy a partially built hotel at the Boardwalk and 3rd Street. It became The Hamilton, a hotel at the center of the resort's summertime social life along with the Atlantic and the Plimhimmon.

Josephine Massey built a cottage on the north side of the hotel, where the family lived. Each year she enlarged The Hamilton, adding rooms, baths, a laundry, a garage, and two more cottages behind it. All the while, until 1905, she operated another boarding establishment in the winters in a forty-four-room house called the Marlboro at Eutaw and Wilson Place in Baltimore.

The Hamilton, like other early hotels on the Boardwalk, was known for its food. This was the era when dinner was served in the middle of the day, from 1:00 to 2:30 P.M., and was what lifetime memories were made of. At her hotel Mrs. Massey presided over a dining room that offered a soup course, four or five meats including fish and crab, four or more fresh vegetables, homemade rolls, and on Sundays, The Hamilton's special, chicken and waffles. An orchestra played at both the midday and evening meals.

The Hamilton became the favored vacation address of some of Maryland's leading political and social figures.

In an old photograph with none of the make-up or poses that enhance women in today's portrait photography, Mrs. Massey looks very attractive. The picture reflects none of the stress that might be expected of a woman who was independent and resourceful enough to build and run a resort hotel.

Mrs. Black remembers that her grandfather had been to college and studied agriculture, medicine, and law, and that he knew a lot and read to her when she was a little girl, but that her grandmother ran the hotel virtually alone. Mrs. Massey had the help of her son and daughter-in-law at the time of her death in 1924. The family sold the hotel five years later to new owners from nearby Berlin.

The Hamilton was a popular hotel until fairly recent years. It burned down in December 1969 in a fire of unknown origin. In its place is a Boardwalk condominium.

ETHEL GRIFFIN KELLEY AND THE ROYALTON

During the fifteen years that Harry W. Kelley was mayor of Ocean City, from 1970 until his death in 1985, a portrait of his mother, Ethel Griffin Kelley, hung behind his desk and dominated his office in City Hall.

Mrs. Kelley was owner and operator, with her son, first of The Royalton and then the Beach Plaza Hotel, and the food from her kitchens was famed from Ocean City to Annapolis to Baltimore. But the good-looking woman gazing steadily from the portrait was as popular for her hospitality and good company as for her cooking.

She was usually in her hotel kitchen by 6:30 A.M. and was often still there at 10:00 P.M. Her hospitality included the children of the town as well as hotel guests. One of the most vivid memories of childhood for some townspeople today is of sticky buns and milk in Mrs. Kelley's kitchen. The late Harriet Showell Bald, who spent her girlhood summers a few blocks away, remembered with special clarity that Mrs. Kelley always made her birthday cakes.

Ethel Kelley's husband, Harry served in the U.S. Coast Guard at the nearby Isle of Wight station.

In 1925 the Kelleys bought a lot on the Boardwalk at 11th Street for $1,800. In partnership with Minnie Lynch, a recent widow, and her son, John B. Lynch, they built a thirty-six room hotel called The Royalton. A few years later, the Lynches sold their share to the Kelleys and built The Commander three blocks away at 14th Street.

In the late 1930s, the Kelleys enlarged The Royalton to eighty rooms, more than double its original size. It had wide porches and white porch railings on two levels across the front and down the street side, and was one of the better addresses for Ocean City vacationers.

Today it is barely recognizable with gaudily advertised commercial establishments on its ground level, a transformation that has taken place on others of the once-venerable Boardwalk hotels.

In 1953 the hotel was so successful that the Kelleys built the Beach Plaza, two blocks away. This hotel continues to be one of the best on the Boardwalk and is now owned by the Brice Phillips family, owners of the famed Phillips seafood restaurants.

Two years after the Beach Plaza opened, Ethel Kelley was fatally injured in an automobile accident while returning from a three-week vacation in Florida. She was fifty-seven. Harry W. Kelley, Jr., her only child, then a city councilman, rushed to the scene and was with her when she died in Waterboro, South Carolina.

Ethel Kelley's obituary in a local newspaper made note of her active community life as a member of the Ocean City Woman's Club and the Methodist Church as well as her ownership and operation of two hotels. Then, in the midst of the somber paragraphs, was what must have been a special memory of the obituary writer: "She became famous for her fine food," it read, "especially her pies, cakes, and rum buns."

SUSIE AMANDA ROUNDS AND THE MAJESTIC

Susie Amanda Rounds and her husband, George William, came to Ocean City toward the end of the last century, when there were only four hotels and a smattering of cottages.

George Rounds was a farmer who owned some land in Pittsville, about twenty-five miles away, but to make ends meet he also did some lumbering and some fishing. His wife was from the Virginia Eastern Shore, and he had met her while working in a tract of timber there.

The young couple had two daughters. When wresting a living from the land became increasingly hard, they moved to Ocean City, where Mr. Rounds worked in the summer in the early pound net fishery. Another daughter was born there.

One of the daughters, Hilda Savage, now age eighty-seven, was a very little girl at the time of the move, but she remembers that there was no insulation in their first home on Baltimore Street and that it was very cold there. But there were extra rooms, and her mother offered them for rent to summer vacationers.

Her father then built his family a house on Talbot Street, and her mother continued to take in boarders. She remembers that "a lot of doctors" vacationed in the early Ocean City and took rooms in the homes there.

"My mother took in boarders all her life," Hilda Savage said. Boarders were so much a part of the family life that when she was once identifying the people in a family picture and referred to one offhandedly as "a boarder," the puzzled friend thought that Boarder was a family name.

Sometime around 1920, the nearby Avondale Hotel on the corner of Talbot Street and Baltimore Avenue went up for sale. Mr. and Mrs. Rounds bought it and went from the boardinghouse business into the hotel business.

The Avondale was typical of early Ocean City, a four-story Victorian structure with gabled roof and wide railed porches on three levels. It no longer exists today.

An early photograph of Mrs. Rounds shows a demure young woman with delicate features, long hair flowing around her shoulders, head tilted forward toward the rose she is holding in her hand. She does not look like a hotel proprietor.

In 1926, Mr. and Mrs. Rounds sold the Avondale and bought the New Avalon Hotel on Baltimore Avenue, which had originally been three houses converted into a hotel by Josephine Hastings. They renamed it the Del-Mar-Va Hotel. Although it is still in business today, it is no longer in the Rounds family.

In 1945, three years after her husband's death, Mrs. Rounds bought a Boardwalk hotel originally called Liberty Farms Hotel but renamed The Majestic. Located on the Boardwalk at 7th Street, it is a five-story, fifty-five-room hotel with wicker rocking chairs on the front porch. Rocking on the porch at The Majestic is a tradition cherished by the summer guests who return to the hotel regularly.

After Mrs. Rounds died in 1955 at the age of seventy-three, the hotel remained in the family and is owned and operated today by a grandson, Bill Savage, his wife, and their son. Hilda Savage is still a very active lady who is on hand to help out when needed.

The American plan, with meals and room a single package, was phased out in 1965. Hilda Savage hated to see it go. Like her mother, she says, "I have always fed people." She recalled the sticky buns that were once a specialty of The Majestic's kitchen and "the best oyster pie you ever had."

Her husband, the late Crawford Savage, operated a grocery store downtown but "despised the business," she said. His first love was fishing, but he did help out in the hotel.

In accounts of the early Ocean City hotels, it is the women who clearly dominate and have been hailed as "pioneers." Some of the men were bossed around, Hilda Savage said. In rebuttal to the famous statement of Ella Dennis about Ocean City's "henpecked men," she added, "But the men did more than they get credit for."

KATE BUNTING AND THE CIRCLE OF CHANGE

Kate Bunting owns and operates the downtown hotel that was built by her great-grandmother in 1905—the Belmont-Hearne, on Dorchester Street. It is one of only two of the old hotels still operating with the

American plan and providing its guests with meals as well as a room. The other is the Commander, a few blocks up the Boardwalk.

Like the other small, wooden frame hotels that remain along the downtown Boardwalk, the Belmont-Hearne Hotel looks like a rambling Victorian house, with porches and porch railings and high steps from the side street. It is as worn and faded and durable as a homespun dress in the attic.

"Ocean City started out with boardinghouses." Mrs. Bunting observes. "Then it went to hotels, and we had 'hotel row' along the Boardwalk from the old Atlantic Hotel north to 4th Street. Then we went to motels, and we had 'motel row' from 15th Street to 33rd Street. Then there were the four-unit and eight-unit apartment houses. Then we went to condominiums—then back to town houses. Now we are getting to the bed-and-breakfast, which is back to the old rooming house again."

Through the whole circle, the Belmont-Hearne has been operated by four generations of women, from its beginnings almost a century ago.

Elizabeth (Lizzie) Harper Hearne and her husband, Dr. Thomas Hearne, moved to Ocean City from nearby Bishopville in 1896. Like Ocean City residents then and now, they had a lot of visitors.

When Dr. Hearne died a few years later, in 1902, Lizzie bought and renovated the Lambert Ayers cottage, renamed it the Belmont, and began taking in summer guests. Over the years she developed a clientele of regular guests who returned summer after summer.

In 1910 Lizzie built a house next door to the Belmont. Her daughter, Minnie, grew up there. (Kate Bunting lives in the house today.) Minnie taught school in Powellville on the mainland and in the Ocean City School.

Minnie married a man as involved with the town as she was—Captain John Burton Jones, who was with the United States Life-Saving Service, later the Coast Guard, and was for a time keeper of the Ocean City station at Caroline Street. For two years, 1916 to 1918, he was mayor of the town. Captain Jones was stationed at one time and another at Elizabeth City and Norfolk, but Minnie would always come back to Ocean City in the summers from wherever they were, to help her mother run the hotel.

Lizzie Hearne died in 1936 at the age of eighty-one and left the Belmont to her daughter. When Minnie Jones took over the hotel, she, like her mother, was a widow; Captain Jones had died in 1932.

During this period, Minnie's son, William Hearne Jones, a metallurgist, had married Dorothy May Brewer of Bethlehem, Pennsylvania, where he was working for Bethlehem Steel Company. Their daughter, Kathryn (Kate Bunting), was born in 1937, the oldest of four children.

"We came down to Ocean City every summer to help grandmother run the hotel," Kate said. Her father was working for the Dominion Steel & Coal Company and the family was living in Nova Scotia when he died in 1954. The family then came back to Ocean City to stay. "I've been here at least part of every year of my life," recalls Kate.

She eventually married Coleman Bunting, who worked for a nearby poultry firm.

In the late 1940s, after World War II, Kate's grandmother bought a property on the Boardwalk called the Laurel House, a summer home that had been turned into apartments. Minnie Jones eventually had it torn down and built the Hearne, part of the old town hotel now known as the Belmont-Hearne. She also bought a lot on the Boardwalk with two stores on it. One of them was rented for many years by a family dealing in fine linens.

The linen shop is fondly recalled by many of the older generation when they speak of the attractions of the old Boardwalk. "The first job I had was working there when I was fourteen," Kate Bunting said. "They had beautiful things. But everything changes. Where do you buy handkerchiefs now?"

The space occupied by the old linen shop is now a fast-food stand called Polock Johnny's. The other space is leased to a gift and variety store called Sunburst Trading Company, Inc.

In 1969, a family corporation consisting of Kate, her brothers and sisters, and her mother bought the Nordica, another old hotel at Talbot Street and the Boardwalk. Then in 1977 Kate bought everything from the corporation. Her daughter, Amy, helps her run the business, carrying the tradition into the fifth generation. Amy is married to Bob Rothermel, executive director of the Ocean City Convention Hall.

A few years ago, Kate Bunting bought the old Mt. Vernon Hotel on Talbot Street and turned it into a restaurant. Her restoration of the Mt. Vernon has been part of a diligent effort to restore some of the old Victorian quality and stability to the downtown side streets, in contrast to the carnival atmosphere at the south end of the Boardwalk.

Kate Bunting traces the big change in the look and activity of the Boardwalk back to one specific occasion: It was the first time a man came into the Belmont dining room for dinner wearing Bermuda shorts—sometime in the early 1950s.

"My mother and grandmother had a fit," Kate said. Guests in the old Victorian hotels on the Boardwalk "had always dressed for breakfast, and then they got dressed for lunch, and then they got dressed for dinner, and that was before we had air conditioning." The man in this case was a long-standing guest, so he was allowed to stay.

Even though the family has laughed about this anecdote in the years since, it marked a turning point. "I really do feel that when Bermuda shorts for men and pants for women came in, it was the start of a big change," asserts Kate. The old formality was gone. People came to Ocean City to escape rather than to tighten the restraints of daily routine.

"I think the old isn't necessarily bad and the new isn't necessarily good, and the other way around," Kate Bunting said. "Most of us just go with the flow.

"I may be looking through rose-colored glasses, but I think downtown Ocean City is great. It has charm and continuity, and you know your neighbors."

MAUDE TRUITT LAWS, A FAMILY LEGEND

Maude Truitt Laws was not among the earliest of Ocean City's remarkable women, but she contributed heavily to the tradition of tenacity and longevity among the resort's female business venturers.

In a beautifully written memoir, Victor H. Laws, Jr., a Salisbury lawyer, describes in detail his mother's move from chicken raising on her Wango farm, to her enterprises in Ocean City, and the verve with which she met the many pitfalls of the resort entrepreneur. He calls his book *Maud and Other Family Legends.*

Maud Laws died in 1983 at the age of 103. She had been born in a time and a region unquestionably male-dominated, but with her bright mind and awesome energy, she did not have to fight for women's rights; she just assumed them.

For the thirty-six years of their marriage, Victor H. Laws, Sr., served as Maud's anchor, a steadying force whose inflexible lifetime rule was never to borrow money. After his death, Maud simply changed the rule.

His mother, Victor Laws, Jr., wrote, "had an instinctive flair for real estate and especially for location." One of her most cherished tenets was, "Bite off more than you can chew and then chew like hell."

That is about what the members of her family all ended up doing in Ocean City.

Emerging from months of depression following her husband's death, Maud Laws's first solo investment was one common to lower–Eastern Shore farmers: two chicken houses, big enough to raise 40,000 chickens under contract to Perdue Farms, Inc. Barely surviving the ups and downs of the broiler business, she hit a bonanza in the spring of 1950, a $500 cash profit.

At the age of seventy, Maud Laws went to Ocean City to fulfill a long-held dream. She put the $500 down on an old two-story, two-apartment wooden cottage at 2nd Street and the Boardwalk and financed the remaining $25,000 purchase price at two local banks. She named the property Beachway Apartments, selecting a name that would put it near the top in alphabetical listings of Ocean City apartments.

For investors in Ocean City real estate, the moneymaking season is short, running from June 1 to Labor Day, with a peak season of only six weeks between July 1 and August 15.

To generate enough money from Beachway to pay off the loans, Mrs. Laws remodeled the building to turn two apartments into four. Then it was discovered that the old pilings that supported the building were almost entirely rotted out at ground level. Undaunted, Maud decided to build a new concrete foundation directly behind it and to move the building entire and intact from the old foundation to the new. In addition, she had the new foundation built high enough to contain two additional apartments.

Mrs. Laws was eighty years old when she decided to sell Beachway and move on to what she believed would turn out to be a better location. She bought and completely remodeled a property at 13th Street into six new Coronet Apartments. This required not only the trials and tensions of extensive renovations, but a hefty $115,000 mortgage.

The first year was good. The second year began with the great storm of March 1962.

At the Coronet all porches, decks, patios, walkways, retaining walls, and railings disappeared in the storm's wake. A picture of its "stairway to nowhere" was so dramatic it was circulated in the national media to illustrate the storm's destruction. The stairway hung in space from the front of the building where it had once led from boardwalk level to the second-story apartments.

Ladies in bathing attire with Thurman Douglas Mason in 1918. (Courtesy Ocean City Life-Saving Station Museum, Mary Lou Brueckmann Collection.)

Maud Laws rallied her forces—her son Victor, daughter Margaret, and their spouses—and with hard physical work and a federal disaster loan, the Coronet Apartments were back in business by July 15, giving Maud the rest of the "season" to recoup her losses. But storm damage totaling $21,750 was added to the unpaid mortgage debt.

The years that followed presented only the normal everyday challenges of managing an Ocean City property—building a returning clientele, cleaning up in the spring, weekly cleanings between tenants, renting, collecting, bookkeeping, taxes, maintenance, and repair.

Maud Laws thrived on it. At age ninety-one she insisted on buying a neighboring property that became available, and launched into more financing and more renovations for Coronet South. Granted, her initiative, drive, and instincts for good investment could carry her son Victor and his wife, Eunice, and daughter Margaret and her husband, George, to the brink of exhaustion. As for Maud, crisis seemed only to refuel her own energy.

In 1980, when Maud Laws was 100 years old, her son Victor persuaded her to sell the Coronet Apartments. They went for $425,000. That was 850 times the original $500 stake, he pointed out in his memoir. But a lot of additional investment and a lot of work had gone in between. The Ocean City years were not easy for the Laws family.

In the memory of this writer, Maud Laws will always be melded inseparably into, of all things, the televised viewing of the first moon walk.

Most of the children who were visiting at Maud's downstairs Coronet apartment that day found the beach more enticing than the chance to watch Neil Armstrong's "giant leap for mankind." Their choice demonstrated Ocean City's always-irresistible appeal. Mrs. Laws, however, sat before the television watching the moon walk with great intensity and excitement.

Maud Laws, born even before the start of the accelerating progress from first flight to space flight, had kept pace with it all. From her perspective of years and innate good sense, she could instinctively keep the triumphs and calamities of national or personal life in the right proportion. The same sense of the truly significant that kept her glued to the television set for the moon landing, shutting out any personal diversion of the moment, had kept her moving ahead, energy and spirits intact, through all the setbacks of Ocean City property ownership.

For her, the Ocean City ventures were as stimulating as the diversions of Boardwalk and beach to the vacationer.

WILLYE CONNER LUDLAM AND THELMA CONNER, TYING IT ALL TOGETHER

Thelma Conner was at first an outsider to Ocean City. She came to town in 1940 as a new bride. When she met her husband in Philadelphia, the only Ocean City she had heard of was the one in New Jersey.

Mrs. Conner arrived too late to be described as one of Ocean City's "pioneer women," but in a town where women have played a peculiarly significant role, hers has been played in both the old town and the new.

She was originally from Texas. In college there, she earned her bachelor's degree as a pre-med student but was discouraged from continuing down a road that was far more difficult for a woman then than it is now. She taught school for a while, then came East to be with her father, who was director of the Bureau of Census in Washington. With his encouragement she went to graduate school, getting her degree in business administration.

"My friends were all in New York," she said. Her father was in Washington. She decided to be independent of both and got a job in advertising in Philadelphia. It was there that she met Milton Conner.

It was perhaps because she had never heard of his hometown of Ocean City, Maryland, that she has worked so diligently to promote it in the years since.

Milton Conner belonged to one of Ocean City's original families. In 1886 his father, George, had opened the first restaurant on the Boardwalk. The sign for "Conner's Restaurant" is evident in yellowed pictures of the old town. His mother, Willye Jones Conner, came to Ocean City from Snow Hill to work in the restaurant, where she met and married the owner.

When George Conner died in 1916, Willye was left with three sons, George, William, and Milton. Six years after her husband's death, the young widow sold the restaurant and bought The Hastings, the small hotel built a few years before by the remarkable pioneer woman, Josephine Richardson Hastings. Mrs. Conner also bought The Hastings Annex, a cottage behind it on Baltimore Avenue.

The year after buying these properties, Mrs. Conner married Captain Charles Ludlam. He and his father, Captain Christopher Ludlam, were central figures in another chapter of Ocean City's history, its fishing industry. The Ludlams came down the coast from Cape May, New Jersey, in 1896 and established the first fishing camp, launching open boats into the surf to harvest pound nets anchored to the ocean floor. It was an industry that continued until 1933 when the Inlet washed away the Ludlam fish camp property and transformed commercial and sport fishing in Ocean City, but that story is to come.

When Thelma Conner arrived on the scene in 1940, she, unlike the women who had built and were then running most of the hotels, had been brought up in boarding schools and had a formal education. "But I didn't even know how to cook. The work was a shock to me," she said.

At The Hastings she ran the office, waited tables, made up the rooms, and cleaned bathrooms. "The family operated everything and did everything there was to do." She hardly knew what went on in the city then, she said. "I never got outside [the hotel] to know."

Her mother-in-law by then had added to her property the Westchester Apartments on the north side of The Hastings, and two houses on the south side which she enlarged and named the Miramar. Next to The Hastings Annex, where Thelma and Milton Conner began their married life, Willye Conner Ludlam built the Jo-Lynne Apartments.

Then, in 1956, just as the whole face of the resort was beginning to change, she built the Santa Maria on the Boardwalk at 15th Street, one of the first big motels in what was to become "motel row."

When Mrs. Ludlam started running the Santa Maria, she turned over The Hastings and its kitchen to her daughter-in-law. "I barely knew how to cook, let alone run a hotel dining room," Thelma Conner said. "The salesmen were real good to me. They taught me how to buy food in quantity, about food preparation, the whole bit. I learned from the salesmen."

The old hotels all had the American plan, she explained. "The people who came to Ocean City selected a hotel and had all their meals there. They did not keep to their rooms, but came downstairs and talked to others in the lobby or on the porches sitting in rockers. Everybody dressed for dinner and to go out on the Boardwalk. It was a lovely time, really."

When she first came to Ocean City, she said, the hotels all had black waiters and kitchen help who came up from Florida, where they worked in the winter. Although it was not a formal thing, most of them seemed to come from around the town of Marianna in the northwest corner of that state. They seemed to know about Ocean City, and they continued to come up until World War II.

During the war Mrs. Ludlam and other hotel owners began recruiting college students as waiters and waitresses. From then on, Ocean City has been a mecca for young people looking for summer jobs combined with a good time.

The public taste, too, seemed to change with the war. People were no longer interested in the American plan. They wanted air conditioning and television and other amenities the old hotels were not equipped to offer.

So, the motels came along—first the Seascape, then Miami Court and Mrs. Ludlam's Santa Maria. In 1966 Thelma and Milton Conner acquired their own motel, the Dunes, at 27th Street.

Mrs. Conner became more and more active in community life. She was involved in the Ocean City Chamber of Commerce and became its president.

Then in 1974 she really broke new ground. She became the first woman elected to the Ocean City Council, holding that seat for eight years. She joined the council before the advent of the city manager system, when each council member served as liaison with one or more of the city departments. Two of her special responsibilities were public relations and "innovative ideas for the good of Ocean City."

In the latter capacity she was the main force behind the Ocean City Centennial celebration in 1975. As an outgrowth of that effort, she shares much of the credit for the Ocean City Life-Saving Station Museum, which now stands at the end of the Boardwalk overlooking the Inlet.

The museum effort began with the threatened demolition of the old U.S. Coast Guard Station that had stood by the Boardwalk at Caroline Street since 1878. With the combined support of the Mayor and Council and a newly formed Ocean City Museum Society, the building was moved to a new location in December 1977.

The exhibits brought together in that building preserve a heritage without any parallel that comes to mind. They include artifacts related to the gallant crews who manned the early Life-Saving Station, to the early fishing industry, to the early hotels, and to the big storms of 1933 and 1962.

The development of the museum was hailed by some as the "coming of age" of Ocean City.

Milton Conner died in 1979. He and Thelma had often talked of the possibilities for a beachfront lot they had inherited next to the Dunes Motel. After he died, "it took a long time to get up the nerve," Thelma said. But, at age seventy-four, she began the most challenging project of her life.

At the north end of the Boardwalk at 28th Street she built the multimillion-dollar Dunes Manor Hotel. It has 160 rooms and 10 suites, swimming pool, jacuzzi, exercise room—all the features vacationers demand these days. But, in architecture, decor, and general atmosphere, Mrs. Conner has tried to keep something of the Victorian style of the old Ocean City.

Every afternoon there is tea in the lobby, with Mrs. Conner presiding in person at the tea table. "The young people who come to the Dunes seem to enjoy the afternoon tea. I think a little of the old formal behavior might be coming back," she said.

Mrs. Conner has been closer than most in the town today to the lore of the old Ocean City, and the Dunes reflects it. There is, for instance, a Zippy Lewis Lounge, named for a legendary figure who lived on the north beach "between the big pines and the little pines" in the earliest days of Ocean City and supported several children by beachcombing.

Stories abound among the old residents here about the Spanish coins that Zippy found and traded for the necessities of life, and there are some here who have never quite given up the idea that there is still, somewhere around Zippy's old haunts, more treasure to be found.

For winter weekends at the Dunes, Mrs. Conner has introduced Victorian round tables in the pattern of Elderhostel, with lectures on selected subjects by faculty members from Salisbury State University nearby.

The big challenge today, she explained, is keeping the resort alive and active in the winter months. "You can't support today's business with just the summer months. The investment is tremendous. Most of the banks lending money now would expect you to stay open year-round. We have become big business. It's not easy."

Mrs. Conner has run one of the earliest of the old hotels on the Boardwalk, a motel, Ocean City promotional campaigns, and now a major new hotel. "The Dunes Manor ties it all together," she said.

FOUR

Men of the Sea

THE FISHING CAMPS

In its early years, Ocean City was about half resort town and half fishing village. While its enterprising women were in the kitchens of their small hotels and boardinghouses, its men were on the sea.

This was no ordinary or relaxed kind of fishing in which they were engaged. Known as pound net fishing, it is just about the most demanding method of fishing there is, one that few people today are likely to have seen. It started off the Maryland coast in 1896, the year Captain Christopher Ludlam and his son, Captain Charles Ludlam, came down from Cape May, New Jersey, with a group of fishermen and put the first pound net in the ocean off the Ocean City beach.

The elder Ludlam was later to be mayor of Ocean City from 1903 to 1908. His son married Willye Jones Conner, who was one of Ocean City's "pioneer women." The younger Captain Ludlam survived the rigors of his occupation, living well up into his nineties and outliving by many years the industry itself.

For thirty-five years the pilings of fish pounds lined the horizon between the sea and the sky. A fish pound was an ingenious structure of pilings and nets built a half mile to a mile and a half offshore in the open sea. It was a huge trap about 40 feet square with netting attached to the pilings of gum or hickory and stretched along the ocean floor 30 to 40 feet down. About twenty-four pilings were required for building each fish pound. The fishermen drove the pilings into the bottom with the help of a pump and a jet of water.

The netting had a funnel-shaped opening. The fish, whole schools at a time, were diverted into it by a weir stretched across the current for as much as 700 feet. Once in, they could not get out again.

The daily challenge of the fishing crew was to get an open dory out to the pound, pull up a net holding thousands of pounds of fish, get them in the boat, and move the heavy boat back through the breaking surf and up on the beach. Each boat required a captain and six to eight men.

There was no Inlet and no harbor then. The fishermen had to launch 40-foot-long open fishing boats directly into the pounding surf. To do this, they placed wooden rollers under the bow and shoved the boat over planks laid under it, one before the other, until it was buoyant. The crew got the boat through the surf by pulling on a heavy rope attached to a piling they had driven offshore for that purpose.

In those days there was a long, shallow bar about 250 or 300 feet off the beach where the waves crashed and broke with their greatest burst of strength before rolling onto shore. The crew in the boat had to catch the right slack in the third, fifth, or seventh wave, to get through. The space between the shore and the bar they called "the gully."

In the gully the crew used oars, and later a small engine, to get the boat turned into the waves crashing onto the bar and keep it from broaching and swamping. The boats were very strong and heavy. They had to be. They often climbed the waves high into the air before crashing down into the slough between.

To harvest the fish at the pound, the crew would remove two ends of the net from the pilings and pull. They did not have hoists, pulleys, or machinery to help. They just pulled.

"We just grabbed aholt and pulled, all seven of us, till we busted. If we had a no'easter and a strong set of current, you can't imagine how busted you were to get that net in." This was Zadock Wallace Sturgis, then seventy-two, describing the days of pound fishing to a local reporter, Orlando Wooten, over twenty years ago. Accounts of the old brand of fishing in Ocean City today must be secondhand, but men who know the sea can describe it with feeling—and awe.

The fish were dumped into the boat loose, piled up as much as 4 feet deep under the feet of the crew. They got butterfish, trout, porgies, hard-heads, a few flounder, and, at one time, sturgeon.

When the heavy boat hit the beach, it was brought in over the runway of planks and rollers, this time by heavy Percheron horses pulling on a block and tackle. Watching the horses pull the fishing boats in was a favorite diversion of vacationers in those days.

At that time, the passenger trains that brought excursionists and most of the vacationers to Ocean City crossed the old railroad bridge and turned north to the station on Philadelphia Avenue. But the freight trains turned south to the old fish platform by the fishing camps at the south end of town. This was the part of town that washed away in the storm of 1933 and now lies at the bottom of the Inlet.

The fish were carted across the beach from the boats to the platform, iced in barrels, sold to buyers on the dock, or shipped on consignment to wholesale markets such as the Gordon Fish Company of Baltimore, the South Street Fish Market in Philadelphia, or the Beyer Fish Company in New York. Prices ranged from 2 cents to 12 cents a pound.

In the heyday of the fishing industry through the 1920s, Ocean City fishermen made about $30 or $35 a month. They came from New Jersey and the Carolinas as well as rural villages closeby. A season at the fishing camps could provide a man with cash to meet a payment on a farm or boat. They worked out of the fishing camps, eating and sleeping there during the season, which ran from about mid-March to mid-November.

The shacklike buildings of the camps were lined up along the beach on both sides of the railroad. Unpainted buildings with dormitory-type sleeping quarters, they also included a room with a long trestle table and benches for eating. The meals served were hearty.

Captains John, Tom, and Joe Elliot operated the Elliott Brothers Fish Company; other camps included the Davis and Henry E. Davis Fish Companies; the L. D. Lynch Fish Company, and the Captain Charlie Ludlam Fish Camp. Ownerships and partnerships for these camps and others—the Quillen, Cropper Brothers, Atlantic, and Thomas and Mumford fishing camps—changed over the years, but the camps continued to be the supporting industry of the town, contributing as much to its population and economy as its infant hospitality industry.

The south end of town, where the camps were located, was very low and often flooded. The flooding was an omen of things to come. When the storm of 1933 cut the Inlet through the island, the railroad, the fish-loading platform, and all the camps except one, the Thomas and Mumford camp, were swept away.

By that time, pound net fishing was already becoming less and less profitable. "Fished out" was how some of the old-timers explained it. The nets trapped small and marketable fish alike, and undersized fish were often simply tossed aside for fertilizer.

Some of the old fishing companies hung on for a while, taking their boats out through the new Inlet and tying up at the new West Ocean City docks. But there was no more pound net fishing after the mid-1930s.

The only company to survive from the original market fishing industry was the Davis and Lynch Fish Company of J. Edwin Davis and L. D. Lynch, which is still in business on the north side of the West Ocean City harbor.

THE MEN WHO SAVED LIVES

Peril on the sea was frequent enough in the early years of Ocean City to be a very personal part of life.

In 1874 the United States government established the U.S. Life-Saving Service to aid seamen and ships in distress along the Atlantic coast. Up to then, help for seamen in trouble had come from volunteers. There were also looters who sometimes made a profession of watching for ships in trouble with more in mind than heroic rescue.

The Act of Congress that established the Service called for stations manned by trained personnel along open coastlines especially hazardous to ships in stormy seas. It specified sparsely inhabited and exposed coastlines with flat beaches and outlying sandbars and no sheltering harbors.

One of the first stations established by the new Service was on Assateague Island at Green Run in 1875. Stations followed at Assateague Beach, Popes Island, and North Beach.

A station was built at Ocean City in 1878 at what was then the northern edge of the village on the oceanfront at Caroline Street. That was just three years after the Atlantic Hotel opened and the first lots were platted. The first keeper of the Ocean City station was William T. West. Six "surfmen" served under him with sleeping quarters at the station.

A bigger station was built in front of the original one in 1891, and that is the building that has now been moved to a new site by the Inlet to become the Ocean City Life-Saving Station Museum.

In the station's days in active service, the surfmen stationed there patrolled the beach on foot and horseback and watched the sea from the watch tower on the Boardwalk and the distinctive tower on the roof of the station. A lifeboat was on the beach ready for use. When the surfmen had their drills, launching it into the surf, "gentlefolk" strolling the Boardwalk enjoyed watching the action.

For rescues at sea, a line was shot from a cannon to a stricken vessel. The line was secured to the beach, and imperiled crew members were brought ashore in the breeches buoy or surf car. The breeches buoy, always a symbol of high drama to any reader of novels of the sea, gets its name from the shape of the canvas seats that are suspended from a large cork ring attached to a hawser and pulled ashore. The surf car is a watertight capsule in which four people can be enclosed and, surviving wind, crashing waves, and claustrophobia, be hauled along the hawser to safety.

To haul heavy equipment down a beach in a raging storm, set up the apparatus of rescue in the face of thundering surf, numbing cold, and driving, blinding rain, is a test of human endurance few people experience. It is a side of beach life seldom associated with a town where people come to promenade the Boardwalk or lounge on the beach.

During the forty years (1875 to 1915) that the Life-Saving Service was in action along this coast, the surfmen stationed at the six stations on the Assateague-Ocean City barrier responded to well over 260 distress calls from ships in trouble off the coast.

A surfman in the 1890s was paid $20 a month. He was also supplied with barracks quarters and food at his lonesome post. In the nearby communities he was regarded as a hero.

Surfmen and their families added to the population and community life of the tiny resort beginning to form on the beach and calling itself Ocean City. Some of its leading business and civic leaders and two mayors were to come from the ranks of the Service.

On early Ocean City postcards, the Life-Saving Station and watchtower on the Boardwalk are landmarks beside the Showell bathhouse, pool, and Oceanic Hotel. In the early years of the Service, the surfmen doubled as beach patrol.

The old Life-Saving Service is merged in the memories of local residents with the U.S. Coast Guard, which came into being in 1915 and in Ocean City was a continuation of the old Service, using the same station until 1964. The Coast Guard then moved to a modern new station on the bayside at the south end of Philadelphia Avenue.

In the Prohibition era of the 1920s and early 1930s, the Coast Guardsmen were alert to more than shipwrecks. From the Caroline Street station a patrol regularly walked the beach, linking with the patrols of stations to the north and south. On one such patrol well preserved in local memory, the men reached the Broadmarsh area, about where the Route 90 bridge

Coast Guard drill by the crew of the Ocean City station about 1920. (Courtesy Ocean City Life-Saving Station Museum, Mary Lou Brueckmann Collection.)

now enters town, at the same time a flotilla of fishing boats was bringing in a couple of thousand cases of bootleg whiskey wrapped in burlap.

As it turned out, a man well-known and liked in town was the local contact for bootleggers from Canada who had hired most of Ocean City's fishing fleet for the job. The men were arrested by the Coast Guard, and the liquor was confiscated and stored in the yard at the Caroline Street station. Many a case of whiskey went over the fence in the night, according to the local storytellers.

As for the men, they were tried, found guilty, and sentenced to several weeks in jail, except that there was no local jail that would hold the number of men involved. The only place big enough to hold them was the fire department building on Dorchester Street.

The best room in the building went to the man who had set up the operation, a courtesy naturally extended to the leader. The others stayed in the meeting hall, which had been turned into a dormitory. Since the government had to feed them and was not otherwise equipped to do so, they were taken down the street to the Del-Mar-Va Hotel for their meals.

This was a group of the town's leading citizens. Since they had their livelihoods to consider, they were released each day to go out in their fishing boats or to whatever else was their occupation, and returned to the firehouse at night.

Other memories of the Coast Guard are told with less jocularity. In the early months of World War II, the Coast Guard saw more action off the Ocean City coast than was generally known.

Fifteen days after the bombing of Pearl Harbor in December 1941, there were signs that an enemy submarine was offshore. The next month, on January 27, 1942, the American tanker *Francis E. Powell* was torpedoed and sunk, with four lives lost. A week later, on the night of February 3, the freighter *San Bill* was torpedoed and sunk, with two crewmen killed and forty rescued by the Ocean City Coast Guard.

On March 10, a Norwegian merchant ship was torpedoed and sunk, and fourteen survivors reached shore in a lifeboat. Three weeks later a tug and three barges en route from Norfolk to New York, were sunk with sixteen seamen killed.

Perhaps the most vivid wartime tragedy remembered in Ocean City was the U-boat sinking of the American collier *David Atwater* on the night of April 2, 1942. The German submarine shelled not only the ship but also the lifeboat in which the seamen were escaping. Three survivors reached shore. Twenty-eight seamen died, and many of the bodies were brought ashore at Ocean City.

That summer, beach vacationers found a subdued resort. The regular force of the Coast Guard had been doubled, and it had taken over the Ship's Cafe on the bay for added space.

So that merchant ships would not be silhouetted against the glow of light from hotels and shop fronts, the Coast Guard ordered a dimout in Ocean City extending for three-quarters of a mile inland. Cars moving at night had to have only the parking lights on and be kept to 15 miles an hour. Jack Lynch, Ocean City's Defense Director, experimented with deep red and subdued lighting for hotels and businesses and called for venetian blinds or other coverings for oceanfront windows.

Fishing boats were handed over to the government. Maryland Senator Millard E. Tydings proposed that Ocean City itself be turned over to the government as a training base. Why this was not done, it was later explained, was because most of the hotels did not have heating plants, and to install them would have cost the army more than building new barracks.

On a visit to Ocean City that year, Hulbert Footner, a reporter for *The Sun*, wrote: "The closely hooded street lights were casting mysterious big circles of light on the ground below, swinging back and forth as the lamps were moved by the wind."

That August, a Coast Guard cutter cruising along the coast at night, found the dimout to be a success. It reported that "Ocean City is not visible from the sea. The U-boats are not getting any help from the Maryland coastline." The dimout continued in the summer of 1943, but the fear of submarines and shelling had subsided.

By bus and train, civilians and servicemen alike continued through the war years to pour into Ocean City for relaxation and fun.

The Caroline Street site was occupied, first by the Life-Saving Service and then the U.S. Coast Guard, from the days of sailing schooners, through World War II, and into the 1960s.

The property had originally belonged to Stephen Taber, the man who turned over fifty acres of his property on the barren barrier reef for the founding of Ocean City. He stipulated at the time that unsold lots blocked off for the original town be used by trustees "in such manner as they shall deem most advantageous to the interests of said Ocean City."

The trustees had deeded the lot for the Life-Saving Station to the U.S. Department of the Treasury with the stipulation that if it ceased to be used for that purpose, it should go back to the owner.

A hundred years later, in 1978, the U.S. Coast Guard moved to its new location on the bay. The Boardwalk site at Caroline Street, by then worth a great deal of money, had been turned over to the city and used for several years as quarters for the Beach Patrol and as a first-aid station.

At this point seven descendants of Stephen Taber claimed ownership of the property on the basis of the original deed and were supported in their claim by the Worcester County Circuit Court and the Maryland Court of Appeals. Under the new ownership, the Caroline Street site of the historic old station and of the town's highest drama, is occupied by a Boardwalk eatery.

THE MEN ON THE STANDS

Up to about 1930, the beach crowd was concentrated at Caroline Street in front of the United States Coast Guard station. This was the block where beach-goers could rent suits at the Showell Bathhouse. It was also where Coast Guardsmen in their Boardwalk tower watched over bathers as well as ships at sea.

Beach Patrol Captain Bob Craig remembers that about a block away was a big double jetty across the beach. It was constructed of wooden pilings with crossbars between, and people kept getting caught between the poles, requiring a lot of rescues.

The surf washed right up to the Boardwalk then and often under it. In 1930 the beach had gotten so narrow that bathers began moving up the beach beyond North Division Street and out of range of the Coast Guardsmen in the tower.

William W. McCabe was the mayor then, and he and Captain William Purnell of the Coast Guard organized the town's original Ocean City Beach Patrol. It began with one man, Edward Lee Carey, who was hired to watch over the beach where the crowd was. He was the son of Savannah Carey, whose mother owned the Del-Mar Hotel on North Division Street.

The Patrol developed year by year. New men were added and supplied with buoys for rescues, first-aid kits, and umbrellas.

Captain Craig remembers well the early members of the patrol: John Laws, whose family had a cottage next to the Del-Mar-Va; Nick Campofreda, an all-American football player for the University of

Maryland; Ned and Tommy Dukehart (Tommy later became a sportswriter for *The Sun)*; hometown boys Milton and George Conner; Gary Todd of Salisbury; Barney McCabe, the mayor's son; Franklin ("Cutie") and Emory ("Huck") Savage; and Bill Pacey of Baltimore.

In 1935 two names of special significance appeared on the roster for the first time. One was Harry W. Kelley, later to become Ocean City's most widely publicized mayor. The other was Bob Craig, the genial, 6-foot man who was still on the Patrol fifty-two years later. From 1946 to 1987 he was its captain.

Bob Craig was born and reared in Wilmington. Ocean City has always been an important part of his life. His father was a school teacher, and the family spent the summers in a cottage at the beach. He married a young woman from nearby Berlin, Virginia Lee Mason.

After he went to the University of Pennsylvania, getting his undergraduate degree with a major in languages and his master's in education, he still returned every summer to Ocean City to be on the Beach Patrol.

His teaching career was in St. Louis, where he taught languages and mathematics to high school students and coached football, basketball, tennis, and golf. He and his wife had two sons and a daughter. All the while, he and his family returned to Ocean City summer after summer.

When he retired from teaching in 1981, after forty years in the same school, he and his wife settled into a year-round home in, of course, Ocean City. He remained Captain of the Beach Patrol, and once described himself as "probably the longest-term temporary employee the city has ever had."

Since Bob Craig started on the Patrol, it has grown to about 140 members. The guard towers kept advancing up the beach as the resort developed. Today the Patrol covers over ten miles of beach from the Inlet to the Maryland–Delaware line. It is equipped with jeeps, Honda quads, walkie-talkies, and the familiar semaphore flags.

Perhaps the biggest change of all, in some ways, is the presence in the last fifteen years of women on the lifeguard stands, as many as twelve a year.

Women have come a long way since the 1930s, when the late Betty Strohecker Gordy worked out with long-distance swims up the beach, out-swimming most of the men on the patrol, but could not be a member. (Betty Gordy, an Ocean City native and later a well-known realtor, was attending Roosevelt High School in Washington then and was the regional backstroke champion. She was in training for the Olympics when her life turned in other directions.) There is no discrimination against women on the Beach Patrol today, nor do they get any special consideration in tryouts.

The tryouts and training are grueling. Even to be considered, an applicant must swim a quarter of a mile in the ocean from the jetty at the Inlet to the fishing pier, keeping his or her stroke through waves and

currents, and come into shore in ten minutes or less. As soon as the swimmer hits the beach, he or she must then run in the sand back to the starting point.

The applicant who survives the initial test—most do not—continues from there with a series of simulated rescues with and without a torpedo buoy, runs a 220-yard course in soft sand in 60 seconds and, if still in action, breaks for lunch.

In a swimming pool there is a test in lifesaving techniques, keeping one's head, and breaking out of the most unexpected holds a desperate swimmer might come up with. Patrol members are taught the semaphore flag signals and first aid, and get intensive CPR training from the paramedic unit.

The lifeguard learns what can be learned about treacherous rip currents, the changing ocean bottom, and how far to let the surf mats go out on different winds and tides. He or she also has to keep an eye out for swimmers who get too close to the long wooden and, more recently, stone jetties that jut out into the surf to help check beach erosion.

Captain Craig has estimated that in a typical season the patrol goes to the rescue of about 2,500 bathers, handles 1,000 lost children, and is called on for first aid about 500 times.

Beyond all that, the Patrol members, generally between the ages of twenty and twenty-three, must have the more subtle skills, or instincts, to deal with all kinds of people. They answer questions, serious and silly, and enforce, as gently as possible, the rules of the beach, such as no alcoholic beverages, glass containers, ball playing, dogs, or loud music.

"A guard needs maturity," Captain Craig has said, "to be able to tell someone as old as his grandfather that he is breaking the law." For his services, he can expect a range of response from intense gratitude to indifference—or embarrassment.

There is, for example, the swimmer washed out in an undertow and nearing exhaustion while making no headway getting back through the breakers. The lifeguard swims out and helps him to shore. Without a word of acknowledgment or thanks, the swimmer walks away as nonchalantly as possible, communicating by his manner, to anyone who might be watching, that he did not really need help at all.

This is one of the most familiar of the small dramas seen by the practiced watcher of a lifeguard on the job.

FIVE

Stormy Times

A GIFT OF THE SEA

The great storm of August 1933 was a turning point in Ocean City history. Firsthand accounts of it, whether recorded at the time or recalled years later, have the elements of life's high moments—vivid language, remarkable detail and clarity, and a sense of calm in the midst of events beyond human control.

The late Harriet Showell Bald remembered how "Daddy hammered wood over everything and people were going up and down the street in boats. But we were calm. We stayed through every storm. We never evacuated."

At the time of the storm, Harriet was very young and was staying at the cottage of her grandparents, the Hickleys, on 5th Street. All the lines were down, and there was no communication on or off the island.

Her grandfather was in Washington, at their home there. He was so worried about his family in Ocean City that he plunged into rain and wind, got across the Chesapeake Bay by ferry, drove across the Eastern Shore as far as the west side of Sinepuxent Bay, found the bridge closed to traffic, managed to find someone to take him across by boat, and then another person to roll him up the sand-choked streets to the 5th Street cottage in a wheelbarrow. There, Harriet said, he found her grandmother calmly playing bridge with her regular group which met that day.

Bill Shreve, whose grandmother built the Plimhimmon Hotel, remembers that he, too, was in Washington when the storm came. It lasted three days.

On the second day he was so concerned about this grandmother and others in his family that he took off for the beach. "I had a hell of a time getting in," he said. "The railroad bridge was totally demolished. The automobile bridge was still there but so weakened that police were stopping everybody. They wouldn't let you cross unless you had good reason. I lied a little bit and said I owned the Plimhimmon Hotel. I had to wait in line, maybe a half hour. They were letting vehicles across one at a time."

Like Harriet Bald's grandfather, he arrived to find the women in the midst of the havoc, coping with the demands of the moment as if with some crisis of daily hotel management.

Meanwhile, the storm was being reported in newspapers across the state as "the most disastrous storm in Maryland's history."

There had been heavy rain for four days when the wind started to blow with force on Tuesday night, August 22, driving the rain in horizontal sheets. "The wind blew a gale and a northeast rain came down, a solid mass of water," Worcester County's weekly newspaper, *The Democratic Messenger,* reported that Thursday. "Big trees in full leaf were easy victims of the wind. Great limbs crashed to the water-soaked earth . . . . Soon roads were dangerously blocked with fallen monarchs . . . . Many stories have been told about Ocean City, scarcely any being alike, but there is no difference in the stories of . . . the mountainous waves that battered down the Boardwalk, smashed in windows and . . . destroyed places of business."

Ocean City was just part of the *Messenger* story. "Farmers will suffer greatly by the storm," it reported. "Most of the late potato crop is ruined . . . . Corn is beaten down and fodder twisted to a bare thread . . . . Peaches, apples and pears were beaten from the trees and many orchards were destroyed by the wind. It was a terrible storm."

Deep down in the *Messenger* account was what turned out to be the storm's most significant legacy. An inlet, it reported, had been cut at Ocean City 50 feet wide and 8 feet deep.

Piece by piece, as the wind and waves calmed, the full story of the storm came out.

The Sun reported on August 24 that "the natives of Ocean City stood fast but visitors had fled. People got out first by automobile, then by foot. The bridge shook under fleeing cars. It was hard to evacuate. People were confronted by waterlogged cars. The electric gasoline pumps were out of commission and there was only one hand pump in town." Automobiles were flooded and stranded in roads. Some people fled by boat: A "primitive ferry system" was set up, with two skiffs hauled back and forth on ropes across Sinepuxent Bay.

Former Maryland Governor Herbert R. O'Connor, who was then state's attorney for Baltimore and a frequent visitor to Ocean City, helped with the evacuation. Thousands of refugees were in the nearby town of Berlin, *The Sun* story continued.

Back in Ocean City, the Boardwalk had been demolished for a mile. "Boards were flying like splinters," one eyewitness reported later.

The best accounts are those of Ocean City residents who described their experiences long afterward.

The late Charles W. Purnell, owner of the Atlantic Hotel, wrote an account of the storm for *The Sunday Sun Magazine* twenty years later.

His hotel and the other Boardwalk hotels had exceptionally big crowds when the storm hit, he remembered. "We all went to bed just like any other night, though . . . . About three o'clock my wife woke me up and told me there was water in our court. Waves have a way of breaking and forming again, you know, and I saw one break right out in my parking lot. I wouldn't have been surprised then if the whole place had washed away. I was a little scared," he confessed.

Mr. Purnell had purchased the Atlantic Hotel ten years before. He had owned it for only two years when it burned down in the great fire of 1925. He had rebuilt it, and now, only seven years later, it was again on the verge of destruction. He wouldn't leave it now, nor would his wife, even in the heart of the storm. "A captain can't leave his ship, you know." he explained.

There were about two hundred guests in the Atlantic Hotel that night. Next morning, right after breakfast, all but about thirty of them "paid their bills and lit out," Mr. Purnell wrote. As it turned out, those who stayed fared better than those who left. With flooded roads and washed-out bridges, many were marooned in their cars.

By Wednesday night, August 23, "there wasn't much left of the storm. We had an orchestra and we had a dance that night. There weren't many people, but we had it just the same." That dance at the Atlantic Hotel—by candlelight—is vivid in other personal memories of the storm.

The next morning, Mr. Purnell wrote, "the bay was quiet and the ocean was quiet," and the new inlet had been cut through.

Annie Bunting has a memory of the day after as vivid as that of the storm itself. "The sun came up so beautiful . . . just a great big ball of red fire, and the wind lulled . . . . You could hear that inlet, and [it] was chopping the bank right off. It had cut the railroad right out. It was just wild. We were panicky then. We really didn't know what was going to happen to us . . . . It turned out to be a godsend, because the Inlet is really Ocean City's lifeline."

As the storm subsided, "aquatic pedestrians," as one account expressed it, began to return to Ocean City. What they found was a resort that was changed forever.

The railroad bridge was gone. The fishing camps, all but one, were gone. The platform along the railroad tracks, where all the fishing camps had their stalls, was gone. So was the C. P. Cropper garage at the lower end of town.

Three entire streets at the south end of town were, in fact, gone. They were, and remain today, under the Inlet that had been cut across the island between the ocean and the coastal bays behind.

Forty years later, in August 1973, Captain John H. Elliott Sr., then eighty-three years old, described the Inlet's creation to a local reporter, Orlando Wooten, as clearly as if the two of them had been standing beside it the day after the storm.

When the storm ended, Captain Elliott's fishing camp was under the water rushing through the awesome new channel. "Water rose in the city streets and waves washed into the bay, but the Inlet was really cut backward," he explained. "It was the bay that cut the Inlet, not the ocean . . . .

"It was a peculiar storm, one the like of which I never really saw in all my years of fishing in Ocean City . . . . We had creations of rain for three or four days previous to August 22, the day of the first high winds. It rained continuously like you never saw, perhaps ten inches a day. Every stream that emptied into Sinepuxent Bay, Assateague Bay, Isle of Wight Bay, and Assawoman Bay was full and overflowing with more rainwater than I ever knew here.

"That, plus what ocean water that did sweep across from the force of the northeast winds, built up a real mountain of water on the bayside. It had to go somewhere, and that somewhere was the lowest spot in south Ocean City, the place where the ocean water had come across, our fishing camp area, just south of the Boardwalk.

"You know, we ordinarily have two tides a day, in and out, flood and ebb, as the level of the ocean rises and falls. But for four or five days after August 23, the day of the real high winds and damage, the tides never flowed into the new inlet. It was all out, or ebb tide. It was a millrace, one way—out—and it never stopped its direction all that time. All kinds of debris were carried out to sea.

"Our buildings were not too severely damaged by the wind at first . . . but as that millrace cut further and further, each went down and was carried out to sea. Railroad tracks could be seen twisting end-over-end. We had a big heavy cement septic tank for our fish camp. The water got to it, rolled it over and over, and the last we saw of it, it was headed out to sea down the Inlet, bobbing and rolling with the tide."

Captain Elliott was a big man, and strong. He had to be, as a pound net fisherman, launching his boat through the surf and pulling up the heavy nets. He and his brothers, Tom and Joe, had a big camp. They operated three boats, sometimes making three or four trips a day out through the breakers to the nets and back.

The inlet being cut during the violent storm of August 1933. (Courtesy Ocean City Life-Saving Station Museum.)

When the storm cut the Inlet, the Elliott brothers did not lose a boat, nor did they lose any of the big dray horses they kept to pull their heavily laden boats out of the water onto the beach. But their nets and other gear were scattered far and wide.

When the tides quieted down a bit, maybe four or five days after the storm, Captain Elliott said, he was the first man to go through the new Inlet.

Fishermen, for sport or livelihood, have been going through it ever since. They could now keep their boats in the sheltering bay and have free access to the ocean.

Ocean City fishermen at first tied up their boats along what was left of the old railroad pier. Later, the West Ocean City docks were built.

But the heyday of the pound net fisherman was over. The row of pilings for the pound nets gradually disappeared from the Ocean City skyline, and an era ended.

AN OCEAN CITY HARBOR

Before the storm of 1933, Ocean City businessmen had been trying for years to get an inlet across the island for access to the ocean from the sheltering bays.

Only a month before the storm, the lead story in *The Democratic Messenger* had been about the status of a proposed inlet project that had been promoted for two years. Senator Millard E. Tydings (Democrat, Maryland) and Representative R. Alan Goldsborough (Democrat, Maryland) had been pressing Congress for authorization of a $281,000 appropriation in a rivers and harbors bill for an ocean inlet into Sinepuxent Bay about five miles south of Ocean City.

This location was a point where inlets had been cut through the island in the past. It appears on historic maps and is identified sometimes as the Sandy Point Inlet and sometimes as the Sinepuxent Inlet. A storm had cut an inlet there as recently as 1920. That inlet had remained navigable by light-draft boats for three or four years, but had shallowed gradually and was last charted in 1929. (It was also near this location that a group of local private investors had tried and failed to construct an inlet in 1907.) The state of Maryland had already appropriated $500,000 for construction of a new inlet at Sandy Point, contingent on approval of the federal share of the cost.

A large Eastern Shore delegation had gone to Washington the year before for the hearing before the Board of Engineers for Rivers and Harbors. Senator Tydings had argued on their behalf that the inlet would provide a safe harbor for about 1,000 fishing boats which came to the fishing grounds off Ocean City from as far north as Massachusetts. An inlet and harbor at Ocean City, he asserted, would make it possible for the boats to ship their catches directly to markets in Baltimore, Philadelphia, New York, and Boston instead of having to return to northern harbors.

This was the Roosevelt era of the New Deal, the NRA (National Recovery Act), AAA (Agricultural Adjustment Act), and PWA (Public Works Administration). It was a time when the United States government was experimenting with program after historic program to lift the country out of the depths of depression. The new inlet was approved by the congressional committee as an impetus to the Atlantic coast seafood industry, but the rivers and harbors bill had not been passed when Congress adjourned. There was now no hope for its passage until the next session.

It was at this point that Nature achieved what the government had so far failed to bring about.

Amid the chaos in the aftermath of the storm, the new inlet was a curiosity thousands of people were coming to Ocean City to see. "It looks as if it came to stay," *The Democratic Messenger* reported.

The week after the storm, Ocean City Mayor William W. McCabe estimated storm damage in the town to be between $350,000 and $500,000. But the main topic of discussion was how to hold the Inlet in bounds and make it permanent. The inlet project on the way toward approval in the United States Congress now had to be changed, and negotiations started anew for emergency funds through the Public Works Administration to stabilize the inlet created by the storm.

It took two years to get the new project through, but in July 1935 *The Sun* reported that work on the Inlet was completed at "Maryland's only Atlantic port." The federal and state governments had put up $781,000 to stabilize it with a concrete seawall on its north side.

The next February, federal funds were appropriated for the two stone jetties which jut into the ocean on both sides of the Inlet to hold back the sand that would otherwise wash in and close the channel.

Besides helping to keep the channel open, the jetty on the north side of the Inlet soon had another, dramatic effect. The sand washed by the ocean's southward littoral drift was blocked by the north jetty and in only a few years filled in the beach behind it to many times its original width. The beach at the south end of Ocean City became so deep, in fact, as to change the elevated Boardwalk to a ground-level promenade, and so wide as to contain a municipal parking lot as well as space for thousands of sunbathers.

During the same time that the south Ocean City beach has been turning into a wide expanse of sand, the northern tip of Assateague Island on the south side of the Inlet has been almost visibly migrating westward. Because of the north jetty's interference with the littoral drifts the sand washed southward from Assateague's northern beaches is not being replaced by sand that, in the natural cycle, would be washed onto the island's shores from the north.

As a result, an air view today shows two segments of what was once a single island, so changed in position that if the two were suddenly pushed toward each other, they wouldn't even meet.

A NEW FISHERY

In the aftermath of the 1933 storm, as the bay waters roiled across the island to join the sea, there were several "firsts."

One of these was the teenage derring-do of Imogene Pierce. When the storm quieted down, Imogene went down to the new Inlet with several of the lifeguards and became the first woman to swim across. Imogene, a native daughter, had deep roots in Ocean City. Her father, Thomas Taylor, who retired from the U.S. Coast Guard, was a partner with L. D. Lynch in the fishing business. Her mother, Kate, ran The Mervue Hotel, and Imogene's husband, Earl Pierce, is the retired Ocean City clerk. The lifeguards were part of the summertime clientele at The Mervue.

More significant in the town's adjustment to its imposing new feature than Imogene's swim, was the gradual realization of what the Inlet was going to mean to the fishermen.

In an engrossing pictorial history book called *Ocean City*, George and Suzanne Hurley identify Captain D. Frank Parsons as the first to use the new Inlet to take out a charter ocean fishing party. It was four days after the storm, when a man and woman offered to pay Captain Parsons to take them out into the ocean to fish. He agreed, against his father's protests that it was too dangerous, and thereby became the first to enter a whole new era for Ocean City's fishermen.

Sport fishing was not entirely new in Ocean City. Some of the commercial captains had been taking adventurous anglers out for years, "adventurous" because the skiffs had to be launched through the surf for sport fishing, just as they were for market fishing.

There was also fishing in Sinepuxent Bay. The bay water was brackish because of inlets in the past and ocean water washing over the barrier island. Fishermen could rent scows from Captain Charles R. Bunting, who had been operating from his Talbot Street dock since 1918. They could catch trout, spot, and small blues. After a particularly severe storm in 1922, the salinity of the bay was changed to the point that flounder and croakers were also being caught there. The new Inlet made this a permanent situation.

With the Inlet came a changed bay and a new breed of vacationer, little known to the beach loungers at the oceanfront hotels. The fishing vacationer is content to spend the nights in the simplest rooms with or without a view or in a cabin or trailer in West Ocean City, and the days in a small rented boat on the bay or casting from the U.S. Route 50 bridge.

For the pleasure seeker, the bay produces not only finfish, but also crabs to be taken by handline and dip net, or hard clams to be felt out by rake or toes and thrown into a basket floating in an inner tube.

For sportsmen on another scale, the most dramatic of the Inlet's gifts to Ocean City was big game fishing. The established fishermen of Ocean City give the credit for pioneering this sport to Jack and Paul Townsend, businessmen of Selbyville, Delaware, and sons of that state's former governor, John T. Townsend.

The Townsends were dedicated sportsmen who had long sought the famed white marlin off the coast of Florida. This species likes warm water and migrates from the tropics with the Gulf Stream. Suspecting that the fish might be found off the Maryland coast, the Townsends chartered a boat during the 1934 season and began the search. That year they located, but did not catch, a marlin at what is well known to fishermen as the Jackspot Shoal.

It was Captain John Mickle of Florida, trolling in Maryland waters, who landed the first white marlin off the coast that same year, an event hailed as a high point by the entire world of sport fishing. The discovery of the heretofore-only-guessed presence of this great fighting fish off the Maryland coast, together with the newly created Ocean City harbor and docks, made the town the "White Marlin Capital" of the world.

As the word spread that the white marlin seemed to favor Maryland's coastal waters, sport fishermen homed in on Ocean City. In 1936 there were 175 marlin landings reported. In 1937 there were 200 landings. In 1938 the figure leaped to 781 landings. To true sportsmen, the figures began to be more alarming than exciting. They began to be afraid that too many marlin were being caught and that a great sport would be destroyed.

In 1939, the figure jumped to 1,343 landings.

To help control the fishery, the Townsend brothers began to offer prizes to the captain and mate of the boat releasing the most marlin during a season. The Game Fishermen's Association was organized by boat captains and other civic leaders to work with the Department of the Interior Bureau of Fisheries on a long-range study of the fishery and the effect of the big catches on the marlin population.

Then, involuntary controls of a different sort—World War II—closed the fishery for three years, from 1942 to 1944.

When the marlin fleet began going out again after the war, there were a lot of changes.

The Jackspot is about twenty miles offshore, a run of about one hour and forty-five minutes. With marlin migrating farther offshore, it is sometimes necessary to go out fifty or more miles. However, a little 40-foot boat with one engine is not much for a fisherman to have under him and his passengers when there is that much ocean between the boat and the nearest land. So, the captains began to modernize their boats with auxiliary engines, safety equipment, and radio transmitters.

To enhance their sport and protect the fishery, a group of experienced marlin fishermen from Washington organized the Ocean City Light Tackle Club in 1947, requiring only lightweight rod and line for taking a marlin. They also have a gentlemen's agreement to release all but trophy or mutilated marlin. Today, an estimated 60 to 80 percent of the marlin caught are released.

To protect the white marlin, federal restrictions were put into effect in 1988, limiting marlin landed and kept to fish at least 62 inches from the lower jaw to the fork of the tail.

The event of the year, in Ocean City's rarefied world of big game fishing, is the White Marlin Open in August. It was started in 1974 by Jim Motsko, owner of Paul's Tackle Shop, near the Inlet. He was just twenty-six years old at the time and had gotten into the world of marlin fishing when he was a mate on an Ocean City boat while a student at the University of Maryland. In 1990 he and his cousin, Chuck Motsko, were directing what has come to be known as "the world's biggest billfish tournament."

Each boat pays a $650 entry fee, covering up to four anglers aboard, and $50 more for each extra angler. There are added entry fees for different divisions, which can push the total well up into four figures. Entrants try for prize money for landings of white marlin, blue marlin, wahoo, tuna, dolphin, and shark.

About 230 boats, carrying about 1,200 individual participants, leave the Ocean City harbor in a predawn stream during the five days of the tournament. For this adventure, boat owners pay $200 and more a day for fuel and about $225 for a captain and mate. Fishermen who don't own their own boats chip in with fishing buddies to charter one for about $850 a day.

The tournament draws boats not only from other states but also from other nations, and thousands of spectators show up at Harbour Island during the tournament for the weighing of the day's catches as the boats come in. The stakes are high; top money winners can take home from $50,000 to $150,000 and more for landing a champion white or blue marlin. There is a post-tournament celebration, as for other Ocean City events from pro beach volleyball to bikini contests—usually a party at one of the big hotels or restaurants.

The big, beautiful fishing yachts that gather for the marlin tournament are a sight to see, with or without prize-winning fish. Besides the marlin fleet going out through the Inlet at the break of day, there are the headboats with a full deck of fishermen-for-a-day hoping for the thrill of landing a bluefish, sea trout, sea bass, or tuna. For those aboard, the words on the window of Paul's Tackle Shop are as apt as for the marlin fisherman: "A bad day fishing beats a good day working."

In the West Ocean City harbor, the sleek private boats with their flying bridges and outriggers tower over the worn and rugged workboats, their decks piled with drag nets, heavy chains, hydraulic rigs, and coils of rope.

The market fisherman spends his life doing for a living what vacationers come to this harbor to do for escape.

A few years ago Clinton P. ("Skate") Redden was interviewed about his rugged life. He had just docked his 56-foot fishing boat in a driving rain after a day out on the ocean. Beside his weathered boat, the *Three R's*, was a gleaming white sportfishing boat which, he said, had gone out only a few days that year. Mr. Redden went out daily at about 3:00 A.M., with a crew of one, and sometimes got home after dark with his catch of flounder, sea bass, and trout. Sometimes the catch was good, and sometimes it was meager. He sold it to a seafood house by the harbor, where it was either packed and shipped to city markets or sold to resort restaurants.

Mr. Redden's father, a market fisherman, started his son with a handline when he was twelve. The younger Redden has been going out for over forty years now and has never tired of it: "I like fishing. It is the only thing I like. Money isn't everything. If I had my life to live over, I'd do the same thing."

THE CLAMMERS

Starting in the 1950s a new kind of fishing boat began appearing along the coast off Ocean City—the deep-sea clammer. The clammers came down from the coasts of Long Island and New Jersey, where years of dredging had just about cleaned out the beds in those waters. The beds off Ocean City, however, were rich and untouched. Local watermen knew they were there, but had believed the huge ocean clams were too tough to eat. The demand for the ocean clams was from big, brand-name companies that used them for canned clam chowder or fried clam strips or spaghetti sauce.

West Ocean City soon became home port to twenty or more big clam boats with their wide, angular dredges and rusty metal net reels towering beside the sport and charter fishing boats.

For an ocean fisherman aspiring to the profits of this new fishery, the changeover meant a major investment and a whole new operation. A crew had to learn to handle a 700-pound dredge and 200 feet of fire hose, which was used to jet water against the ocean bottom and loosen the clams embedded in the mud. Clams are dredged at depths of 45 feet and more. It requires a 70- or 80-foot boat to carry the heavy dredge equipment and operate ten or twenty miles offshore.

In spite of the hazards of weather and economics, so many clammers were working off the mid-Atlantic coast in the 1970s that the National Marine Fisheries Service imposed a moratorium on licenses for additional clamming vessels and a quota system for the harvest. Each clam boat was registered and limited first to four days a week, and then to two, that it could work. Clammers complained that to make a living and meet payments on their boats, they sometimes went out on their assigned days in weather that would otherwise have kept them in port.

For the vacationer watching idly from the beach, the clam boats, with their tall rigging, that pass across the skyline in the late afternoon and turn in at the Inlet, can be brought to a very personal level with the story of just one.

When Robert L. Martin, in partnership with family members in the Martin Fish Company, bought an all-steel, 75-foot ocean fishing boat in Mobile, Alabama, in 1978 and brought it home to Ocean City, *The Daily Times* in Salisbury ran a feature about the young captain and the new addition to the local fleet, *Atlantic Mist*.

Captain Martin, a graduate of Stephen Decatur High School, was the third generation of his family to fish the ocean out of Ocean City. His grandfather was fishing out of Carolina ports in 1933 when the Inlet was formed at Ocean City. He moved to the Maryland port, and the family has been there ever since.

Atlantic Mist was built in 1973 and had been operated as a shrimp trawler in the Gulf of Mexico before Captain Martin bought her for $195,000. She was equipped to go out for three to five days at a time and was intended initially for ocean fishing.

In February 1985, Captain Martin and *Atlantic Mist* were again in the news. His boat, now rigged for clamming, had gone down in high seas in the night, taking one crewman with her. The captain and the three other crewmen floated in icy water for twelve hours before being rescued by fellow clammers. They were wearing survival suits, but one died before the rescue while the others held him in their arms.

It was the third fishing boat in three months to go down off the Eastern Shore, sending crew members to their deaths. The tragedies brought wide but brief attention to the ocean fishery and its hazards in the shadows of vacationland.

Captain Martin has since left Ocean City for a new life in Hawaii.

"THE TIDES OF MARCH"

Sitting as it is on the outer rim of the continent, Ocean City is part of the constant drama of the meeting of land and sea. That is its attraction. Even on the calmest days, when gently rolling swells spread soft sheets of water across the sand, there is an awareness of high drama and pent-up strength in those gentle splashes.

It takes an event such as the great storm of March 1962 to remind us just how high that drama can be, and that when we establish ourselves at the edge of the sea, we remain there only because of Nature's restraint and not because we have prevailed against her.

The amazing thing about the historic storm of 1962 is that it took everybody by surprise. It was so unexpected that most in the Ocean City community of 1,500 year-round residents were still caught up in the routine of daily living, right into the heart of the storm.

The even more amazing thing about the aftermath is that in no time at all, the town not only had bulldozed off the sand and rubble and returned to "booming normalcy," as one newspaper put it, but was on the way to an all-but-overwhelming new burst of growth.

The storm of 1962 did not bring to Ocean City a concrete and lasting result like the Inlet created by the 1933 storm. But it was a turning point of another kind. This storm's legacy was less obvious, but maybe even more significant in the long run: It ushered in an era in which the cherished rights of the private property owner, rights defended with a special fervor on the Eastern Shore, ran head-on into the fast-developing ethic of the environmentalist.

In this new ethic, the importance of beaches, dunes, and marshes in the cycle of natural and human life, overrides the right of a property owner to do with them what he wishes. The environmental ethic places on land a value of natural significance far beyond its immediate market value as building lots.

In Ocean City, as in resort communities up and down the coast, the belated recognition of the place of barrier islands in the natural scheme of things has created an ongoing and still unresolved dilemma. And yet, the dilemma had been scarcely recognized before the storm of 1962.

The great storm was expected to be a routine northeaster. Such a storm usually lasts for three days with winds less than gale force, reaching a peak on the second day and diminishing on the third.

The storm began as predicted on Monday night, March 5. But two lows merged off the Maryland coast and coincided on Tuesday with the new moon, when tides are highest. Tides were 7 to 9 feet higher than usual, and the wind did not shift. It stayed northeast for more than forty-eight hours. Six high tides built up water in the bays, and the high winds kept it there.

Tuesday's high tide leveled the protective dunes. For two days after that, the ocean washed across the beach, meeting with a crash the water spreading over the barrier island from the swollen bays on the west side.

The storm reached its peak on Wednesday morning when the high tide rose to 9 feet 4 or 5 inches above mean low water. (In the 1933 storm, the peak tide was 7 feet 1 inch above the mean low tide level.) The ocean surf pounded the town. As it receded, it undercut the foundations of buildings and washed so much sand from the beach that the front steps of oceanfront buildings were hanging in space higher than a man's head.

When it was over, Maryland Governor J. Millard Tawes flew over the town in a helicopter and then came into the city by car, wading to the City Hall in knee-high boots. "This is the worst disaster in Maryland's history," he said.

One native of the area who had flown fifty missions out of North Africa in a B-17 in World War II, viewed the devastation with quiet astonishment and said it was worse than anything he had seen in the war.

The cold statistics were fifty business establishments, including apartment houses, and fifteen homes destroyed. Crippling damage occurred to 250 other homes and 105 businesses.

The city line was at 41st Street then. The area above that was hit especially hard. A temporary inlet had been washed across the island at 71st Street, taking with it the buildings in its path.

The beach level had been reduced in some spots by 6 to 8 feet. Some beaches had been narrowed by 100 to 250 feet. Property owners thus lost not only their summer cottages, but the lots on which they stood.

At the north end of town, people who could not see the ocean before because of the high, protective dunes, had an unobstructed view across flattened beaches. One out-of-towner who came after the storm to check on his North Ocean City house looked for it in vain until during a lull in the crashing waves, he spotted the foundation stones out in the surf beyond a whole, new mean low water line.

On the north beaches, the leveled sand had to be surveyed to locate platted streets and lots. Some of these lots today lie beneath giant condominium complexes.

The storm of 1962 raised legal issues of public and private beach rights that have since taken years to resolve. At the time, the storm's havoc was more immediate.

In the weeks following, *The Sun Magazine* brought out a special issue on the storm. *The Eastern Shore Times* published a book called *The Tides of March,* a title supplied by the publisher's teenage son who had just read Shakespeare's *Julius Caesar* in school.

In a small community where most of those who experienced the storm knew each other, the local publication, especially, brought it to a very personal level. Some of the local children, for instance, not only had to be carried from flooding homes by fire engine, dump truck, or an

Damage to beachfront property caused by the storm of March 1962. (Courtesy Ocean City Life-Saving Station Museum, William and Beryl Dryden Collection.)

amphibious Coast Guard vehicle called the Duck, but were just coming down with chicken pox.

Among the stories told in *The Tides of March* was the account of several women who taught in local schools who were planning to attend a weekly class in Salisbury that Tuesday night. Kitty Purnell, who lived on the bayside just south of the airport, was slated to drive that week.

A little after 5:00 P.M. she drove out of her lane to pick up Dot Mumford at her house. By the time she got there, the wind was getting so high that the two phoned the others and decided they better not make the thirty-mile drive that night because there might be trees or electric wires across the road.

About fifteen minutes after leaving her house, Kitty Purnell started back. In that short time, the bay had risen so high that waves were lapping at her car as she approached her lane.

Her husband, Bill, was one of about twenty men in the Ocean City area who had citizens band radio equipment. It was a hobby that turned out to be crucial to the rescue operations in the hours ahead. By walkie-talkie, Bill Purnell advised his wife to park her car on the highest spot in the road and walk the rest of the way up the lane, a distance of about two city blocks. By now there was a swirling current up to her knees.

Home was not a safe haven. Water was rising rapidly all around it. The couple started to wade toward the main road, but before they got very far the water had risen up to Kitty's neck. They tried wading out in another direction across a field. Again they turned back.

Back home again they were drying themselves off, when a wave crashed through their picture window.

Bill Purnell got on his citizens band radio and called the Ocean City fire hall to ask his friends there for advice. The fire company dispatched a light, tracked vehicle called the Weasel to pick them up. But the Weasel never made it. The vehicle was knocked out of commission when it ran into an unlighted parked car in the road, in sight of the house. The Purnells were now joined by their two would-be rescuers, and the four awaited help in a house which now looked like a foundering ship at sea.

Rescue came later by three friends in a 16-foot aluminum outboard which they had maneuvered through deep water made hazardous by floating debris, whole parts of houses, and outbuildings.

When they went back to their house at low tide the next day, the Purnells found the front room with all the furnishings completely gone and water standing throughout. It was many months before they could move back in.

Beulah Eby, another of the teachers who was planning to go to the adult class in Salisbury that night, lived in town at 49th Street with her husband and six children. Two of her daughters had gone to a Brownie meeting at the Presbyterian Church that evening, even though the wind was "blowing up a storm."

After Beulah talked to the others in the evening class and decided not to drive to Salisbury, things began to happen fast. By a little after 8:00 P.M., there were 3- and 4-foot waves in the Eby yard, and sleet was hitting the house like BB pellets. The wind was blowing harder than they had ever heard it before.

"About midnight we knew this was the worst storm by far that we had ever experienced," Mrs. Eby recounted afterward. "As the sky lightened Wednesday, we had an ocean view as far as we could see. The Coronado [a luxury apartment building on the beach at 47th Street] lost some of its roof as we watched."

At about 7:00 A.M. on Wednesday, the Coast Guard Duck pulled up to their house, and the family, with blankets, some food, and son Ronnie's beagle dog, waded to it. Others were picked up along the way. People needing rescue had been told by radio to hang white sheets from their windows. At the bridge they were met by school buses and taken to Buckingham School in Berlin. The Red Cross had opened an emergency shelter there and the regular cafeteria workers were on the job at the school to feed the Ocean City families.

The Eby family was invited into a Berlin home and had only been there a half hour when two spots appeared on the face of one of the children—chicken pox. It was one of the many cases making the rounds.

At 5:30 P.M. that Tuesday, Mayor Hugh T. Cropper asked the volunteer firemen to assemble at the fire hall. It was the regular meeting night, and some had come early to play pool. Soon the distress calls started coming in from people trapped by rising tides, and the firemen had all ten of their vehicles in action.

The citizens band radios that kept Bill and Kitty Purnell in touch with friends and rescuers, saved the day for unknown numbers of other people.

When he realized on Tuesday night how serious the storm was getting, Bill Bunting took his parents, Mr. and Mrs. Levin J. Bunting, across the U.S. Route 50 bridge to safety and then went back and got on his CB radio. Soon a network developed between Bill and about twenty other ham radio hobbyists in the beach area.

When a house owner was stranded, he would telephone the firehouse for help. The calls would be relayed to Bill Bunting, who would dispatch the word to other radio operators in touch with volunteers and vehicles that could be used for evacuation. Pressed into service were outboard boats, fire trucks, dump trucks, and finally the Duck, sent by the Coast Guard from Cambridge about sixty miles away.

Mr. Bunting stayed on his radio from Tuesday evening until Thursday afternoon and handled about two hundred calls.

At the St. Paul's By-the-Sea Episcopal Church on 3rd Street and Baltimore Avenue, the Reverend William L. Dewees appeared for the 7:30 A.M. Ash Wednesday communion service. He read the traditional service to an empty church, as far as the creed. (In the Episcopal Church it is canon law that a rector may stop the service at this point if no communicants are present.)

With most of the town already evacuated, Reverend and Mrs. Dewees boarded the next fire truck that came by for the sad ride along Baltimore Avenue to the bridge. Also on the fire truck were the Russ Cullens, owners of the Hamilton Hotel, and six of their seven children, one only eight months old. All boarded the school bus at the bridge for the ride to Berlin and went to the homes of friends there.

Other vehicles arriving at the bridge were loaded with people, dogs, cats, and caged birds.

The Ocean City people were leaving behind a strange world where landmarks had changed, familiar buildings were gone, and houses had moved to locations where houses had not been before.

The Coronado, which the Ebys saw beginning to blow apart on Wednesday morning, was subsequently reduced to rubble. The seven people who lived there lost just about all of their personal belongings. Two of them, Gail and John Whaley, were newlyweds. When they returned to the island on Wednesday after the height of the storm, their furniture, clothing, and wedding gifts were somewhere under tons of sand or scattered along the beach. Still reeling from their loss, they turned to leave and found their car so bogged down in sand that they had to walk for help to pull it free.

Among the many stories of the storm is one told by Fred Brueckmann, which offers some reassurance about the much-maligned U.S. Postal Service: An Ocean City resident had posted a letter to Mr. Brueckmann in a 26th Street box that Tuesday and later watched the same mailbox float down the street. The mailbox was found near 7th Street and Philadelphia Avenue, and the mail inside was dried, readdressed by the men in the post office, and sent on. Mr. Bruechmann got his letter only about one day later than usual.

The late Edgar G. Gaskins of Berlin wrote his memories of the 1962 storm over twenty years later. On March 9, after the winds died down and the tides receded, Mr. Gaskins drove up the beach in a high-wheeled dump truck to the Carousel Hotel, then being built at 118th Street. (He was supervisor of construction for George Bert Cropper, a local engineer and developer who was building the hotel for the notorious Bobby Baker and his partner.) Rooftops, doorsteps, porches, and furniture were scattered along the route. The Carousel was the only building left standing in "the vast wasteland" of North Ocean City, he wrote.

Henry, the night watchman, had come to Ocean City from Washington and had never seen the ocean until he took the job. He came out of the building waving his arms and calling, "Come get me." It developed that when the tide started rising on Tuesday, Henry had packed up food, candles, and blankets and gone to the elevator tower, where he had stayed through three nights. He had thus weathered the storm, Mr. Gaskins said, but he had had enough of Ocean City. He left for Washington "on the first bus out of town."

For many children in Ocean City, the storm was an adventure heightened by the ride on a fire engine or the Duck and the fact that there was no school in Ocean City for eight days.

The Maryland National Guard took over the Ocean City Elementary School as headquarters. About 275 men were stationed at the school, at one time; the first unit arrived on Wednesday afternoon from the Salisbury and Crisfield area. The National Guard helped bring order to the rescue and cleanup and guarded against looting. The school gym was the mess hall, and classrooms, library, and halls were sleeping quarters. When Mrs. Eby returned to her classroom on Monday, March 19, she was surprised and delighted to find that the occupants had fed the goldfish and watered the plants every day.

At the emergency shelter at Buckingham School in Berlin, school teachers and other school personnel pitched in to keep track of refugees and their needs.

After the storm, the National Red Cross set up a disaster headquarters in the Villa Nova Hotel in West Ocean City and helped over a hundred families get resettled with food, clothing, and household supplies.

In the aftermath of the storm, President Kennedy declared the Worcester County coast a disaster area to make property owners eligible for federal loans. An emergency office of the Small Business Administration was set up in City Hall and offered the possibility of 3-percent-interest loans for rebuilding and repair to those with the endurance for the application and follow-up process.

Property owners faced other complications because hotels, rental apartments, and homes were not insured against water damage, only wind, and to prove that destruction was caused by wind rather than water was a long, drawn-out, and often losing proposition.

More immediately, the Maryland State Roads Commission moved in more than a hundred bulldozers and other heavy equipment for the cleanup. Through the Civil Defense organization, people registered for temporary jobs in the cleanup and were referred to employers. Privately operated bulldozers, mechanical shovels, and graders were hired by property owners, along with just about anybody who showed up with a shovel and the willingness to use it.

For Ocean City Mayor Hugh Cropper, this was the most challenging period in his ten years in office. In the midst of devastation, he predicted Ocean City would be open for business as usual by Memorial Day, the traditional start of the beach season.

He was right.

Almost before the wind died down, the shoveling and hammering were underway, and wind and wave began to wash back onto the beaches what they had taken away.

On March 19, the first day of school after the storm, several teachers asked their students to write about their experiences. *The Eastern Shore Times* included passages from some of the papers in its book about the storm.

"We saw a house float down the bay and many other sad sights," wrote Robin Garlick, who lived on the west side of the bay. There were also "a wheelbarrow, chairs, wood paneling, two boats, and a part of an attic" in her yard.

"Boards, pieces of Boardwalk, toys, and bricks were washing down our street, " wrote Sally Rayne, whose house was in downtown Ocean City.

Barbara Suit, who lived on the oceanfront, wrote that "chunks of furniture washed by, pieces of boardwalk rammed against the fence. Dad had nailed a white flag up. An army truck came."

Gregory Carey's conclusion said it all: "It was a frightening experience. I wouldn't have missed it for the world."

SIX

Coming of Age

"THE VICES OF OCEAN CITY"

Ocean City in the 1950s and early 1960s was like an adolescent in the midst of a growth spurt. At heart it was still more small town than booming resort. It was self-conscious, worried about its image, and sensitive to every slight.

The sensitivity was not a subtle undercurrent. It has been expressed in this town since the dawn of the century in the simplest and most direct terms: "Why don't they like us in Baltimore? Why do the papers always want to write bad things about us?"

Now, more than ever, there was some basis for this feeling. Ocean City had become a small town with big city problems to handle, and the whole state was watching.

Up to the storm of 1962, and for some years afterward, the issues covered with the most diligence by the Baltimore and Washington papers were the wild activities of young people in Ocean City (and sometimes adults as well) and the shortcomings of local political and law enforcement figures in coping with them.

In the late 1930s and early 1940s the stories getting the most statewide attention were stories of illegal slot machines that were widely evident in Ocean City but only spottily discovered and seized in periodic raids by local authorities.

Visitors to Ocean City in this era still recall playing the slots in hotel rest rooms or in back rooms where doors were quickly shut when the word spread, as it always seemed to, that the authorities were coming.

The attendant newspaper coverage of this situation brought complaints from Ocean City fathers that the resort was being "singled out." Three city councilmen issued a statement in August 1947 asserting that "much publicity has been given to the vices of Ocean City," but "similar conditions believed to exist openly in Baltimore continue unabated there year around."

By the following August there had been no change on all fronts. In a feature on Ocean City a *Sun* reporter described a much-frequented teenage hangout where "police on the way to the gambling room have to pick their way between tables around which are anywhere from five to ten underage drinkers.

"It is not an uncommon sight," the story continued, "to see a 'sick' youth being walked up and down the Boardwalk or being helped into a washroom. But it would be uncommon for authorities to question the youth and find out where he purchased and consumed the liquor."

Then in May 1951 the season opened with a *Sun* story reporting that "the slots are gone," and that two big night spots had been closed for selling beer to minors.

"Teenagers can't buy beer and their fathers can't find slots," another story reported that July. At a Boardwalk bar once popular for the under-twenty-one set there was now a turnstile, the story went on to say. A customer had to prove that he was twenty-one before a "watcher" pushed a pedal to open it.

Credit for the turnaround was given to a new Worcester County state's attorney, John L. Sanford, who acted with no-nonsense authority. To the wide applause of the elected Ocean City officials then in office, and much of the citizenry, Mr. Sanford mobilized the local law enforcement departments for a crackdown on illegal gambling and drinking.

The mayor then (1944 to 1959) was Daniel Trimper, Jr., a highly respected man whose father had been one of the first to settle and invest in the town when it was only a few wooden buildings in a vast expanse of sandy wilderness.

A recently elected member to the city council had based his strenuous campaign on the need to crack down on the sale of liquor to teenagers. The spectacle of intoxicated youngsters was not doing the town or business any good, was the vigorous argument of Harry W. Kelley, a man who was later to personify Ocean City.

Early in the 1960s, while the town was fighting its "vice" image with much publicity and some success, its law enforcement authorities began to be aware of "youths with a peculiar glassy-eyed look." This was the dawn of a new challenge, the drug culture, and the partiality of its adherents for the resort atmosphere. *The Sun* ran weekly lists on Monday mornings of drug arrests in Ocean City.

Throughout the decade when the public and the media were still focused on the riotous behavior of young people, another element was beginning to come to the fore. Young businessmen, some almost as young as those who staged the annual Labor Day riots on the beach, were beginning to appear in the chambers of the Ocean City Council and the Worcester County Commissioners. They wore tailored cashmere jackets and flared pants and were attended by a phalanx of designers, engineers, and public relations people with flip charts showing plans for big splashy developments and graphs showing how their plans would enhance the local economy and lead Ocean City to a bigger and brighter future. Some of the proposals put forth by these men were to change Ocean City forever, but at first they attracted little attention beyond the city officials and property owners directly involved.

Words and phrases such as "wetlands," "dune and marsh ecology," and "environmental controls" were still not the stuff of which headlines were made or issues that would draw packed houses to public hearings. All that was to come.

But before that awareness developed, and only five months after the storm of 1962, the new era of big-time development in Ocean City was ushered in by the most colorful opening in the resort's history. With lavish festivities and a barrage of publicity there burst upon the scene on July 22, 1962, Bobby Baker's Carousel.

BOBBY BAKER'S CAROUSEL

Robert Gene Baker was born on November 12, 1928, in a village in South Carolina. His mother had been a clerk in a department store when she married at the age of eighteen. His father was a millhand and was only twenty years old when Bobby, the first of eight children, was born. His father got a job as a mail carrier in the nearby town of Pickens, and then an appointment as postmaster, and Bobby grew up there.

In his teens, Bobby worked in a drugstore and liked the job a lot better than he liked school. He was an outgoing boy, mingled with adults easily, and was happy with his job and with life in his small town. His father was ambitious for his son and urged Bobby to grab the opportunity when he was offered an appointment as a page boy in the United States Senate. And so, in December 1942, at the age of fourteen, Bobby Baker left by Greyhound bus for Washington.

Thirty-six years later, he was to tell his story in a book called *Wheeling and Dealing, Confessions of a Capitol Hill Operator,* in which he describes himself as "a kid up from scratch and a compulsive hustler." While going about the routine duties of errand boy, the rookie page took note of the habits and special preferences of key senators. He attended Capitol Page School and at the same time learned the unwritten workings of the Senate and how its individual members operated.

His long and close working relationship with Lyndon B. Johnson, he wrote in his book, began by phone. "Mr. Baker," said the voice on the other end, "I understand you know where the bodies are buried in the Senate." The future president was then a congressman and had just been elected senator from Texas. Bobby Baker was twenty years old, had been working in the Senate for six years, and had been promoted to chief telephone page, a post which gave him professional staff status. As a Southern boy, Bobby had become especially close to Southern senators in powerful seniority posts. He knew their personal interests. As Senator Johnson rose in power, so did Bobby Baker.

In 1949 he married Dorothy Comstock, another congressional employee working for Rosemary Wood on the staff of Senator Richard Nixon of California. Their combined salaries were about $30,000 a year.

During this period Bobby Baker got his law degree at night from American University Law School. And he began to make investments on the advice of friends. "I have always been fond of money and of making it," he wrote in his book. "I like, too, the wheeler-dealer aspects of business, putting people and deals together." He also liked "being a viable part of the political process, plotting strategy."

Senator Johnson advanced in the Democratic leadership, first as minority leader, then as majority leader in the Senate. Bobby Baker became assistant secretary to the Senate minority in the Eisenhower years and then secretary to the majority and right-hand man to Lyndon Johnson.

After the election of 1950 when John F. Kennedy became president and Lyndon Johnson, vice president, Bobby Baker continued in his Senate post under Senate Majority Leader Mike Mansfield. He became, in his own description, "advisor to the mighty, political mover and shaker" and was rumored as possible future governor or senator in his native South Carolina. He "cavorted with lobbyists and show folk and athletic heroes" and became a "paper millionaire."

Then his world came crashing down. It began in a small way. With a $400,000 loan arranged by his good friend, Senator Robert Kerr of Oklahoma, he started Serv-U Corporation to handle vending machines at various companies with defense contracts. Then in late August of 1963, a rival vendor claimed that Bobby Baker was involved in influence peddling.

During this period, Senator John J. Williams of Delaware had assumed a watchdog role in the Senate and had already brought about the downfall of Sherman Adams, President Eisenhower's top White House assistant, for accepting furs and other gifts. He pressed for a Senate investigation of the charges against Bobby Baker. News stories fed the fires. The nation was regaled with stories of the town house Mr. Baker had bought for his girlfriend, Carole Tyler, of big parties and big spending.

Meanwhile, Bobby Baker was pursuing a long-held dream. He felt, "an increasing urge to begin to accumulate and build for the future as rapidly as possible." As a means to that end, his idea was to build and operate a motel-nightclub in Ocean City, Maryland. Ocean City was less than a three-hour drive from Washington, he reasoned. It was growing by leaps and bounds. Bobby Baker believed that within a few years its oceanfront property values would zoom out of sight. "Given the general prosperity of the period and the trend toward increasing leisure time for most Americans, I calculated that a first-class resort complex could not help but be a profitable venture."

In 1961 his dream was about to come true. He had borrowed money, bought two blocks of beachfront property at 118th Street and Ocean Highway, then far up the beach from the rest of the resort, and gone into partnership with two friends, Alfred and Geraldine Novak. Construction began that October.

Then there were bad weather conditions, contractor delays, and a down-turning economy. By March 1962, cinderblock had been laid and brickwork started when the partnership ran out of money. The business ventures Mr. Novak was counting on to finance the Carousel did not materialize, and on March 3 at his home in Washington, his wife, Geraldine, found him dead in the garage with the car motor running.

The next day, the great storm of 1962 swept across Ocean City. The storm left the partially built motel in ruins, and drifts of sand 14 feet deep extended across the building site. There was no storm insurance. Bobby Baker owed money for work that had been destroyed by the storm, and he needed still more money to clean up and continue.

His old friend Senator Kerr came to his rescue. He arranged $300,000 in bank loans and made a personal loan of $50,000 taken from his Senate safe. That personal loan was later to figure heavily in the criminal charges of fraud that brought Mr. Baker to trial in 1967.

The Carousel was completed and ready for its grand opening in July 1962. Bobby Baker knew that if it were to catch the attention of the Washington clientele he hoped to attract, the opening had to make a big splash in the news media, so he hired a Washington public relations man.

Vice President Johnson and Lady Bird came to the opening in an official limousine. Bobby Baker rented a fleet of limos for other celebrity guests, including some well-known senators and representatives, and the "hostess with the mostest," Perle Mesta. Seven buses transported about two hundred other guests, congressional staffers, lobbyists, and friends. The buses featured bars serving champagne.

The Carousel has since been transformed into a high-rise among high-rises, but in the Ocean City of 1962 it was impressive even though it was only a three-story building. It offered a heated pool and two cocktail lounges; there were hostesses in formal black outfits; and the guests were put up in roomy suites. It was a high moment for Mr. Baker, except that, he wrote later, his head was "barely above water."

His troubles continued to mount. The following August, Senator Williams began his drive for the Senate investigation of Mr. Baker's activities. In October 1963 Bobby Baker resigned his Senate position. The hearings began in 1964 amidst a continuing barrage of media exposure.

Then in May 1965, his longtime friend, Carole Tyler, who was working at the time as the Carousel's bookkeeper, left the lounge with a male guest about 2:00 P.M. one Sunday to fly over the resort in his single-engine private plane. They buzzed the Carousel at low altitude, pulled up suddenly, and banked over the ocean, never came out of the turn, and hit the water nose-first at high speed only a few hundred yards from the hotel.

The tragedy is still remembered vividly by vacationers who were staying nearby, and to the local populace it seemed to have come from a lifestyle new to the experience of the town. It was accompanied, of course, by another round of publicity.

The Senate hearings led, in January 1966, to a nine-count indictment against Mr. Baker in the federal district court in Washington. He was charged with income tax evasion and fraud in connection with money received from Senator Kerr and from savings-and-loan moguls in California. Senator Kerr had died of a heart attack on New Year's Day in 1963 before he could testify in the case.

Through all his troubles, Bobby Baker still hoped to enlarge the Carousel into a high-rise of twenty-five to thirty stories with luxury condominium apartments and indoor parking. He visualized Ocean City as a year-round resort and predicted that it was about to bloom into a second Fort Lauderdale. He became a full-time resident of the town and worked night and day at the Carousel as everything from manager to bookkeeper to bartender to driver of the equipment that cleaned the beach in front. The five Baker children worked as bellhops, busboys, and front desk clerks.

Bobby Baker projected energy. He was affable, good company, a lively talker, open and well-liked. There was even talk among some Ocean City residents of getting him to run for mayor, a proposal he quickly put to rest. His notoriety enhanced the glamour of his motel and brought attention to Ocean City. When he was convicted, the prevailing reaction in the town was regret.

Even after the failed appeals and his months in federal prison from January 1971 to his parole in June 1972, and even though the Carousel was sold during that time, it was still identified as "Bobby Baker's Carousel."

What he predicted for the Carousel and for Ocean City has come true, but Bobby Baker has seen it only as an occasional visitor.

BEACH RIGHTS, WETLANDS, AND JAMES B. CAINE

On the north side of the Carousel, in 1968, stood a beach house constructed on high pilings and extending, on some tides, into the surf. It was called Crystal House and had been built by a developer whose name appeared on real estate signs up and down the beach—James B. Caine—for his family.

The living room of the house faced into the sea like the prow of a ship. It was visible from far up and down the beach, because it stood alone in front of the line of structures on the oceanfront. Beach walkers had to go under it or wade into the surf.

Shortly after the house was completed, Bobby Baker and two other neighboring property owners filed suit to have it removed on grounds that it interfered with their right, and the right of the general public, to use the ocean beach.

Mr. Caine seemed deliberately to fan emotions aroused by his house. He ran a picture of it on the cover of his catalog of rental properties. In a rare interview for a local radio station, he asserted that he had built his house to show everyone "that you can build a house on the beach legally."

From the Carousel to the Delaware state line, he said, the beach was owned by individuals and was not a public beach, as most people thought it was. He had bought "over 600 acres of land on the bay side of the ocean highway from the Cropper boys for over $3 million, and one of the biggest problems that was in my mind was, when I developed said property, where and how were these people going to utilize the beach."

He built his beach house, he said, to impress upon the people that there was not a public beach in North Ocean City, and that if there were going to be one, the state or county or city would have to buy the ocean-front lots from the owners or build a beach out in front of them. The better idea, he insisted, would be to build a beach by constructing stone jetties projecting into the ocean, and pumping sand to the beachfront from the bays behind.

Public beach rights had been provided for in the plans for the old town of Ocean City in 1876. Old plats show that the Atlantic Hotel marked the easterly line for building lots and kept the beach east of Atlantic Avenue (the Boardwalk) as public domain.

Later, in 1891, The Sinepuxent Beach Company acquired a large area north and south of the old town and subdivided it into lots. The Sinepuxent Plat retained the designation of a beach area between Atlantic Avenue and the ocean as far north as 33rd Street.

From 33rd Street north, this was not the situation. The next segment of beach, from 33rd Street north to about 109th Street was not platted until 1917. This was called The Isle of Wight Plat. A later revision of this plat subdivided the area into blocks and lots on both sides of a roadway to be called Maryland Avenue and now called the Coastal Highway.

When a local engineer, George Bert Cropper, surveyed the area in 1939, he found that the area designated as "beach" on the plat did not actually exist above mean high water. He deleted the front lots in each block in order to have some space between platted lots and ocean.

The next big stretch of beach to the north was known as The Fenwick Plat. It extended from about 118th Street north to the Delaware line and was first platted in 1902 and replatted the following year. It also was subdivided into blocks and lots on both sides of the street that became the Coastal Highway.

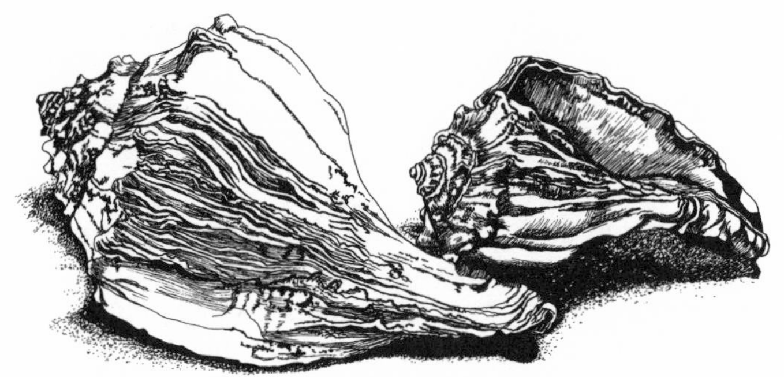

In 1940 Mr. Cropper surveyed this property and found that the shoreline shown on the plats "didn't conform to what was found on the ground." The beach shown did not exist. It was his opinion that the early plats were the result of no more than a "horseback" survey and that if the "beach" shown on the plats existed in 1903, it did not exist in 1940. Development north of 33rd Street proceeded slowly.

Mr. Cropper belongs to a family with roots in Ocean City from its earliest years. His own long life has been interwoven with the resort's history as engineer, surveyor, developer, businessman, and much respected participant in local public affairs. He and his two brothers, Robert Cropper and Harry H. Cropper, bought the Fenwick property from The Fenwick Corporation and tried to sell lots at auction in 1941. They did not sell enough to cover the auctioneer's $25 fee. In the 1950s, North Ocean City was still a desolate stretch of beach.

Then in 1960 James B. Caine bought The Fenwick Plat from the Croppers.

Mr. Caine had come to Ocean City from Delaware. Reared in Delaware City, at the eastern end of the Chesapeake & Delaware Canal, he had contracted polio as an infant, and he worked hard the rest of his life to overcome his handicap and to keep in shape.

His father was a barber who made enough in his profession and through other enterprises to send his son to Friends School in Wilmington and later to Washington College, a small but highly respected liberal arts college on the Eastern Shore in Chestertown. Jim studied accounting and business, and was graduated in 1945.

The beach area had always held an allure for him. In his college years he worked summers as a lifeguard in Rehoboth.

At college he met and married Joyce Walker, the daughter of a private-school teacher from Washington. After college, the Caines lived in Wilmington for seven years, where Jim worked as an accountant, first for Hercules, Inc. and then for the DuPont Company. They had two children: a daughter, Bradley, and a son, James.

At the same time, Jim started going to Ocean City in the summers, working weekends and developing a small, seasonal real estate business, concentrating on the barren and mostly untouched expanses north of town, which then ended at 41st Street. One local businessman remembers Jim Caine doing business at first from a table under a beach umbrella beside the Coastal Highway. Jim then established an office on the highway at 53rd Street. His wife and two children stayed in an apartment above it.

A friend of his wife who visited there remembers that she saw little of Jim Caine. He made an occasional pass-through, saying "Gotta make a dollar."

And make a dollar he did.

Mr. Caine did not invite close personal association. In fact, he often rejected it so abruptly that the overtures were not attempted again. When he began making waves in Ocean City real estate, one well-established native of the town, who had known Joyce Caine in Washington, called to say that he and his wife would like to give a cocktail party to introduce the Caines to some of the townspeople. Mr. Caine's response was that he and Joyce did not smoke, drink, or go to parties, and that ended *that* gesture.

But if he was not visible in the town's social scene, the Caine Real Estate signs were visible everywhere. At first they were visible mostly on two-unit, four-unit, and six-unit simple frame apartment buildings built on pilings along North Ocean City beachfronts and side streets for summer rental. Mr. Caine convinced builders, correctly, that such rental properties would be a good investment, and then he handled their rentals.

He recognized the local people who could do the best job in whatever line he needed, and offered them more than they were making either on their own or working for someone else, to work for him. One of them was Roland E. Powell, who would later become mayor of Ocean City. Mr. Powell made more money selling real estate for Mr. Caine than he had ever made before, he said. Jim Caine could see ahead; he believed in what he was doing and convinced others it would work, Mr. Powell said. "He helped a lot of people make a lot of money."

The man himself remained elusive, and appearances at any public gathering were rare. On occasional appearances at one of the always-crowded bimonthly meetings of the Ocean City Mayor and Council, Jim Caine would show up in work clothes, looking as if he had just come in from one of his construction sites.

Up to the time that Mr. Caine arrived in Ocean City, there had been little interest shown by the state of Maryland in what was going on in the coastal area. Ocean City fathers had felt through the years that they were regarded on the western shore as outsiders.

In the early years of this century, Captain William B. S. Powell, who was then mayor, filed a complaint with the Public Service Commission asserting that the railroad beds and equipment serving the Eastern Shore were neglected and that the railroad system favored Rehoboth and Atlantic City. Later, in 1934, local papers published accounts of a campaign to be launched by the Ocean City Chamber of Commerce for better understanding and closer commercial and social ties between the two shores of Maryland. The eminent writer for *The Sun*, Gerald W. Johnson, described the Eastern Shore as "an economic stepchild."

There were a number of excuses for this attitude. Ocean City then was inconvenient to get to. Until the first span of the Chesapeake Bay Bridge was completed in 1952, visitors had to cross the Bay by ferry or travel around the northern end of the Bay and down the Shore over secondary roads. Then, too, very little economic value was attached to the lowlands and marshes and barren sand along the coast.

"One shining light in this broad expanse of indifference was the State Roads Commission of Maryland," a local lawyer, L. Hollingsworth Pittman, wrote in a professional journal in 1961. The reason was the Coastal Highway. Delaware had built a highway from Rehoboth to Bethany Beach to the Maryland line, and Maryland completed a six-mile link from the north end of Ocean City (then 41st Street) in 1939, using workers paid by the New Deal's WPA program. It is recorded that a Delaware farmer with a load of vegetables was the first to travel down the new highway.

The State Roads Commission soon became aware that to protect the road, it had to keep the ocean from washing back and forth across it or breaking through the barrier reef. To do that, the Commission would have to maintain nature's own line of defense, the sand dunes washed up by wind and wave to form a natural barrier. Where the dune line was weak, the Commission, through the 1940s and 1950s, constructed sand fences to catch and hold the moving sand. Only casual and often oral permission was needed from the owners of what was then considered to be land of very little value to build these fences.

The dunes, constantly building and shifting and rebuilding, had created this barrier reef through the sweep of geologic time and kept it above sea level, protecting the mainland beyond from the full force of storms and erosion. But the dunes were on private property, with all the emotional and economic protectiveness that implies. Neither the state nor the county governments had any jurisdiction over them. Until 1961, when Maryland passed a permit system for grading and altering natural dunes, there was no permit system for changing the topography of the beach and no zoning regulations. The dunes were not protected by any law.

The issue of public and private rights to the beach was to take thirty years to resolve.

Even before he built his house on the beach beside the Carousel, James B. Caine had brought the issue to the fore, although not yet to wide public attention, when in 1960, he began to acquire and build on the undeveloped expanses of North Ocean City.

The area consisted of wide sweeps of sand blown into dunes, low sand mounds, and depressions in which water, washed across by the tides, formed pools and rivulets. To prepare the land for development, Mr. Caine leveled it with a bulldozer and moved sand from the beach to fill in the low places.

The State Roads Commission filed for an injunction against the developer to stop the dune destruction on grounds that it exposed the state highway to flooding from the sea. The county commissioners of Worcester County followed suit, filing for an injunction on grounds that by altering the beach, the developer was endangering other private and public property.

In July 1960, Mr. Caine reached an agreement with the State Roads Commission and Worcester County on specifications for grading and filling on the beach. He agreed to build sand fences and to plant beach vegetation to hold the dunes in place.

It was at this point that the 1962 storm leveled the North Ocean City beaches, changed the boundaries of sea and land that separated private property from public domain, and brought the whole issue of beach rights from legal debate to high drama.

At the time of the great March storm, there were just forty-two buildings between 119th Street and the Delaware line.

After the storm, the U.S. Army Corps of Engineers proposed the construction of a protective dune line from the Delaware state line south to 41st Street. Because it had to be built on privately owned beachfronts, the Worcester County Commissioners obtained easements from lot owners to build it, and stabilized it with sand fences and beach grass.

In the summer of 1964, a group known as the North Ocean City Improvement Association began to press for annexation by the town of Ocean City and the extension of public sewer and water facilities. The annexation, in 1965, brought a burst of development. It also brought to a head the unresolved issue of a public beach north of 33rd Street.

By the time the significance of the dunes had begun to be realized, the value of beachfront property was also beginning to be realized.

There is always resistance to any government regulation controlling the use of private property. In Ocean City, the resistance was especially strong because proper dune preservation would have deprived some owners of any profitable use of their land at all. To establish public beach rights for the full length of the resort was to require years of decision making by the courts and action by the Maryland legislature.

Although Mr. Caine forced the initial round by building his beach house, it was ten years before the Caine beach house made it through the court process, and the Maryland Court of Appeals, in March 1977, passed down its ruling. The court decided that only about a 5-foot portion of the overhanging front porch of Mr. Caine's house extended over publicly owned beach, and ordered it removed.

The ruling was anticlimactic, because by that time, two other beach houses had been challenged in the courts: one built by George Bert Cropper at 138th Street, and another by Emil Germanos, a Severna Park engineer, at 70th Street. The rights of both owners to build on their properties were upheld by the lower courts and the Maryland Court of Appeals.

In March 1975, the Maryland legislature passed a bill protecting Ocean City's open beaches from further development by establishing a building limit line and a beach erosion control district between the dune line and the surf. It was the first step in what was to be a long beach-acquisition process.

In the summer of 1990, Mr. Caine's house on the beach, which by then had been sold to someone else, was bought by the state and at last removed from the beach. For over twenty years it had been a symbol of the issue of public and private beach rights.

The tempest over the Caine beach house was as nothing compared to the whirlwinds arising simultaneously from Mr. Caine's activities in Ocean City's bayside wetlands. Mr. Caine's oceanfront developments had forced the beach rights issue, and his bayside developments, as much as any other, led directly to the Maryland Wetlands Act of 1970.

In one of his first deals, Jim Caine acquired from three well-known and affluent Salisbury and Ocean City businessmen an undeveloped expanse of property in North Ocean City extending from oceanfront to bayside. It was on this property that he developed the bayside communities called Caine Keys I and Caine Keys II. He developed them in the established pattern being used up and down the coast in this period: Artificial canals were dredged and bulkheaded (stabilized with wooden walls on each side) and the spoil spread behind the bulkheads to raise the wetland to building elevations, thereby creating "waterfront" lots with adjacent boat docks.

These developments coincided with an issue then building in the public conscience both locally and nationally—the preservation of wetlands.

To most Marylanders up to this time, "wetlands" and "worthless" were synonymous. In colonial times, a landowner on the lower Eastern Shore was considered a man of industry and worth according to the acreage of marsh he had filled.

In the early fifties the Chesapeake Bay Bridge had put the Shore and its thousands of miles of waterfront on bays, rivers, and ocean into easy reach of the rest of the world. The era of the "second home" and the "planned vacation community" dawned. Big-time developers began to appear before rural county officials who had never before had to deal with the scale of construction they proposed or the size of the figures they presented to show how private investment could produce public economic gain.

The pattern of development they proposed for Ocean City bayfronts was much the same as development then in progress on the fringe of barrier islands down the whole Eastern Seaboard. The value of "unproductive" marshland was being doubled many times over by dredging, bulkheading, and filling land. The practice created rich profits for developers and investors and greatly enhanced the tax base for rural counties, which could use the money. In Ocean City, Mr. Caine was but one of the developers and property owners reaping profits from this practice.

He and other developers who began rushing to this virgin vacation land then began to run afoul of the new and at first widely denounced group of adversaries—the environmentalists.

The most dogged, vigilant, and effective environmental activists on the local front, in the years that followed, were Ilia and Joe Fehrer of Snow Hill and Judy Johnson of Towson.

The Fehrers had moved from Baltimore with their family of eight children because they wanted the natural setting, the untouched cypress swamps along the Pocomoke River, and the wild shores of coastal bays. When these were threatened with what they viewed as wanton destruction, Ilia and Joe Fehrer organized the Worcester Environmental Trust. Together with Judy Johnson and her Committee to Preserve Assateague, they defended the marshes in legislative halls, at public hearings, and in courtrooms. Through the years they were more determined and unrelenting than most government agencies.

At first they were dismissed as, in the words of a former Ocean City mayor, "a bunch of bird watchers and clam diggers." Their complaints seemed trivial beside the scale of development and profit promised by the burst of construction. They were like a canoe beside a 50-foot yacht.

The wetlands, the local environmentalists argued, were even more productive than a similar acreage of farmland. They were the very basis of the food chain that supported the fisheries of bay and ocean. They filtered runoff, protecting the water quality of the bays. They were an essential part of a complete ecological system, absorbing flood waters and replenishing underground aquifers.

Up to this time, the right of property owners to fill their land had not been challenged. Landowners were assumed to have historically recognized riparian rights to fill submerged land adjacent to their shorelines so long as they did not block boating channels.

In 1965 several big dredging and filling projects were in progress, and Mr. Caine was planning one that would have extended two-thirds of the way across Assawoman Bay. Because of the extent of the proposed projects and the cloudiness of the legal issues involved, Maryland Attorney General Thomas B. Finan was asked by state authorities for an opinion on public and private rights to underwater property. The ruling from his office was that the state of Maryland had title to all offshore land dating back to the seventeenth century, and that before filling any land, a property owner would have to secure the right from the state "for a consideration adequate in the opinion of the Board of Public Works."

The ruling threw dozens of Ocean City property titles into question and its realtors, developers, and builders into a tizzy. It was challenged by the Larmar Corporation, one of the firms developing a bayside property, in what was expected to be a landmark case. When that suit was finally decided in 1971, the Maryland Court of Appeals upheld the right of the Larmar Corporation to fill land in front of its shore to the extent that the fill did not obstruct navigation. It was a ruling in direct conflict with the opinion of the attorney general six years before, but it was after-the-fact. By that time a series of actions had further complicated the issues leading up to the Maryland Wetlands Act of 1970.

Before the Wetlands Act established the state controls over dredging and filling that exist today, the developers and political leaders of Ocean City and Worcester County had attempted to establish their own local controls. The Worcester County state senator, John L. Sanford (who was the Worcester County state's attorney both before and after his terms in the state legislature), got two bills passed by the state body. One bill created a Worcester County Shoreline Commission to approve dredge and fill projects; the other established a bulkhead limit line to control how far a developer could go into the coastal bays.

The creation of the commission "put the rein on Caine," as one local lawyer put it.

George Bert Cropper (the double name is always used, never simply one or the other) was the man chosen by the Worcester County Commissioners to head the new commission. He had a lot more respect in Ocean City than any state or federal official could ever hope to have. His family history and the history of his own long life, weave in and out of the story of Ocean City from its earliest days. He was born on 3rd Street in the old downtown in 1902. Now retired, he and his wife live in a home on Ocean City's bayside with his oceangoing sailing yacht docked beside it.

When Mr. Cropper was growing up, his father had a hardware store down near the old fishing camps, an area that now lies under the Inlet, and was one of the principal players in the affairs of the old town. There were three brothers, George Bert, Harry, and Bob. The family owned a great deal of land both in Ocean City and on the mainland, and particularly the big and at one time worthless holdings in North Ocean City that were to be acquired by James Caine.

Mr. Cropper graduated in engineering from Duke University and early in his career worked for the United States Army Corps of Engineers, an agency at which he was later to direct some heavy criticism. In 1938 he, as so many native sons before and after him have done, returned to his hometown to build his future. It was a future that brought him local prominence and wealth. He established a consulting firm that figured in a variety of resort real estate, insurance, and business ventures.

After World War II, when Ocean City really began to take off, he saw the need for new foundations (literally) for the old resort, and established George Bert Cropper, Inc., a concrete and construction company. The concrete plant looms directly to the left as one enters the resort over the U.S. Route 50 bridge. His company built one of the first big motels, the Santa Maria, for Willye Conner Ludlam, and the original Carousel for Bobby Baker, and poured the concrete foundations for most of the construction in Ocean City. Because he was an engineer and resort native, his expertise and judgment were relied upon by local officials and developers in many a confrontation with "outsiders" representing state and federal agencies.

Within a few years of its creation the Worcester County Shoreline Commission became a superfluous agency superseded in its functions by the Army Corps of Engineers, the Maryland Department of Natural Resources, and state and federal health agencies newly aroused to the urgent need for wetlands and beach preservation. (Among the commission's approvals during its active years was some wetlands filling along the shore of a 3,500-acre project on the west side of the coastal bays which has become today the thriving community of Ocean Pines.)

During the period of legal uncertainty about state and local rights, Mr. Caine, impatient to get on with development of another huge project of 3,000 mobile home lots called Montego Bay on the bayside in North Ocean City, negotiated an agreement with the state to fill 160 acres of wetlands in Assawoman Bay, paying the state $100 an acre and 10 cents a ton for dredge material from the bay bottom to fill them. This deal became a running story in the statewide press and soon made the destruction of wetlands and the lucrative deals of Ocean City investors the biggest issue in the state.

It was then discovered that a few years before, in 1964 and 1965, the Maryland Board of Public Works, under Governor J. Millard Tawes, had made similar agreements with Mr. Caine and other Ocean City developers with no payment to the state and no public notice at all. The right of ownership to over 900 acres of filled wetlands had been granted to private owners by the state simply on the basis of the property owner's unquestioned riparian rights at a time when all but unrestrained development was the order of the day and the curtain was rising so slowly as to be almost imperceptible on the new era of environmental awareness. The biggest single operation in this period had been some 330 acres for Mr. Caine's bayside development called Caine Keys.

Condominium row at North Ocean City in the eighties. (© 1991 TADDER/Baltimore.)

"Wetlands," a term seldom heard in Maryland before the big dredging and filling projects in Ocean City, became a valued resource in the public mind almost overnight, and with it came the recognition that long-term values for the many were being destroyed for the personal gain of a few. This was a period of general disenchantment with people in high places, and the possibility of wrongdoing brought to the issue a barrage of media coverage.

Feeling was so high in Ocean City and Worcester County that John L. Sanford, now the county state's attorney, initiated a Grand Jury investigation of the charges, summoning an editor and three reporters from *The Evening Sun* for questioning. He then released a Grand Jury report calling the articles on the Ocean City wetlands deals "erroneous, scandalous, and based mostly on hearsay," and exonerating all local officials of any wrongdoing or conflict of interest.

An activist lawyer in Baltimore, Leonard J. Kerpelman, filed suit against the state Board of Public Works, seeking to have the wetlands that it had allowed private developers to fill, returned to public ownership. He made his wife the plaintiff in the suit on behalf of the Maryland taxpayer and argued that the state Board held the lands in public trust and had no right to convey them to private owners.

Mr. Kerpelman lost his lawsuit, but during the two years it was in the courts, titles to undeveloped lots in a 122-acre tract called Addition to Caine Harbor Mile, remained in question. Some were still underwater, and without clear deeds Mr. Caine could not continue with the streets and utilities promised to the buyers. Before Mr. Kerpelman's suit was resolved, Mr. Caine was forced to liquidate two of his corporations. The Caine Harbor Mile property was sold to pay off the buyers who could not build on their lots.

The Maryland Wetlands Act of 1970 was the lasting thing to come out of all this. The Act established a legal definition for public and private wetlands, mandated a mapping system to identify them, and created a permit process for any activity that would alter them.

State regulation of privately owned wetlands was no better received in Ocean City than government regulation of privately owned beaches.

Jim Caine had brought about more of the rapid development of North Ocean City than any other single developer, and it was Caine developments, as much as those of any other developer, that had forced public regulation of unbridled alteration of sand and marsh.

During this same time, Mr. Caine launched into some of the most flamboyant spending the lower Eastern Shore had ever seen.

Mr. Caine had not been in Ocean City long before he moved his family out of the 53rd Street apartment to a fine new home in one of the best residential neighborhoods in the nearby town of Salisbury. He bought a double lot so that his property faced one street in front and another in back. Residents on the street in back were soon nonplussed to see a sign go up on the Caine property reading "Stable Entrance."

There were at first just a pony for Bradley, then age six, and, for Joyce, a mare that was the great-granddaughter of Man O'War. Then there appeared on a Caine-owned tract along U.S. Route 50, just east of Salisbury, the buildings that were to become in just a year and a half one of the best-known stables in the nation—Winter Place Farm. It was a phenomenon the like of which had not been seen either on the Eastern Shore or in the world of show horses.

The farm buildings themselves were opulent. There was a coliseum-sized 175-by-200-foot indoor riding arena. Around its edges forty horses could be housed in pine-paneled and carpeted stalls and soothed by piped-in music. The arena floor was of chips, sand, and clay. A sprinkler system kept the dust down. Overhead were three enormous two-tiered brass and crystal chandeliers in the pattern of the famed Lippizan stables in Vienna. At one side, a nymph rose from an elegant horse fountain. A separate building housed an exercise pool curved to allow a horse 120-foot laps.

Another long building contained Mr. Caine's unparalleled collection of antique carriages. Lighting the exhibits were a dozen crystal chandeliers. The central one—2 tons of crystal and brass, with 450 lights—was so big, it almost touched the Florentine fountain on the carpeted floor below. The carriages on display more than lived up to the decor: over eighty of them, exquisitely refinished by an Amish craftsman who had done similar work for the Smithsonian Institution but had been hired to work exclusively for Mr. Caine for five years. There were runabouts, surreys with fringe on top, a row of sleighs, an elegant double brougham from Denmark, a milk wagon, children's tub carts in wicker and wood, a Victorian lady's phaeton. Accessory items by the score—coach lamps, horse bells, and whips—added to the quality of the display.

Outside, the grounds were laced with concrete-post-and-wood-rail fences. There was a go-cart track for son Jamie, who preferred motors and ocean racing boats to horses.

In the horse world, the most astonishing and, in fact, unprecedented aspect of Winter Place Farm was a stable of horses that had not developed over the course of many years, as such stables usually do, but had emerged full-blown all but overnight.

Winter Place Farm achieved a far-reaching reputation for extravagant purchases of horses and was soon being written about and talked about from the Eastern Shore to London. The Caine horses were transported through the show circuit in heated and air-conditioned vans. They were transported by ocean liner to shows abroad. An especially fine horse, Southside, was ridden in the 1976 Olympics by a member of the United States equestrian team. The trophy room at the farm displayed championship ribbons and cups from some of the most prestigious shows in the world.

A resident trainer and staff of about twenty riders and grooms were gathered from all parts of the country to work with the horses of Winter Place.

Mr. Caine did not ride. Mrs. Caine had been grounded some years before by a back injury and could not ride, but she loved the horses and accompanied them to the shows in this country and abroad.

Winter Place Farm rose and fell with Mr. Caine's fortunes in Ocean City. Only six years after its astonishing appearance, the horse farm, along with his Ocean City empire, began to come apart.

In the spring of 1974, farmers along Isle of Wight Bay, just west of Ocean City, complained to Worcester County officials that a steady stream of dump trucks thundered past their homes night and day, including weekends and holidays.

By this time, a row of high-rises had bloomed along the skyline across the bay and had become the Ocean City Gold Coast. The new Route 90 Expressway crossed the bay to a new entry to North Ocean City at 62nd Street, passing though Ocean Pines, a vacation community with a bigger population than those of the old, established Worcester County towns.

As it turned out, about 200 dump trucks were rolling from 6:00 A.M. to 1:00 A.M. and working under floodlights at night, hauling and spreading hundreds of thousands of cubic yards of fill dirt for a $10-million bayside recreational complex called Lighthouse Sound Country Club.

This fast-moving project was planned for over 700 acres of marsh-fringed farmland and woods owned by a Caine corporation in partnership with another local corporation and an individual investor. Lighthouse Sound was to have had two eighteen-hole golf courses and a tennis complex with thirty courts, indoor and outdoor swimming pools, a marina, and winter storage for a thousand boats.

It was not to be.

The project had been engineered by wetlands experts to conform to regulations established by the U.S. Army Corps of Engineers under the federal Clean Water Act of 1972. The Environmental Protection Agency was stymied in its attempt to stop it.

The Maryland Department of Natural Resources watched the operation carefully and in August 1974 found that about seven to ten acres of the project had been filled in violation of the Wetlands Act of 1970. At perfunctory court proceedings in March 1976, Mr. Caine's lawyer, Raymond S. Smethurst of Salisbury, entered a guilty plea with no elaboration and paid a $500 fine already agreed to by the state.

By that time, the project had already been bought to a standstill by economic rather than environmental difficulties. A recession was bringing almost every high-rise across the bay in Ocean City to foreclosure.

Lighthouse Sound's first eighteen-hole golf course was finished, and the irrigation equipment was in the ground when construction came to a halt. By the start of the vacation season the following spring, 1975, the site was desolate and deserted. The only sign of the extravagant complex that was not to be, was the aqua siding of the unfinished indoor tennis building. Weeds covered the sculpted mounds of the abandoned golf course. The only activity was county roads equipment resurfacing the St. Martin's Neck Road, worn down by the heavy trucks carrying fill dirt the summer before.

Lighthouse Sound was one of nineteen major developments that were planned for the bayside west of Ocean City. All had failed either to get wetlands permits or to meet other state environmental standards for sewer and water systems. The Caine development got more attention than most because of its extravagance and fast-moving pace and because it got further along than the others.

Its demise was to have a domino effect.

The lawsuits of creditors began to mount. They were filed by contractors who had worked on the abandoned Lighthouse Sound project and by buyers of unfilled lots in Montego Bay Mobile Home Park who claimed they were unable to get either title to the property or their money back.

In March 1977, Mr. Caine's Montego Bay Development Corporation filed a petition for reorganization in bankruptcy in the Baltimore federal court, citing debts of over $25 million owed to 128 creditors.

That June, the wonderful collection of antique carriages at Winter Place Farm was seized by a creditor, the Peninsula Bank of Princess Anne, and scheduled for auction on July 16. The auction was conducted by the Kruse Auction Company of Auburn, Indiana, a firm specializing in antique and classic cars. With a flourish of showmanship seldom seen on the Eastern Shore, the collection was presented to a crowd of about 500 collectors and onlookers from many states. It was sold piece by piece, for a disappointing total of $323,000.

The following spring, in March 1978, the land and buildings of Winter Place Farm went up for auction and were bought for $400,000 by the firm that held the mortgage, C. I. Mortgage Group of Boston. The day before, C. I. Mortgage had bought at another auction a property at 55th Street and the Ocean Highway where Mr. Caine had intended to build a Holiday Inn, and farther up the beach, seventy-three acres of undeveloped land known as Caine Harbor Mile.

At another foreclosure auction, the firm had also bought the Lighthouse Sound property for $1.8 million. It later sold the property to Jeffrey Levitt, of the Old Court Savings and Loan, who was later to be at the center of Maryland's savings and loan scandal. When the Maryland Deposit Insurance Fund took over Old Court, it also took over Lighthouse Sound and sold it for $3 million to a plumbers' union pension fund. It remains much as it was when Mr. Caine's grand project was abandoned.

Mr. Caine was down but not out.

His real estate firm still flourishes in Ocean City today. He has big new projects in the offing and a magnificent new home on the west side of the bay, where he lives with his second wife and former secretary, Mary Lou Taylor. He remains, as he has from his arrival almost forty years ago, an enigma.

He shuns society and continues to be an intensely private person. At the same time, the scale of his beach projects, his horse farm beside U.S. Route 50, and his new home, floodlighted at night, have been like trumpet blasts on the landscape.

His impact on Ocean City might have been even more visible than it has been. Back in the mid-1960s, he had been planning a thirty-story luxury apartment complex that would have been Ocean City's first high-rise. The city had not dealt with anything like it before, and Mr. Caine, who always worked fast, grew impatient while officials were still trying to cope with water extensions and summertime construction noise. He abandoned the project.

It remained for others to change the skyline of Ocean City.

HIGH-RISE ROW

When Bobby Baker staged the grand opening of the Carousel in July of 1962, he was teetering on the edge of financial disaster. He hired a Washington-area promoter and obscured his situation with glitter, extravagance, and celebrity guests. "From that moment, Ocean City came of age," Warren Adler, the promoter, said then.

Eleven years later, in December of 1973, Mr. Adler was back in Ocean City for another campaign. Towering new structures of concrete and glass were rising like Jack's beanstalk on the oceanfront of the north beach. Ocean City had been discovered by big-time developers. They were building luxury condominiums so fast that they rushed headlong into a recession. Metropolitan newspapers were running big, splashy stories about empty high-rises in an overbuilt resort. Like Mr. Baker, the developers were facing financial catastrophe, and like him a group of them had hired Mr. Adler to counter the negative stories with a positive approach.

The group of eight developers met in near secrecy at the Braemar, twin condominiums at 132nd Street. Mr. Adler said afterwards that Ocean City was not as well known as it should be in Washington, and he planned to remedy that with seminars and bus caravans bringing prospective buyers to the beach. It only takes a tank of gas to get here, and there is only one beach this close to Washington, he said.

In less than a year Mr. Adler had dropped his promotional efforts because support for them had died. "Sales are off because we're in an economic slump," one developer explained. "You can't change that with promotion."

Time was to achieve what promotion could not. When the economic upturn came a few years later, the Ocean City boom revived with a momentum that was to carry it to new heights.

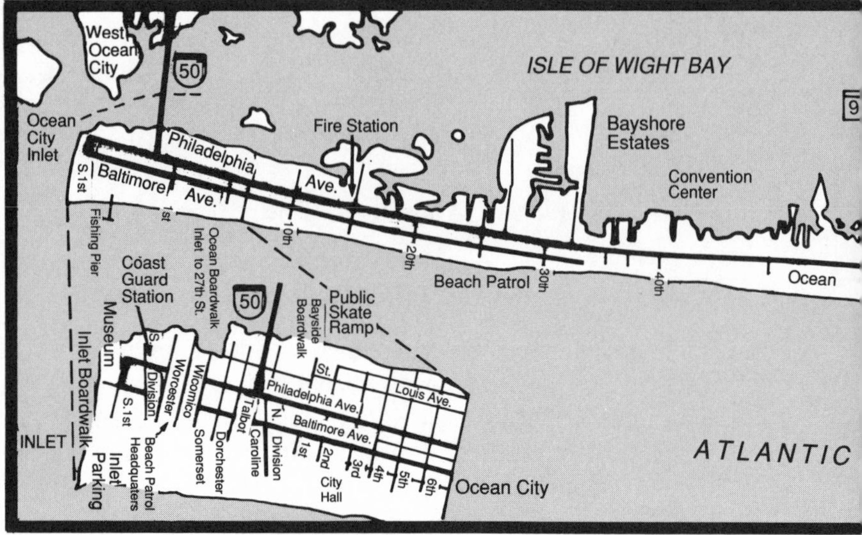

Ocean City's coming of age, whether or not it was one of maturity, could be said to have begun with High Point, the resort's first high-rise condominium. It was built in 1970 by a local developer, John Whaley. High Point was a great curiosity standing alone on a north beach and fifteen stories high, more than double the height of any other building on the whole Eastern Shore of Maryland.

Not only did its model units give the visitor a view of ocean and beach from a whole new vantage point, but they brought to an area dominated by period design and conservative tastes, the informal lines and bright colors of contemporary decor. The condominium units sold out in three months.

A key to the burst of development that was to follow was an Ocean City sewage collection system and treatment plant which had been completed a few years before and later expanded. Waste water was carried a mile out to sea through an outfall pipe at 64th Street.

Ocean City's zoning ordinance established a height limit of 45 feet for buildings, but unlimited variances were being granted by the Board of Zoning Appeals for construction of high-rise condominiums up to 200 feet, or twenty or more stories, and no protesters were showing up for the hearings. High-rise construction was concentrated on undeveloped tracts in North Ocean City above 94th Street where the tall buildings would not cast shadows or block the ocean views of existing buildings.

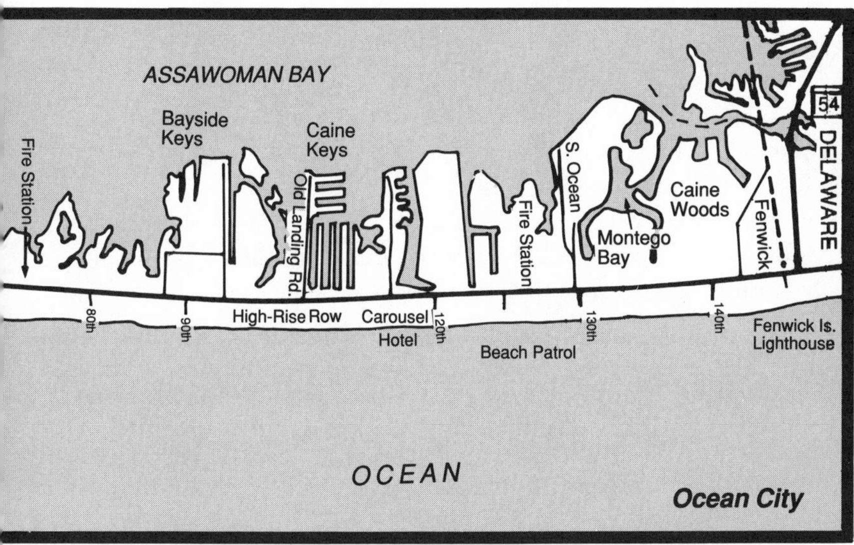

"The pressure for development in Ocean City is like water coming out of a spillway," in the words of one resident. "Miami Beach here we come," a local official exulted.

Close on the heels of High Point came a whole line of construction cranes along the skyline of North Ocean City. The first luxury high-rise motel, the Sheraton Fontainebleau, was soon booked solid every weekend. The Fountainhead, a $4.5-million, eighteen-story condominium at 100th Street, followed soon after. Then, before the Fountainhead was finished, the same developer, Max Berg of Chevy Chase, started construction on the even taller (twenty-one stories) and costlier ($5.5 million) condominium next door, named the Irene, after his wife.

The construction mortgage for the Irene was said to be the biggest ever transacted in Worcester County. Mr. Berg reported that 70 percent of the condominium units in the Irene had been sold before construction began. They sold for prices ranging from $45,000 to $62,500.

Mr. Berg, then age forty-five, was a remarkable man. He had come to this country at the age of eighteen with no money and no family. When he was twelve, his family was massacred by the Nazis. Left for dead, he crawled out of a mass grave and survived. He found refuge with a group of Polish partisans before coming to America by way of Bucharest, Budapest, and Torino, Italy.

In his imagination, he once said, America was a place where money would just be lying on the ground. "All you had to do was lean down and pick it up." When he got here, he said, he had found that to be true.

Mr. Berg's is a classic success story. He started out in Washington, D.C., washing dishes in a restaurant for $15 a week. He invested in a small store, then a restaurant, and eventually owned ten restaurants and nightclubs in various parts of the city.

Then he got into real estate. He built two luxury apartment houses in Prince George's County, one in Frederick County, and beach condominiums in Norfolk and Virginia Beach. At the start of the Ocean City boom in 1972, Mr. Berg sold his Washington restaurants and became the biggest single investor in condominium development.

With the Fountainhead and the Irene still under construction, Max Berg launched into the development Bobby Baker had dreamed of. While Mr. Baker was in federal prison in Lewisburg, Pennsylvania, for influence peddling, Mr. Berg bought his four-story, seventy-six-unit Carousel Motel for $2.5 million, then moved ahead with construction of the most elaborate hotel and condominium complex to be built in Ocean City. Attached to the original motel was a 21-story structure of masonry and glass containing 155 hotel rooms and 189 condominium units. The complex also included an indoor swimming pool, an ice-skating rink, convention and exhibit rooms, and a five-story garage for 535 cars.

Mr. Berg soon sold his interest in the venture to a group of stockholders.

Then, in the fall of 1975, the Carousel went the way of about every high-rise under construction in Ocean City: It went to foreclosure. The Carousel had the distinction of being the biggest foreclosure of all. The Alison Mortgage Investment Trust of California alleged a total indebtedness of $16 million. The lending firm was the only bidder at the auction in December 1975, and possessed the property for $5.1 million.

The Carousel complex continued operating without missing a beat and remains active year-round, with a lot of bookings for conventions. Its history followed a pattern that the new high-stakes developers were trying to break out of when they hired Mr. Adler, the Washington promoter, two Decembers before.

When the high-rise boom was at its height in 1972 and 1973, condominium units were being bought in blocks by investors at the start of construction and sold at a profit by the time the building was completed. Developers borrowed to build, and lending firms across the country were eager to get in on the boom. The same thing was happening during this period from the Maryland to the Mediterranean coast.

Ocean City was wide open to big-time development. It had one of the last developable oceanfronts in the mid-Atlantic coastal region close to two major cities, Baltimore and Washington, and it was a town which, from the beginning, had existed as a seaside resort. The people lived there, and their families had before them, to make a living in tourism. Even so, the town was not prepared for the scale of activity that suddenly hit it.

An article in *Forbes* magazine in October 1975 places much of the blame for what happened next on the banks and moneylenders. "Instead of blowing the whistle on this frenzy, they encouraged it, sometimes lending more money than the builders had even dared to ask for," *Forbes* reported. Resort areas were favored by lenders because the deals there were riskier and could bring in an extra point or two of interest.

In 1971, 1,258 condominium units were under construction in Ocean City. In 1972 the figure continued to rise to heights undreamed of in a resort which up to then had seemed, to residents and vacationers alike, to be on a home-town scale. Big-time developers from Washington and Baltimore and out of state had projects going in Ocean City. Local entrepreneurs, some still in their twenties and early thirties, were also getting into the action. They were vacationing in Florida and the Bahamas and coming back with new and flashy ideas of what Ocean City could be.

James English, Jr., a former restaurant owner in nearby Salisbury, was building English Towers on an open expanse of sand and dunes at 100th Street, which had been up to then the special domain of surfers and picnickers. Next to that he built Century I, twenty-eight stories high, and he had two other condominiums underway.

John Whaley built a companion to High Point called High Point North. Then he launched into the Pyramid, a project in which he took special pride because of its innovative architecture that did not cast the long, early-afternoon shadows on the beach that the other high-rises did.

By late 1973 and 1974, the resort was overbuilt, the market glutted, the money market tight, construction costs rising, and sales all but halted. Both the builders of high-rises and the buyers of individual units were unable to sell in time to pay off the lenders. And banks and other lending firms were forced to foreclose, take over unfinished high-rises, and go into the real estate business.

The first big foreclosure auction was held to unload the Capri, a twenty-one-story beachfront condominium built by a Prince George's

County developer who was also building a condominium called the Aquarius. It was by far the biggest foreclosure sale in Eastern Shore history. The Capri was bought by the lending firm in North Carolina for $5.85 million. A few months later there was a second big foreclosure auction at which the twenty-one-story Atlantis, being built by a New Jersey firm, went to a Philadelphia mortgage company for $7.7 million.

One by one, the new high-rises were either foreclosed, reorganized, or taken over by lending firms by negotiation with the defaulting builders. The *Forbes* magazine article estimated in 1975 that there were by then 3,000 unsold condominium units in Ocean City, "more than enough to provide each of its 2,500 year-round residents with a second home." By that time, only three builders still held title to the projects they had started.

Mortgage companies and banks, which by then owned most of the buildings, were advertising condominium units like fast food. Along the Ocean Highway big, brightly colored signs, one after the other, read: "Lenders Close Out," "Models Open," "Reduced." In huge letters they competed with cut-rate terms: "10% down, 8% interest, 30 years to pay"; or "95% financing, 6% interest." All offered the same luxuries—ocean view, wall-to-wall carpeting, air conditioning, swimming pools, tennis courts.

It was four or five years before buyers caught up with construction. In the years since then, the building and the buying has continued with an impetus that sometimes seems unstoppable.

When Mr. Adler was hired by worried developers in 1973 to promote condominium apartment sales, he proved to be absolutely right about one thing. There may be hundreds of unsold condominiums in the resort, he said then, "but there is only one beach."

In 1979, only four years after the height of the overbuilding in Ocean City, there was more construction than ever before, with $33 million in building permits issued.

The surge continued in the year that followed. The high-rise era had ended, but everywhere there were new oceanfront mid-rises, motels, malls, and restaurants. New luxury town houses on the bayside were selling for $130,000 to $170,000. In a town in which enterprises had in the past generally been small, independent, and seasonal, there were now supermarkets, chain drugstores, fast-food chains.

Tony Barrett, the new city manager, pointed out that the narrow barrier reef contains only 3.8 square miles of real estate. The real estate in that space was now worth $1 billion.

Mayor Harry W. Kelley's years in office coincided with the boom, and he reveled in it. "She's hot," he would say in his exuberant way when he spoke with pride of his city. In the city's long-running struggle with building controls, his spirit was in general that of the developer eager to forge ahead without the hindrance of blanket restrictions.

Mayor Kelley personified the place and the time. For the people of Ocean City and Worcester county, in which it was located, the resort's rapid rise meant prosperity in a rural and job-poor region. The big-time development in Ocean City resulted in the lowest tax rate in the state for the property owners of Worcester County. The imposition of controls at any level was resisted with emotional outbursts against the intrusion of outsiders in local affairs or threats against private property rights, which were generally regarded as being as sacred as freedom of speech or religion.

In the early stages of the Ocean City boom the Ocean City Mayor and Council and the Board of Zoning Appeals were all but overwhelmed by the pace and scale of development. But as the population increased, so did civic involvement, and dissent. Residents filled the council chambers to overflowing for the bimonthly meetings of the mayor and council. Newly organized citizen groups pressed for action to improve the aesthetics of crowded and quickly put together, prebuilt housing units, and to resolve the increasing problems of traffic, noise, lack of parking, and overcrowded beaches. They pressed for revisions in the zoning code and for density controls.

One of the young businessmen who were beginning to become active in city affairs declared Ocean City to be "one of the most dense seaside resorts in the United States or the world."

It was not until 1985 that the Ocean City Mayor and Council, after two years of public hearings and debate, approved the first new comprehensive plan in eight years and a revised zoning code. The new ordinance reduced by as much as 66 percent, in most zoning categories, the number of dwelling units that could be built in the future. Although Ocean City would seem to most eyes to be solidly developed from ocean to bay for its entire 10-mile length, maps in the planning office showed a total of 286 undeveloped acres still scattered through the resort and now subject to the new density regulations.

Four years before that, in 1981, the mayor and council had, after long debate, passed a safety ordinance that would apply to high-rise structures already built and to come. The big problem they had wrestled with was how high-rises completed in the big boom ten years before could be refitted with safety measures not required when they were built.

The new ordinance requires that partial sprinkler systems and smoke detectors be installed in all existing buildings 75 feet or more high and sprinkler systems in all the units of new high-rises along with smoke detectors, voice-activated alarm systems, and pressurized stairwells.

The density controls and safety measures came at a time when a new trend was beginning to overshadow even the continued development of Ocean City: redevelopment of the old town became the big concern. The simple frame apartment houses and hotels of the old resort were vanishing one by one to be replaced by sleek, modern, and more lucrative condominiums and businesses. The old Ocean City was disappearing, not before the onslaught of shifting sands and stormy surf, but beneath the waves of new tastes, desires, personal values, and economic pressures.

A lot of people miss it.

A JUDGE OF FIRST IMPRESSION

From 1964 to 1982, Worcester County had a judge to remember—Daniel T. Prettyman. During his years on the bench, Judge Prettyman, Chief Judge of the First Judicial Circuit, was presented with more precedent-setting cases, or cases of first impression, than any other judge in the state.

His years coincided with the big boom in Ocean City. As builders rushed to establish claims to beachfronts, he was confronted, for instance, with the first court rulings in Maryland on the bounds of public and private beach rights. Coming before his court was the first case, the Larmar case, in which the state defended its vested rights in navigable waters and the land under it (wetlands).

Most memorable of all was Judge Prettyman himself. He was round and pleasant, with his own contagious and inimitable laugh which came through his teeth like a breeze. When a lawyer's questioning seemed to obscure more than clarify the issue at hand, he often startled witness and lawyer alike by taking over the questioning himself.

His natural wit was never dulled by heavy issues. A lighthearted quip or bit of wordplay would come so quickly from the bench that only court spectators unburdened by participation in the proceedings might catch it and smile.

Judge Prettyman was born in 1919 in the isolated Eastern Shore village of Taylors Island. He attended schools in the rural villages of Stockton and Trappe and got his law degree from the University of Maryland School of Law in 1948. Before his appointment to the judgeship, he was Worcester County state's attorney for nine years. He died in 1982.

One of the first in a series of cases before Judge Prettyman's court, to be followed statewide, was a citizens' appeal of the rezoning by the Worcester County Commissioners of 3,200 acres of farmland, woods, and wetlands on the west side of Chincoteague Bay near Ocean City. The massive rezoning was granted for a developer planning a new vacation community to be called Harbour Towne. It was to be a planned community of homes for 40,000 residents and would have tripled Worcester County's population if completed.

The rezoning was challenged by a group of about fifty county residents who were the core of an organization that later became the Worcester Environmental Trust and fought other planned subdivisions perceived to be in defiance of local zoning or state wetlands regulations. The group filed suit against Harbour Towne on grounds that there was no legal basis for it. The suit argued that there had not been enough change in land usage in the immediate area to warrant a rezoning and that there was no mistake in the original zoning, which had been adopted in 1965. This case was the first challenge to rezoning in the Worcester County Circuit Court.

The case brought statewide attention to other big-scale vacation developments then in the planning stages for the rural shores along the coastal bays west of Ocean City. The local elected officials saw change as inevitable and desirable and supported the planned projects as an economic boon to the county.

In a long-awaited ruling, Judge Prettyman upheld the rezoning. His opinion was an astonishing 108 pages long. In the middle of the tedious pages on the legal issues raised by the appeal appeared an unexpected segment:

> The court, like the protestants, could lapse into nostalgic euphoria and reminisce at length about "the good old days."
>
> The court could easily revive memories of selling fresh vegetables from the garden out of an "express wagon" along the streets, of poling a bateau at George Island landing, riding a bicycle to a remote mill dam or along a highway for 3 miles and back again

during a school lunch recess . . . hauling barrels of potatoes from the field to a waiting line of box cars for shipment to "the city," men fighting in the legislative halls for money to build "farm-to-market" roads, tramping over acres of strawberry plants in search of Japanese beetles, young married couples in a Lions Club having a beach party north of Ocean City and sitting and singing around a bonfire during the early evening . . . telephone operators that knew where you might be at any given hour of the day . . . fresh eggs from the hens in the backyard and frying chicken only in the spring and summer . . . barrels of Chincoteague oysters . . . winding through lush apple orchards and peach orchards on a "trip" to Ocean City, there to enjoy a picnic basket and change into a "bathing suit" in a "bath-house". . . dancing at the "pier ballroom" when it was "big" and one knew everyone else in the hall . . .

But to what avail does one dream of what used to be? Now, a young person does not even know that word "huckleberry," much less the fun and enjoyment of searching for and eating them. Telephone numbers now have seven digits . . . farm-to-market roads now bring people to do their weekly shopping at the supermarket, not to transport truck crops. There are no apple orchards and only two small peach orchards. There are no more fields of strawberries. There are no more potato crops. Ice is purchased only for a party, not for the preservation of daily food supplies. A mason jar is a collectible.

Laws prevent beach parties with fires, and there isn't any beach with such a degree of solitude, except Assateague, and that is closed at night. The main highways are too dangerous to ride a bicycle.

Fried chicken is promoted year-around by big corporations that control the chicken from the egg to the table. The cost of equipment makes every farmer a big businessman. There is no labor to pick the garden vegetables and the fruit . . . the supply of clams is limited by pollution restraining orders; and a wild duck or wild goose is a delicacy because of restrictive regulations and the enforcement of complicated laws.

The court might like to indulge itself in the dreamy philosophy of a 16-year-old when she offered the suggestion that new people could only move into Worcester county as the older people died off. Neither reality nor legality, however, can implement that dream . . . .

The Maryland Court of Appeals later struck down the rezoning for Harbour Towne, and it was never built, but neither the courts nor memories of things past have blocked for long the relentless pressure for growth and development in the beach area.

SEVEN

On the Map with Mayor Kelley

A FUNERAL TO REMEMBER

In the decade of the 1970s, Ocean City became a city. In the same decade, it had a mayor, Harry W. Kelley, Jr., who could only have been molded by the intimacy of small-town life. By simply being what he was, he gave the town an identity that millions of dollars' worth of contrived public relations could not have achieved.

It is hard to explain the man except to say that his artless openness, his unrestrained emotions—whether anger or exuberance—his obsessive love of Ocean City, and his always easy accessibility made him a reporter's dream. His name in the lead of a story, especially if accompanied by one of his always-colorful quotes, gave it immediate assurance of good position in a Washington or Baltimore newspaper. And, he attracted television cameras like a pop celebrity.

Perhaps the most likable thing about Mayor Kelley was the fact that his public and private life were pretty much the same. His life merged with the story of Ocean City in his time and came together at his funeral. To describe that funeral is perhaps the best way to describe the man.

Mayor Kelley died February 13, 1985, at the age of sixty-six. He was in Pompano Beach, Florida, at the time, attending a convention of horsemen in keeping with his lifelong interest in harness racing.

He had been rushed to the hospital six months before with blood clots in both lungs, and, he said afterward, he was "the sickest I have ever been in my life." He went on to be reelected to his eighth term in office on October 16, but was on strong anticoagulants and was plainly unwell. His death was not unexpected. He had known it was coming and planned for it, even to listing the pallbearers he wanted.

When his body was returned to Ocean City, it was driven the length of the town, starting at the Inlet at the south end and moving through the old town, past "motel row," the big new hotels, the line of high-rises on the Gold Coast, the new malls and developments, to the Delaware line. An escort of police cars was arranged in the "missing pilot" formation, with one car missing.

Before the two memorial services on Monday, February 18, the mayor's body lay in state in an open coffin in the rotunda of City Hall, a building which, in an earlier time, had been the Ocean City school where the mayor entered the first grade. Contingents from the American Legion and the city's police and volunteer fire departments served as honor guards.

Onlookers and reporters from across the state began crowding the streets outside City Hall long before the mayor's coffin arrived at noon. The entrance was draped in black bunting supplied by the city of Baltimore through its mayor, then William Donald Schaefer.

An hour-long memorial service in the gymnasium at City Hall included three eulogies and was followed by a religious service at the Atlantic United Methodist Church. Then the long funeral procession drove to a cemetery eight miles away on the mainland.

Both the gymnasium and the church were overflowing, and the services were broadcast outside by loudspeakers.

"This town is putting on a first-class wingding of a ceremony for you, and this town knows that's the way you want it," Judge Dale R. Cathell, an old friend of the mayor who was as close to him as a son, said in one of the eulogies. Throughout his presentation, Judge Cathell addressed the mayor as if he were present. "There will be laughter and tears," he promised.

After the services, the mile-long procession to the cemetery was led by a city flat-bed truck carrying a black-draped bulldozer topped by a hard hat labeled "Bully." This was the hat the mayor had worn some years before when he summoned the media and drove a bulldozer into the surf to push sand onto an eroding beach. "Bully" was the symbol of his much-publicized demonstration of defiance of the U.S. Army Corps of Engineers, which had prohibited the practice. In the funeral procession, the bulldozer was followed by city police cars, a garbage truck, beach patrol vehicles, fire engines and rescue trucks, and six municipal buses carrying mourners.

Riding with the family in the funeral limousine was the mayor's wife, Constance Quillin Kelley, for thirty years an invalid suffering from lupus and confined to bed and wheelchair in a Salisbury nursing home. Behind the limousine were cars bearing Maryland Governor Harry Hughes, Senator Paul R. Sarbanes, Representative Roy P. Dyson, Mayor Schaefer, Former Baltimore Mayor Tommy D'Alesandro, and Maryland Comptroller Louis L. Goldstein.

The mayor's coffin was carried by three Ocean City policemen and three firemen. There were also about twenty-five honorary pallbearers, whose names the mayor had written on the back of an envelope after his visit to the hospital a few weeks before. Among them were Former Governor Marvin Mandel; Brice Phillips, owner of the Phillips seafood restaurants; Clinton P. ("Skate") Redden, an Ocean City fisherman; Howard ("Jake") Shaffer, retired head of Ocean City maintenance; and the seven members of the city council. Another of the honorary pallbearers was Verson Purnell, whose tenure as a City Hall maintenance man paralleled the mayor's fifteen years in office. Mr. Purnell was wearing, by special request, a gift from the mayor—the famous pink suit Mayor Kelley had worn during much of his campaign for Maryland governor two years before.

At the Evergreen Cemetery, near the town of Berlin, the long procession entered under crossed ladders raised from Ocean City fire trucks. There was a twenty-one-gun salute.

Afterwards, much of the crowd returned to City Hall for a post-funeral reception. The chairs for the funeral service had been removed, and a long table extending the full length of the room was laden with crab balls, chicken wings, and sandwiches.

From the color of this day-long event and the people who came, a total stranger could have learned a lot about Harry W. Kelley and the town he was reared in and served for fifteen years as mayor and sixteen years before that as a member of the city council.

One of the three eulogies at the City Hall service was delivered by Mayor Kelley's son-in-law, Jack Collins, whose wife, Connie, is one of the mayor's two daughters. Ocean City was also family to him, Mr. Collins said of the mayor. "It was the son he raised and catered to . . . . He lived it, breathed it, and loved it."

Representing the media, Susan White Bowden, then of WMAR-TV in Baltimore, recalled the mayor's "special relationship with the press." In her eulogy she said she had been covering the mayor for eighteen years and described him as "the best P.R. man I ever met. He served up the city on a platter of personality, and we in the press devoured it. He did use us, but we loved being used."

Judge Cathell's was the most intimate eulogy. He was then a Worcester County circuit court judge, later to be a judge in the Maryland Court of Special Appeals. He was a personal friend and had been Ocean City solicitor and right-hand man to the mayor during his first eight years in office.

Judge Cathell's remembrances of Mayor Kelley at that unparalleled funeral in February 1985 make a good framework for the story of the man and of a whole era in the resort he came to personify.

FIGHTS AND TRIUMPHS

In his eulogy addressed to the mayor, Judge Cathell spoke of "the fights you had and those you invented."

Mayor Kelley himself had once said, "I will be the first to admit that I can be cantankerous, difficult, and hard to work with . . . hot-headed and impulsive."

The mayor loved a good party. During his years in office, the parties given by him and for him were Convention Hall–sized. One of them was given by a group of friends in 1978 right after he had been reelected mayor for the third time by a margin of three to one. There were 3,200 people at the party, more than the number of voters in Ocean City.

William Kelley, a cousin of the mayor and one of the resort's leading businessmen, introduced the guest of honor at the party as "abrasive, opinionated, hard-headed, and irrational. These are his attributes," he said.

Mr. Kelley said that the mayor had tangled with the attorney general, the state Department of Natural Resources, the federal Environmental Protection Agency, the Army Corps of Engineers, and the Department of Commerce. "What it means is that these agencies are still answerable to the man in the street. Around here, Harry Kelley is our representative—and represent us he does." He then led the party crowd in three cheers of "Give 'em hell, Kel."

At the funeral Judge Cathell remembered that the first major triumph for Mayor Kelley and the council after he took office in September 1970, had been the passage by the Maryland legislature of a room tax that would give Ocean City badly needed financial stability.

Then, and throughout his fifteen years in office, Mayor Kelley fought against strong and relentless pressures for legalized gambling as a road to prosperity for the resort. His adversaries pointed to Atlantic City as an argument for the blessing of gambling. The mayor used that town as an argument against it. Ocean City was and would remain, if he had anything to do with it, a family resort, the mayor kept insisting. During some crucial years for the city, he was the main barrier against the gambling interests.

He was outraged when a delegate in the Maryland General Assembly from Prince George's County, on the west side of Chesapeake Bay, introduced a resolution promoting gambling in Ocean City. The resolution quickly died when, to widespread hilarity, the Worcester County delegate introduced a resolution promoting legalized prostitution in Prince George's County.

"Now it can be told" who was the author of the prostitution resolution, Judge Cathell said in his eulogy at Mayor Kelley's funeral. "Even his practical jokes were man-sized."

Mayor Kelley, photogenic and quotable, took on the Army Corps of Engineers in the spring of 1977. In defiance of the agency's prohibition, he called the press and television people he had come to know by first name, donned the hard hat labeled "Bully," got into a big city-owned bulldozer, and personally drove it into the surf to push sand onto an eroded beach at 13th Street. The city had bought the bulldozer the previous summer and used it to restore badly eroded beaches after a series of northeasters. The Army Corps of Engineers had granted the city a temporary permit to do the bulldozing the previous fall, but would not renew it.

Mayor Kelley asserted that beaches could be restored by bulldozing at a fraction of the cost of the beach restoration projects being studied by the Corps and supported by the Maryland Department of Natural Resources. Furthermore, they could do it on the spot without the long and cumbersome bureaucratic delays encountered when dealing with government agencies.

The Corps's proposed multimillion-dollar project involved bulkheading, dune-building, and beach replenishment by pumping sand from offshore, and was a long way in the future. Mayor Kelley defended the city's bulldozing program because the beaches were eroding severely, "something had to be done," and "nobody's doing anything."

In his gesture of defiance, he made one run into and out of the surf, dropping and lifting the machine's giant blade under the direction of Alex Johnson, the regular operator. The press loved it, and so did the public.

Eight years later, in his eulogy at Mayor Kelley's funeral, Judge Cathell said, "It's time, Kelley, for the whole truth of that ride to be known. The truth is that you were gallantly backing into the surf by yourself in a bulldozer in reverse without the slightest idea of how to get it out of reverse or to turn it off. Thankfully, it choked out before you and the dozer disappeared beneath the sea." The mayor had then gladly yielded to the expertise of the driver who stood by on the beach.

Two months after the mayor's bulldozer ride, the Corps reconsidered a permit at a boisterous hearing at Ocean City Convention Hall at which most of the 215 people in attendance supported the mayor's stand at shouting level on the grounds that "he is doing something." Biologists testifying for the Corps argued that bulldozing causes unacceptable biological disturbances and offers only temporary benefits.

That fall, a series of northeasters severely eroded the beaches, and surf washed up around the foundations of beachfront buildings. The

Mayor Kelley's infamous ride on the bulldozer. (Photograph by the author.)

Corps issued an emergency permit for bulldozing in limited areas. After another series of storms that December, the mayor's bulldozing program was strengthened by a government-surplus bulldozer obtained from the Department of Defense and two more on government loan. At one point, eight bulldozers were at work on the beach.

That January, in what was hailed as a great victory for Mayor Kelley, the Corps issued a full-scale permit to the resort to bulldoze sand.

The mayor had just been reelected and was at the height of his popularity, when, less than a year later, and to the surprise of many, a newly elected city councilman expressed doubts about the bulldozing program. At the first city council meeting after his election, Hale Harrison, owner of several resort hotels, suggested that bulldozing be "re-examined" as a method of beach preservation. He said that he and other resort property owners had had a change of heart about beach building by bulldozing. He was backed by another new councilman, Guy Ayres, who had a letter from a property owner who believed that bulldozing was damaging the beach in front of his property and suggested a lawsuit against the city if it continued.

The mayor eventually reached an agreement with dissenters on the council that he would order bulldozing of sand only when necessary to keep the surf from reaching the Boardwalk or other property and not to push sand in front of property if the owner objected.

The wisdom and folly of the bulldozing or other of the city's beach-preservation methods have been argued ever since. But none of the highly credible scientific studies on beach dynamics or the long-range proposals for land-use controls and erosion control, has attracted even a fraction of the public response that Mayor Kelley did when he put on a hard hat and drove a bulldozer into the surf.

It was Mayor Kelley's response to the gasoline shortage in the spring in 1979 that put him in the national media.

"We were the only city in this whole country that benefited from that shortage," Judge Cathell said in his funeral eulogy.

As Memorial Day and the opening of Ocean City vacation season approached, the mayor let it be known far and wide that he had a "secret plan" to ensure that everybody who came to the resort could find enough gas to get home.

A picture of the mayor holding a gasoline hose and grinning broadly was flashed across the country. It brought the resort "a million dollars' worth of publicity," but he did not initially plan it that way, the mayor said at the time.

The "secret plan" turned out to be a cache of gasoline the mayor had started buying at spot markets that April at higher than market value and storing in city tanks. He had arranged for the rental of a tank truck to deliver it, at cost, to filling stations that requested it. The mayor had bought the gas with city money. It was his plan to sell to service stations at the going rate, with the city subsidizing the rest.

The city council had favored the plan in a vote of five to two. One of the dissenters, Granville D. Trimper, and some of the station operators as well, called it a "black market" deal. If it isn't black, "it's a gray market," Mr. Trimper said.

The mayor's secret supply was sold and pumped.

By the Fourth of July weekend, dissenters had been shouted down by local businessmen at a crowded and emotional council meeting, and Mayor Kelley renewed his gasoline supply to reassure vacationers and keep them coming to Ocean City.

By the end of August, the mayor's plan had cost city taxpayers $30,000 to $40,000, but he was able to report "the biggest season we've ever had." The lines of cars in Ocean City were not waiting for gasoline, but to move in the solid streams of traffic that continue to plague the city.

Mayor Kelley's most heated fight was the long-running one with the city of Philadelphia and the Environmental Protection Agency over the dumping of sewage in the ocean.

Year after year through the 1970s, in what became a ritual of frustration, Maryland and Delaware officials and ocean resort towns fought the annual renewals by the EPA of the permit allowing Philadelphia to dump its sludge off their coast. Since 1960, Philadelphia had been disposing of its sludge by transporting it down the Delaware River on barges and dumping it at two sites southeast of the mouth of the Delaware Bay.

In 1972 the mayor and four councilmen chartered a prop-jet and went to Washington to protest the dumping before two subcommittees of the House Merchant Marine and Fisheries Committee. "Out of respect for the United States, we cannot physically stop a barge operating under a federal permit," the mayor told the congressmen. "But if you remove the federal permit, our seamen and our watermen—our commercial fishermen—will turn the barges around."

The congressional panel and spectators applauded, and television cameras homed in on him in the hallway. That year, Congress passed the Marine Protection Act, establishing standards and requiring annual permit renewal by the EPA for ocean dumping.

The Philadelphia dumping continued.

At a hearing in Rehoboth Beach in 1975, a Maryland assistant attorney general, Warren K. Rich, accused Philadelphia of dumping contaminated sludge, and Mayor Kelley accused the EPA of "not having the guts to say no" to Philadelphia.

In Georgetown, in 1976, Mayor Kelley told the officials at a heated hearing that he had protested the dumping at thirteen hearings so far, and it was time "to get rid of the experts and get back to some common sense." That was the hearing at which Mr. Rich offered to punch the Philadelphia water commissioner in the nose, a response which so pleased the mayor that the two became close friends.

It was not until the fall of 1980 that Philadelphia developed new means of land disposal for its sludge and the dumping ended.

The long fight had established a rapport between the mayor and the Maryland Department of Natural Resources, which had not been the case during the years of dissension over the best way to save Ocean City's eroding beaches.

In 1970, about the time Mayor Kelley took office, construction was accelerating on the North Ocean City beaches, erosion was a continuing problem, and the bounds of public and private beach rights had not been resolved.

The mayor and city council traveled up and down the beach, considered the dune line, existing buildings, and public access and established a building limit line. They passed an ordinance prohibiting any building between that line and the surf. It was the first step toward an open-space plan and the acquisition of public easements from beach-property owners to the portion of their lots that extended east of the established building line. If an entire lot were east of the line, the city hoped to acquire it outright as a part of the public beach with money from federal and state agencies.

The mayor, Judge Cathell said at his funeral, considered the assurance of the public beach to be his major achievement.

In 1975 the Maryland legislature, with some revisions, established the building limit line by state law and created a beach-erosion control district. The state then began the long beach-acquisition process. (It was a process not to be completed until the summer of 1990, a story to be continued under another mayor in another chapter.)

Although their aims were the same, the long relationship between Mayor Kelley and the Maryland Secretary of Natural Resources, James B. Coulter, was passionately adversarial. Mayor Kelley felt for Ocean City all the possessiveness of a settler for his homestead, and his differences with the secretary were often marked more by bristling hostility than by rational argument.

The mayor defended to the end the jetty-building program he set in motion on the public beach. (His program has since been replaced by the long-studied beach-erosion control project of the U.S. Army Corps of Engineers, a program the mayor had resisted with characteristic fire.) The mayor's program was viewed by Mr. Coulter as an interim beach-preservation effort until the long-range project being studied by the Army Corps of Engineers could begin. The mayor saw it as an effective and far less costly substitute for the Corps plan.

The state of Maryland financed on a year-to-year basis the mayor's building of wooden jetties, or "groins," and later jetties of giant granite rocks, into the surf to catch and hold sand on the beaches. Mayor Kelley insisted on selecting the jetty sites and supervising their construction himself and could hardly bear the intrusion of federal and state officials into Ocean City's beach-erosion problems. Nor could he bear lightly the criticisms made by professional engineering and geological studies of his jetty-building program.

When, after three years of putting up state money to build jetties where and how the mayor wanted them, Mr. Coulter withheld approval of state expenditures unless the jetties were built to state specifications, Mayor Kelley, in characteristic style, began to work anyway on a stone jetty at 87th Street. He used city labor and money appropriated for jetty building by the Worcester County Commissioners. When the jetty was completed, he celebrated with country music and waving flags.

An agreement was eventually reached with the state to build future groins using the costlier but more solid construction methods recommended by an engineering consulting firm.

During the years that Mayor Kelley resisted the state's supervision, twenty-three stone groins were built into the surf, either from scratch or by adding stone to existing timber groins. Less than ten years later, these groins have sunk into the sand and are almost lost to view and, in the public mind, are covered and overshadowed by the multimillion-dollar beach-replenishment program that has widened and deepened the beaches.

In 1981, Harry W. Kelley declared his candidacy for the Democratic nomination for governor. He was then 62 years old. People in all walks of life from all over the state had known him as "Harry" or "Kel" since he and his mother ran the Royalton hotel and knew most of their clientele personally. There is no question that he had a wider identity than almost anybody in the state and unfailing media attention any politician would envy.

"Even if you disagree with him on some issues, think what it would mean for Ocean City," Guy Ayres, an Ocean City councilman, said of the possibility of the mayor's being elected governor.

The mayor's first hurdle will be credibility, said Charles ("Buddy") Jenkins, a resort businessman and old friend at the candidacy announcement party. "The answer to that is money." Mr. Jenkins and other friends then set about to raise it.

Like all the mayor's parties, his big fund-raiser at Ocean City Convention Hall a few weeks later was big, splashy, and fun. There were 3,000 guests at $50 a couple, 5,000 balloons, two orchestras, and great quantities of food and drink.

The big kickoff raised about $70,000. The campaign hired a professional staff and pollsters. But, by the following April, poll results and little continued financial backing gave his candidacy low credibility. The mayor's advisers gave him "no shot," and he reluctantly let his staff go. Then, against all advice, he decided to stay in the race after all and began on his own, the second stage of his campaign. "I always wanted to serve the state," he explained at the time. "Suppose we beat the system? Suppose we can win without money?"

Connie Collins ran her father's campaign from her home in Catonsville and a small office in town. She enlisted friends as volunteers. For the mayor's running mate for lieutenant governor she and her husband, Jack, enlisted Mark Vincent, a thirty-nine-year-old lawyer who was a friend and neighbor.

The mayor traveled the state, buoyed everywhere by recognition from the crowd and shouts of support. He loved it.

When it was over, and he was defeated by the incumbent governor Harry R. Hughes, Harry Kelley went home and filed three days later for his seventh two-year term as Ocean City mayor.

It turned out to be the most challenging election in his career in city politics. He was opposed by a city councilman, George Feehley, who had stressed his independence from the "good old boy" network and built a following among senior citizens and new North Ocean City residents. Mr. Feehley even challenged the mayor's pride and joy, his personally supervised jetty-building program. It did not, he said, meet spacing and design requirements that are supposed to be a prerequisite for state financing.

"It used to be his town," Mr. Feehley said of the mayor in his campaign. "It's not that way anymore. It's a new era. But it's hard to fight a legend," he admitted with a touch of resignation.

Mayor Kelley won reelection, but by the narrowest margin ever.

And it really was a new era. Two years before, after a voter referendum, the city council had developed and passed a charter amendment creating a city manager form of government and substantially reducing the mayor's power.

Two years later, in 1984, Mayor Kelley was unopposed when he ran one more time for his eighth term. "The fact is, I'm in love with Ocean

City, Maryland. And let's face it. I don't know how to do anything else," he explained. In his usual open way, he also admitted that he liked being recognized and welcomed in the offices of senators and representatives in Washington and the state officials in Annapolis. "I've loved it." he said.

Whatever differences with the mayor there might have been in his many years in office, neither friend nor foe could deny one unfailing instinct—his "nose for a storm." Whatever the reports of imminent disaster in the news media or the uncertainty of the populace, he seemed to have a special sense that a hurricane was not going to make its landfall at Ocean City. He never panicked.

"We wish you, Kelley, a heaven free of northeasters," Judge Cathell said as he ended his eulogy of the mayor, "and a heaven where hurricanes always head out to sea—and wish you heavenly weathermen who agree with you."

EIGHT

Samplings of Success

THE HARRISONS, MAKING GOOD AT HOME

The modest headquarters of the Harrison Group, inside a white picket fence by the Plim Plaza in downtown Ocean City, looks like a classic hometown business office.

For Hale and John Harrison, Ocean City is home. Hale and John, both still in their forties, are small-town boys who, in a reversal of the traditional success story, have stayed home and made good. Today their firm owns more of Ocean City than any other business venture in town. They own seven major Ocean City hotels and five restaurants; they have an eleven-story high-rise called Sandpiper Dunes at 58th Street; and they have completed an expansion of the Holiday Inn at 67th Street to include a 600-seat banquet hall to serve the resort's growing convention trade. They have made the circuit of the town's growth up the beach and down again.

They speak modestly of their business success. "We were fortunate enough to have the opportunity," Hale explains in his characteristic and sometimes deceptively low-key manner. "It would have been a shame to let it pass."

Their growing-up years paralleled the period of most rapid growth in Ocean City, and their business ventures have matched the pattern of its development step by step, from the Boardwalk stands of their boyhood to downtown hotels, the motels of the 1960s, uptown luxury hotels, and high-rise condominiums.

When they tell their story, two themes emerge that are repeated in almost any local recital of the history of Ocean City.

One theme is the influence of a mother who was among the many women who played a strong role in the town's early development. "Women ran this town for decades," John declares. "Women were running Ocean City long before it was in vogue for women to work. When I was in college, every mother worked and did something. I didn't know anybody who was 'just a housewife.' "

The late Mayor Harry W. Kelley, whose own mother was an energetic Ocean City businesswoman and hotel owner, described Lois Harrison as "a hard worker. I had a very deep respect for her." She gave Hale and John "a lot of rope," he said.

"She always had a sense of knowing when to let us try," Hale says of his mother. "She could have said 'no' " to one of their early ventures, "when it must have been the hardest thing to say 'yes.' "

A second and equally dominant theme is what Hale Harrison describes as the "fertile environment for young entrepreneurs in this town. There are opportunities for business experience at a very, very young age. You get a taste of it, and it whets the appetite.

"When older people see kids applying themselves, they take to you," he continues. "Ocean City has a lot of friends." For instance, when the brothers went to the bank for a loan for one of their ventures, "the executive loan officer had been a waitress in Ocean City," in the days when they were boys working the Boardwalk stands.

In the early part of this century, when Ocean City was mainly sandy lots and pine barrens, the Harrison family owned 5,000 acres near Berlin a few miles west on the mainland. It was land that was said to be the biggest producer of fruit trees and ornamental shrubs in the world. Harrison Brothers Nurseries was established there by Hale's and John's great-grandfather. Their grandfather was a state senator, and their father "liked to dabble in politics," as Mayor Kelley put it.

The late Hale Harrison, father of Hale and John, was operating the Harrison nurseries with three brothers and two cousins when he met his future wife, Lois Carmean, who had come to Ocean City from Raleigh, North Carolina. She had been sent there by a hotel chain to manage the old Shoreham Hotel.

Mrs. Harrison left her hotel career when she married, but in 1951 when John, the youngest of her three children, reached the age of two, she wanted to get back to work. So her husband built a hotel for her to manage. Harrison Hall, at 15th Street, was the first hotel to be built in Ocean City in twenty years.

During those years, the Harrisons lived half the year in Ocean City and half in Berlin. When Hale was fourteen and John twelve, their father died. The two boys both worked at the hotel, and operated soft-drink stands on the Boardwalk in the summer.

"Our mother encouraged us to try things and never to be afraid to fail," John says. By the time they were seventeen and fifteen, too young to sign the papers themselves (their mother signed for them), they had bought their own apartment house, a nine-unit building rented to young people who worked at the beach. "It was our first big thing," Hale says.

Both studied the business, Hale at the University of Maryland and John at Cornell University School of Hotel Administration.

At ages twenty-three and twenty, they bought the old Plimhimmon, the landmark Victorian hotel built by Rosalie Tilghman Shreve in 1893. They didn't consult their mother before buying it. "It was more like we brought it back home and said, 'Hey, Mom. Look at this!' " Hale recalls, "She was surprised but saw that it was fine and that the price was good." They changed the name to Plim Plaza and remodeled it. Today it has 181 rooms with amenities unknown in earlier years—heat, air conditioning, and television.

Moving up the beach with the changing resort, in 1973 they bought one of the motels that had been built in the 1960s—the Quality Inn at 54th Street. They have since expanded it from 47 to 130 units and added a five-story atrium, complete with tropical birds and palm trees.

The brothers next bought the Diplomat, a fifteen-year-old motel at 26th Street that had gone to foreclosure. It became the franchise Best Western Flagship, with ninety-three rooms and the Jonah and the Whale restaurant attached.

The first hotel they built themselves was the Holiday Inn at 67th Street, a luxury hotel which, since expansion, has 216 efficiencies. It opened in 1981 along with the elegant Reflections restaurant.

Their ventures, they say, have not always been impulsive. Their expansion has been "methodical, one foot at a time," John says. "It has been carefully orchestrated." And, he adds, "It has been a lot of fun. I get bored when things are not happening. It is just the way we were brought up."

He foresees for Ocean City "an economic shift downtown." With that in mind, he and his brother built the new Harrison's Harbor Watch restaurant, overlooking the Inlet. They also bought the existing Quality Inn and its restaurant at 17th Street on the Boardwalk and the Quality Inn Stardust at 32nd Street.

In what Hale describes as "a high-decision-type business, with hundreds of decisions to be made in a day," the brothers continue to operate from the crowded quarters at the Plim Plaza. They have not moved, nor have they given their offices the sleek decor encountered in real estate and other offices uptown. "There is always something more important to do," John says.

In their cramped office space, the two brothers do not seem to step on each other's toes, literally or figuratively. How, they are asked, do they manage to achieve what rarely seems possible—a good working relationship between two family members in business together? "We very seldom have differences of opinion," Hale says. "But when something goes wrong, we don't argue in front of employees. It's like in a marriage—you don't argue in front of children.

When involvement in the town's development inevitably led to involvement in local politics, it was Hale who ran for the city council and won handily.

How did they decide who would run? "Hale had more political ambitions. It was an aspect that didn't appeal to me," John replies. Besides, John lived in Berlin and wasn't eligible. Hale lived in Ocean City.

In the city council, Hale pushed for Ocean City to enter the bond market to pay for needed improvements, and for a city manager. His opposition to beach bulldozing often led to clashes with Mayor Kelley. By the time he left office in 1982, Hale said, "I felt like I had been in the U.S. Marine Corps for four years."

Do the two brothers feel that development in the resort might have gotten out of hand?

"My only regret is that I wish we had bought more land," is John's instant reply. "The good old days are not as good as made out," he adds.

"I don't miss the time when Ocean City was shut down between Labor Day and Memorial Day and didn't really come to life until the Fourth of July."

"There are certain things we wish hadn't been built," Hale said. "Some would like to close Ocean City down, and there are some who want to build on every inch. But the majority fall somewhere between these two equally illogical views.

"Ocean City has evolved naturally. Starting as a small town, there is a lot of community spirit here. There have been mistakes. But Ocean City has done a high percentage of things right."

John's wife, Karen, has contributed to the Harrison Group her talents in promotion and interior decoration. Hale's wife, Alberta, managed the group's restaurants until the arrival of their baby.

For the Harrisons, there is little or no time for the beach that is just a few hundred yards from any of their operations. In the off season, they vacation briefly in the Caribbean or Hawaii.

"I don't want to learn tennis," John says. "I'm afraid I would like it."

THE PHILLIPS RESTAURANTS, A FAMILY AFFAIR

"We are still dependent on the place where we started. We like to think of Hoopers Island as home." Restaurateur Brice Phillips had touched the heart of the matter. During over thirty years in business, Brice and his wife, Shirley, owners of three restaurants and a hotel in Ocean City and seafood restaurants at Baltimore's Harborplace, Norfolk's Waterside, and on Washington's Potomac waterfront, have never separated themselves from the Eastern Shore fishing village where their story begins.

Hard work, family closeness, and loyalty to friends are virtues taken for granted as much now as when the family first moved to Ocean City.

Hoopers Island is a community of watermen on a narrow strip of marshy land between the Honga River and the Chesapeake Bay, in the lower reaches of Dorchester County. It is one of the most isolated peninsulas on the Eastern Shore, separated from Cambridge, the nearest town, by about thirty miles of marsh grass and loblolly pine forests.

Here on Hoopers Island, Shirley Flowers, whose father was a pleasure-yacht captain, had "a wonderful childhood," and graduated from high school in a class of eight. Here she married Brice Phillips, who was working in, and later inherited, his father's seafood packinghouse. And here they had two sons, Steve and Jeffrey.

Their life on Hoopers Island was disrupted by World War II when Brice Phillips went to Baltimore to work for Bethlehem Steel before being drafted into the army. Shirley got a job in Baltimore with the Chesapeake and Potomac Telephone Company and was able to get job transfers and follow her husband from camp to camp.

After the war, there was a change in the crab business; the big demand was for steamed crabs. Brice Phillips trucked "the big ones" to Dave Gordon's in Baltimore and kept the smaller ones for picking and packing at the Hoopers Island plant.

Then they decided to try their own outlet for steamed crabs, which Shirley would run as a supplement to the packinghouse. She chose Ocean City, she said, because her two sons, then four and eight, could enjoy the beach. It would be "a fun place."

That was 1957. Ocean City was still a small, seasonal resort that came to life on Memorial Day and was shut down after Labor Day. The "shack" where the Phillipses set up a carryout for steamed crabs was located "up the beach" at 21st Street.

The demand that first year was such that "we didn't get to the beach at all," Shirley recalled. She spent the summer in the kitchen steaming crabs.

Early in the venture, Shirley and Brice Phillips lost their fathers in the same year. Brice's mother, Leone Phillips, and Shirley's mother, Lillie Flowers, joined them in Ocean City and began working in the kitchen. The demand kept growing for crab cakes and for crab imperial and soft crabs, which were now offered in addition to the steamed hard crabs. The Phillipses like to call the two mothers "the first Phillips girls."

For twelve straight years, a dining room was added every year to the original Phillips Crab House at 21st Street. It grew to a seating capacity of 1,400 and a staff of more than 400.

Both Leone Phillips and Lillie Flowers are now dead. Mrs. Flowers made crab cakes until the age of ninety when she retired to an apartment at the Beach Plaza, the Boardwalk hotel the Phillipses had added to their holdings. She died two years later.

The year Phillips Crab House opened, 1958, a sixteen-year-old from Hagerstown, "Semore" Dofflemyer, came to Ocean City looking for a summer job and was hired by Shirley Phillips who wondered at the time whether extra help would be needed. Mr. Dofflemyer was still with the restaurant thirty-two years later with the title of executive chef.

"Seafood," Shirley Phillips believes, and many would wholeheartedly agree, "is at its finest with little preparation." The original simple menu grew simply to meet the requests of customers for more elaborate dishes such as crab au gratin or crab thermidor.

A high point for the restaurant was a visit by the famed gourmet, the late James Beard. He returned twice more and wrote about the Phillips Crab House in his syndicated newspaper column and in two of his cookbooks. Letters and customers from all over the country followed.

At the time, "I wouldn't let a platter get out of the kitchen that I didn't see," Shirley recalled. "The hardest thing to adjust to," as business grew, was "leaving it to others." The adjustment had to be made as the Phillipses acquired the Beach Plaza and its dining room, Phillips-by-the-Sea, in 1973 and a Phillips Seafood House and CarryOut at 141st Street in 1977.

Such was the celebrity of Phillips restaurants among Ocean City vacationers from Baltimore that when Harborplace revitalized the Baltimore waterfront, the Phillips restaurant there was a centerpiece. Young people who learned the business as waitresses and busboys in Ocean City supervised the food preparation and service for between 7,000 and 8,000 customers a day at the Phillips Harborplace in Baltimore.

Soon to follow were Phillips Waterside on the revitalized waterfront in Norfolk and, on a waterfront in Washington, a restaurant seating 1,400 diners.

The restaurants continue to be supplied—as they were from the beginning—by watermen who sell their catch to Phillips seafood houses at Hoopers Island and Deal Island in Somerset County. Here the bushel baskets of live hard crabs, soon to be steamed in the restaurants' "crab departments," are unloaded.

The lively Victorian decor, which is as much the mark of Phillips restaurants as fresh seafood, began "because we didn't have the budget for new things," Shirley Phillips explained. She "shopped around" and picked up authentic Tiffany lamps for as little as $2 apiece, beautiful stained-glass windows from a Victorian house that had been torn down in Salisbury, chandeliers, and a hodgepodge of other Victorian items that, she pointed out, were not being collected twenty-five years ago. The Victorian theme "has been successful for us," she said, and the theme was continued in Phillips Harborplace, which opened on July 2, 1980. Shirley added big rag dolls representing Baltimore personalities.

Along with fresh seafood and an original decor, the Phillips Ocean City operation has been distinguished from the start by a staff of attractive young people who vie for the chance to work there as waitresses, busboys, and cooks. In a rambling structure spreading out from the original carryout shop, about 2,000 young people are interviewed at the start of the season for about 350 openings that are not already filled by returnees. Such is the camaraderie among the young people that they publish a yearbook every two years, edited by members of the staff in the pattern of a high school yearbook. To house its young staff the Phillipses now own four Ocean City apartment houses.

Steve Phillips, who, at the age of eight, used to sit on the steps of the family's newly opened crab shack in Ocean City, is now, over thirty years later, president of the family business. His wife, Olivia, a local woman and a former Phillips hostess, handles the hiring and organization of waitresses. The couple have four children.

It was Steve's idea to open the Baltimore Harborplace restaurant and the others in Norfolk and Washington. He now also owns a crab plant in the Philippine Islands which supplies a California plant where canned soups and microwaveable seafood products bearing the Phillips label are produced.

Shirley and Brice Phillips's younger son, Jeffrey, was a student at Cornell University's school of hotel and restaurant management eighteen years ago when he was the victim of an automobile accident. Shirley describes it as the worst thing that has happened to the family. Jeffrey was in a coma for three months and had to learn anew to walk and talk. "My parents gave birth to me twice," he said years later. The second birth, he explained, has been the struggle to regain his faculties since the accident. Jeffrey is unable to take the active role he might have had in the family business. He has been married twice and has four children.

At the heart of the 1990 summer season, Shirley and Brice Phillips are in and out of the office, the six kitchens, and the maze of twelve dining rooms at 21st Street constantly. TV monitors keep track of the long line that forms outside the Phillips Crab House doors every evening and the rate at which it is moving.

An IBM system records and prints out checks for a payroll that reaches about $200,000 a week at the Ocean City restaurants. Some of the staff here began with summer jobs and have stayed on for twenty or more years.

The Phillips home on the bayside of Ocean City has the colorful and delightfully distinctive decor that is Shirley's style and, with its indoor swimming pool, is at once luxurious and homey. Brice and Shirley spend about half their time there, and the other half in apartments they now own in Washington and Baltimore and a beautiful old house in Norfolk.

The Phillipses have a place among the leading figures in Maryland business and industry. Brice has been in the official state delegation on four trade missions abroad—one to Canada and three to Europe, including Russia and the newly emerging Eastern bloc countries.

Shirley Phillips, with her dark, shoulder-length hair and alert and responsive face, and Brice Phillips, with his open and good-natured manner, both look as slim and vital as if they were just starting a new venture.

Shirley's formula for success is two-fold: "We were willing to start at the bottom," she said; and she has always liked to entertain.

"It kind of grew," Brice Phillips said of his crab business. He and his wife give much of the credit to "a lot of wonderful young people. This is the smartest generation this county ever had," he said.

NINE

An Interlude on the Ocean

Fish and clams are not the only quarry that bring visitors to Ocean City's harbor.

"Fishing or birdwatching?" a worker at the dock asked one arrival as the charter boats revved for departure at 5:45 A.M. on a Sunday in June. "Birdwatching," was the answer.

The other parties were loading up at the Talbot Street dock for a day of marlin or blue fishing. It was clear from the studied indifference of the boat crews and dock workers that the party of birdwatchers was an oddity. Captain Howard Cleaver's 55-foot cabin cruiser was rigged for marlin, but for this day it would take a party of twenty-four on one of the nine or ten annual pelagic trips that go out from Ocean City.

Pelagic means "belonging to the ocean surface or open sea." On this occasion, it was hoped, the term would apply to shearwaters, storm petrels, and other birds that live and migrate at sea and are still regarded as one of the frontiers of field biology in North America. As a bonus, the adventurers aboard Captain Cleaver's boat hoped to glimpse a whale or dolphins or even a loggerhead sea turtle.

"Welcome to the biggest gamble in Ocean City," was the greeting of Richard A. Rowlett, the trip organizer. The group was headed straight out into the ocean, to go about seventy miles to the rim of Baltimore Canyon, then back—a trip that would take about fourteen hours and might yield nothing but a prolonged view of open sea.

For the Ocean City fishing captains who take the expeditions out, the birdwatchers are still regarded as offbeat and a little embarrassing, Mr. Rowlett said. But Captain Cleaver obligingly maneuvered his boat for close views of bird concentrations and watched the horizon for the plume of a whale.

The party, of all ages, included a group of four from Akron, Ohio, and a couple from Brooklyn, New York; the others were from Virginia and the Baltimore–Washington area.

A heavy early-morning rain had subsided to a drizzle as the boat left the harbor and lurched through the colliding currents of the Inlet.

The boat is small enough to put its occupants close to the surface of the sea—so close, in fact, that in the rough waters of the day, waves slammed across the bow, streaming over the sides like a waterfall, and flowing across the deck and out the openings in the stern. The boat rose high on the swells and descended with a suddenness that had much the same effect on the stomach as some of the thrill rides in the Ocean City amusement area, which was receding into the distance. At once, the heavy spray penetrated openings in rain gear that had not been known by the wearer to exist. Jeans clung chillingly to the legs.

The heaving boat produced in some passengers glazed expressions and slow-motion movement; in others, flat-out surrender. By the end of the day, the deck and cabin would look like a battlefield, with bodies stretched out on any flat surface or slumped in deck chairs. Little of the food brought so festively aboard was ever eaten.

But the spirits of birdwatchers are not easily defeated. An hour out from the Inlet, the cry went out, "Shearwater at nine o'clock." The deck came to life with a rush for binoculars and cameras.

The time called by the spotter indicates the location of the bird in relation to the stern or the bow. Within the next few hours, shearwaters and petrels glided and skimmed across the water in such abundance that no location signals were needed.

The greater shearwater has a wingspan of up to 45 inches. It breeds in our winter months on remote islands in the South Atlantic and migrates north in spring over the western Atlantic, feeding on small fish and crustaceans, resting on the surface of the sea, and never going ashore. Seen in fewer numbers than the greater shearwaters, were the Cory's shearwaters, which have a darker plumage than the brown-gray and white of the greater, and the sooty shearwater, which is also a darker, slender-billed bird of slightly smaller size.

The shearwaters sweep across the water with a long, graceful glide, banking beside the boat and gaining momentum with deep wing beats. Petrels are small birds that flutter, hop, and dance across the waves with long legs and quick movements, much like the familiar sandpipers that run along the edge of the surf in early mornings on Ocean City beaches.

At about fifty miles out to sea, the pelagic birds suddenly took second place to an adventure hoped for but only half expected—the sighting of the misty plume of a whale.

As the boat circled, first one and then another of the awesome mammals curved above the water, great white undersides clearly visible. They left the greenish prints of their bodies like giant footprints on the sea as they vanished below the surface. They were fin whales, estimated to be up to 70 feet long—longer than the boat. With each new appearance of a whale above the water, excitement surged among the watchers.

The boat passed among fin whales twice that day, with a total of about fourteen sighted. There seemed to be a resident population, Mr. Rowlett said, that had been sighted by the pelagic expeditions at about the same location out from Ocean City for the last couple of years.

For those still able by midday to stand and focus, there was another thrill—an exhibition by about twenty bottle-nosed dolphins, exciting creatures about 12 feet long, rushing near the surface of the water, first directly in front of the boat, then rolling in the waves as they broke before the bow, then arcing above the water.

Besides the bonus of the dolphins and whales, the score of pelagic bird sightings by the end of the day, Mr. Rowlett estimated, totaled 2,200 Wilson storm petrels, 225 greater shearwaters, 70 Cory's shearwaters, 10 sooty shearwaters, 2 Manx shearwaters, and one possible arctic tern.

Eleanor Kendell of Ohio, a veteran birdwatcher at age seventy-seven, was one of the minority still alert and mobile as the boat pitched from side to side and dusk fell. Had the trip been rewarding? It had, she said. She had seen her first Cory's shearwater on the Ocean City trip.

There has been a recent surge of interest in pelagic birds off the mid-Atlantic coast, Mr. Rowlett said, and it started with field expeditions from the Ocean City harbor. He said he was first attracted to pelagic birds when he went on a fishing trip from Ocean City and saw birds nobody had supposed were around the area, such as the Cory's shearwater, from the west coast of Africa, and the sooty shearwater, which breeds in the Antarctic and is considered uncommon along the East Coast.

He had been doing research for the United States Fish and Wildlife Service and organizing periodic pelagic tours, and people from as far west as Texas attended his tours.

Starting about the mid-1970s, the whale and seabird expeditions off the Maryland coast became known for more sightings of whales and dolphins, seabirds, and marine life than any other similar ocean ventures in eastern North America.

After fourteen hours at sea on this rougher-than-usual expedition, the skyline of Ocean City emerged against a mixture of dark clouds and sunset.

As the boat neared the harbor at 8:30 P.M., late-hour fishermen still stood along the stone jetty at the Inlet, a cluster of surfers bobbed in the chill water nearby, and cars were streaming into the Inlet parking lot for an evening among the Boardwalk amusement rides, arcades, and food stands.

The birdwatchers, Mr. Rowlett believed, might be gaining acceptance in this setting as no more of an odd breed than any other.

TEN

In Full Bloom

A NEW SEASON

It is mid-May 1991. The Ocean City season, once just getting started in late June, is already in full bloom.

All across the Eastern Shore, people are planning their lives to avoid the beach traffic. On weekends traffic is solid for miles at the Chesapeake Bay Bridge, slowed down to the speed limit and below on U.S. Route 50, and stopped interminably when trying to enter the highway from a side road.

A new four-lane bridge across the Nanticoke at Vienna was at last completed last year, as the final link in a dual highway from west to east across the Eastern Shore. A new bridge over the Choptank at Cambridge was opened in the spring of 1988. And a new bridge across Kent Narrows is now completed, arching high above that busy waterway so that boats can go through without creating the familiar miles-long lines of idling cars on each side of an open drawbridge.

All this has been brought to pass mainly to get ever-increasing multitudes to the ocean beaches. Getting people to Ocean City is an effort that has been in process since the Wicomico & Pocomoke Railroad brought the first visitors to the newly opened Atlantic Hotel in 1875.

Back in 1934, the Ocean City Chamber of Commerce campaigned for a bridge across the Chesapeake. It was a project long talked of then and at last completed in 1952.

In support of the link between Maryland's eastern and western shores and an easier journey to the ocean coast, Gerald W. Johnson, the eminent columnist for *The Sun*, wrote in 1935: "Most Baltimoreans have for Ocean City the sort of affection people usually cherish for any place they have had a good time. The windswept beaches and the sparkling water of the bay have furnished a gigantic amount of human happiness for the inhabitants of this town; and any event that promises to contribute to the well-being of Ocean City and the region around it cannot be a matter of indifference to Baltimore."

Mayor Kelley never said it better.

Before the Bay Bridge was completed, vacationers headed for Ocean City rolled their cars off the Sandy Point ferry at Matapeake after a leisurely (too leisurely, for most travelers) Bay crossing.

The dual highway was built across the Shore patch by patch. It was not until 1967 that the links were completed between Salisbury and Cambridge and Salisbury and Ocean City.

By the time the Chesapeake Bay Bridge was completed, the traffic was backed up at its approaches in such density that the pictures and stories of the endurance of ocean-bound motorists were standard Monday-morning features in the metropolitan newspapers. Pressure for a second span began almost immediately; it opened in 1973. But for years, until the new Cambridge and Vienna bridges opened, the familiar orange cones of highways under construction funneled traffic from four lanes into two to cross the Choptank and Nanticoke rivers.

In 1987, under Governor William Donald Schaefer, a lifelong Ocean City vacationer, the state began a $2 million "Reach the Beach Campaign." To help whisk traffic across the Shore to the beach, five low-powered radio stations issued traffic information; express lanes and eventually one-way tolls kept cars moving more steadily across the Bay Bridge; thirty state police cruisers were fitted with push bumpers to aid stalled vehicles; and electronic message signs warned motorists of tie-ups and suggested alternate routes.

Widened roadways, cloverleaf approaches, and elevated crossovers have changed beyond all recognition the once rural, bucolic, peaceful entry to the Shore at Kent Island. The Eastern Shore driver, who could once breathe a sigh of relief when at last reaching the east side of the Bay Bridge after the long bout with city traffic, now remains as tense, alert, and combative on one side of the bridge as on the other.

Growth and progress in Ocean City have been hailed, condemned, or simply accepted, according to the bent of the person experiencing them.

Back in the 1960s another (then) *Sun* columnist, Russell Baker, whose point of view was a bit different from Gerald Johnson's, described Ocean City as a "typical American place by the sea where typical Americans come to do typical American things." Being as typical as possible, he ate a submarine sandwich, and while waiting out the twenty-four hours it took to digest it he drove up the Ocean Highway to "behold what man has done to nature. Up the road a piece, towering out of the dunes," he wrote, "there is a splendid new Swiss chalet. It gazes down, not on the Jungfrau, but on a trailer park fringed with plastic palm trees."

Later, after a bout with steamed crabs served by "beautiful young girls in very tight shorts," he at last went for a dip in the ocean. "On the cool Atlantic green . . . floating serenely in the surf," he found time "to think calmly and murmur, 'Thank God, no power on earth can resist this awful ocean if it decides to go for those plastic palm trees.' "

A surfer who shall be nameless has described a recurring dream. He is swooping in to shore on the crest of the most magnificent wave he has ever encountered. It carries him right across the beach with all the new stone jetties, and then it keeps going and carries him right over the top of "all those condominiums."

The motorist entering Ocean City at the north end by the Route 90 Expressway and crossing the long bridge to 62nd Street has a spectacular view of "all those condominiums." Outlined against the sky, sometimes they seem as stark and clear as a line drawing and sometimes they are hazy and blurred, but always they are startling.

One who has known Ocean City for a lifetime will still, after more than a decade, gasp a little when that skyline first appears from a rise on the bridge. There is the row of high-rises to the north, and to the south the great bulk of the Ocean City Convention Hall projecting into the bay. In either direction, as far as the eye can see, the line of buildings is unbroken.

The view is particularly impressive when the surf is high and can be seen breaking just over the roofs of the dense cluster of buildings directly ahead at the end of the bridge. In some storms, the breakers, as seen from this bridge, look as high as the buildings, and the motorist has the feeling that he is driving with foolhardy recklessness directly into the sea.

Entering the town at the south end over the U.S. Route 50 bridge, the visitor sees a completely different Ocean City. Until recently there stood on a point of land to the right, just before the bridge, the shell of a house that had been built for the filming of "Violets Are Blue." This was a simple and unpretentious film starring Sissy Spacek and Kevin Kline as two young people who had grown up in the real Ocean City—the old town, that is. There was a premiere and lots of fanfare when the film opened here in 1986, but although the movie showed the two stars racing sailboats on the bay, just like the catboat races of local memory, and although Sissy Spacek rode on the familiar Trimper rides on the Boardwalk, most of the local people who attended the film found it hard to recognize the Ocean City they knew.

Just about everyone, it seems, gives this town a character shaped by his or her own memories.

Crossing the bridge and turning to the right toward the Inlet, the visitor will see at the southernmost tip of the town, looking out toward Assateague Island, a towering Indian head carved in wood. In the summer of 1976, a twenty-seven-year-old Hungarian-born artist, Peter Toth, came to Ocean City and carved the head as a gift to the city and his personal tribute to the American Indian.

Peter Toth lived in a van and traveled with a friendly sheep dog named Smoke, supporting himself with temporary jobs and the sale of small wood carvings. It was his intent, he explained at the time, to carve similar monuments to the Indian in each of the fifty states. He chose resorts when he could, because more people would see them there. In a letter about ten years later he reported that he had realized his goal, or almost. He had completed fifty-eight monuments, at least one in every state and one in Ontario, Canada. His remaining desire was an Indian memorial in Washington, D.C., carved from "a gigantic redwood or sequoia log."

At the end of the Boardwalk, not far from the Indian head, the Ocean City Life-Saving Museum recaptures a past that is still visible around it in the old downtown, if one looks beyond the gaudy facades to the weathered wooden buildings behind the shops and eateries and flashing lights of video games.

It is an excellent museum, bringing to life the exploits of the early Life-Saving Service, the ocean fishermen, and the homey, wood-shingled Victorian hotels. For many, the Life-Saving Museum is a lot more fun than the jangling arcades outside its doors.

Beside the museum, cars cruise the vast blacktop parking lot between the Boardwalk and the ocean, looking for space. There are heavy, jacked-up pickups with holders for fishing gear on their front bumpers, and a line of anglers standing on the huge boulders that form the Inlet jetty. There are compact cars, luxury cars with fancy hubcaps, rusty cars with dented fenders, RVs, and the small buses that replaced the station wagon as family vehicles. To get to the water's edge, their occupants trek across the wide expanse of sand at this end, carrying beach chairs, sand toys, towels, blankets, coolers, and umbrellas.

Here in the old downtown the steady roar of the surf, the moan of the foghorn near the jetty, and the shrieks of sea gulls merge with the clatter of thrill rides and the barkers in game booths. In the background are the brightly colored towering structures of amusement rides, looking like the skeletal framework of futuristic high-rises. From them come the screams of thrill seekers plummeting on mats down the bright blue fiberglass chutes of water slides, or plunging down tracks at only slightly less than 90-degree angles while strapped into open cars.

Some of the old-timers of Ocean City get their hackles up when the old downtown is described as "honky-tonk." To others, that is its appeal.

In 1978 Dennis Devlin, a young businessman from Atlantic City, paid $1 million for a lower Boardwalk property with 100 feet of frontage. It contained five or six small gift and candy shops downstairs and eight one-bedroom apartments upstairs. "The Boardwalk is my cup of tea," he said at the time. "You can shop in malls at home, but there is only one Boardwalk."

A stroll on the Boardwalk is not an even-paced amble. One must weave a path through the mass, watching out for the Boardwalk trains that move slowly by, for the long line of people waiting for Thrashers fried potatoes, or for children with fast-melting ice-cream cones.

The first impression of the total stranger to this scene would be that this is a town of perpetual youth. Those who do not qualify in years seem determined to qualify in manner and dress. It is a city of illusions—illusions of fun, illusions of progress, and most of all, illusions of people about themselves and how they look in shorts or bathing suits.

The real youth form most of the resort's summertime work force. They drive the Boardwalk trains, augment the police force, operate the amusement rides, cook the fast food, man the lifeguard stands, rent the umbrellas and surf mats, perform in summer theaters, wait on tables, clerk in stores, work on construction crews, bait hooks on party fishing boats, rent motel rooms, tend bar, and play in nightclub bands. In the spring of 1990 there were an estimated 11,000 summer jobs being offered in Ocean City, most of them filled by high school and college students.

When the colleges and universities start their fall terms in late August and early September, Ocean City is like a balloon with the gas leaking out. "Help Wanted" signs appear in greater number in September than "No Vacancy" signs in July.

Up the Boardwalk at 12th Street, the venerable old Commander Hotel, which served its first dinner in 1930, still includes meals with a room and caters to a clientele that returns year after year. The Commander's guests rock in high-backed chairs on the hotel's wide front porch and watch the endless parade on the Boardwalk below. By contrast, the same old hotel offers in its dining room a seasonal Cabaret Theater generating the energy and vitality of youth, exuberance, talent, and thoroughly contemporary performances.

For the young summer workers, whatever the job, Ocean City offers more than extra money for college. "I could never go back home," said one young operator of a children's amusement ride. "There is nothing there."

From early spring to late fall, there are, suspended in the sky in perpetual flight on the beach beside the Boardwalk, a wondrous array of kites. There are the ones with thick wire crossbows and long streamerlike tails that are operated with two strings, fast reflexes, and skill, to dive and recover, swirl and loop in mesmerizing figures. There are four or five kites on one string, swooping and rising like the Blue Angels in precision flight. There are fish and dragons and huge boxes and supersonic jets.

Kites began to be really popular in Ocean City in the mid-1970s, and in 1977 Mayor Kelley proclaimed his town to be the "Kite Capital of the World." The kites have remained in the Ocean City sky longer than many fads have lasted at the beach.

Skateboards came and went and came again, and the feats of the helmeted daredevils in the skateboard bowl in back of City Hall at 3rd Street have become even more awesome the second time around.

Surfboards, a symbol of youth in the late 1960s and 1970s, projecting from windows or tied to the roofs of vehicles on the way to the beach, still bob in the surf offshore, but not in the numbers that used to be. The wave action, some say, has been altered since sand has been pumped from the ocean bottom for the beach-replenishment program, now underway after years of debate.

Bill Shreve, who spent his summers as a youth in Ocean City in the 1930s, is pretty sure that he and a group of his friends had the resort's first big surfboards. Bill remembers a fellow summer vacationer named Watt Smyth, whose family came from St. Louis and who had spent a couple of summers in Hawaii, where he learned how to surf. Watt helped him build his first surfboard, and "it was heavy as lead," he remembered. "There were about four boards in Ocean City that summer," Bill Shreve

Ocean City shown "in full bloom" in this 1990 aerial photograph. (© 1991 TADDER/Baltimore.)

said. "I had one, and Harry and Bert Cropper [natives still attached to the town] and a guy named Neal had boards."

Daniel Trimper III remembers those wide, heavy early surfboards, too, and Watt Smyth's expertise both on the board and in the Hawaiian techniques of body surfing. He also remembers that two other friends, sons of William W. McCabe, who was then mayor of the town, had been to Hawaii—a place he had barely heard of then—and had come back with surfboards.

Today, new adventure is sought in high-speed boats and jet skis, which hum down the oceanfront, or by dangling from billowing parachutes rising high as a plane on a speedboat's tow rope.

But the diversions that occupy the most people are simple and timeless—fishing, and crabbing, and the softball games behind City Hall between the teams of summer workers.

Up the Ocean Highway, huge plastic animals and Russell Baker's plastic palm trees are still proliferating at miniature golf courses and amusement parks.

In 1977, McDonald's was the first national fast-food chain to open a restaurant on the Ocean Highway. Since then, just about all the familiar chains have come in.

That same year, 1977, the $6-million Gold Coast Mall, the resort's first big indoor shopping center, opened with forty-five stores. Its two anchor stores, the A&P supermarket and the Drug Fair, reported the biggest opening days in the history of their chains. Since then, the small, independent, seasonal commercial enterprises that had characterized this town have been swamped by big chains and big malls.

In April 1970, Ocean City's $3.5-million Convention Hall was dedicated. The big hall, standing on 20-foot pilings beside Isle of Wight Bay between 39th and 42nd Streets, was built by the state of Maryland as a stimulus to tourism and hence to the state economy and as an impetus to year-round activity in Ocean City. The Convention Hall has brought to the town the Maryland Bar Association (which before that had held its annual conventions in Atlantic City), the state's classified employees, firemen, American Legion, Veterans of Foreign Wars, Association of Counties, and Municipal League. Here are held the annual East Coast Commercial Fisherman's Expo, St. Paul's Episcopal Church Antique Show, Bavarian Festival, and World Championship Wildfowl Carving

Competition; monthly Big Band Dances from October through March; and weekly flea markets all year.

Small conventions and gatherings and fleets of tour buses come and go from the Sheraton Fountainebleau, the Carousel, the Holiday Inn, and the Dunes Manor Hotel.

From the Convention Hall north, the image of Ocean City is of the plush and affluent resort life, with transplanted palm trees, piña coladas on outdoor decks by swimming pools, high-style beachwear in carpeted shops; of socially connected groups gathering at the beach, as they do at home, in clusters of chairs on the sand or for cocktails on condominium terraces.

It is impossible to explain Ocean City dispassionately, objectively, with the view of an outsider. That is because whether one is on the beach with a family and a picnic basket or at a party on the twentieth floor of a condominium looking out over the lighted city at night, one gets caught up in the place.

Life boils down to the moment, to the tiny space you have blocked out for yourself on the beach, to the particular character of the particular situation of which you are a momentary part.

Asked why he had driven for three hours in uncertain weather on a mid-May weekend to get to Ocean City, a young man with a group of fellow teenagers on the Boardwalk came close to a definitive answer: "The excitement of the crowd," he said, "the flash and flare of it all."

A NEW MAYOR AND A NEW BEACH

When Roland E. ("Fish") Powell became mayor of Ocean City in a special election in April 1985, he was surrounded by television cameras and reporters the moment the results were announced.

It was not the kind of attention normally expected for a municipal election in a town with fewer than 3,500 registered voters, and it showed the kind of celebrity status Ocean City has come to have in Maryland. In contrast, the grand opening of the Atlantic Hotel and the official founding of the resort just 110 years before had created barely a ripple in the stream of Maryland history, as recorded by either journalist or scholar.

Now, Ocean City property owners and vacationers from far and wide were following the town's election and feeling that they had a personal stake in it. For one thing, Mr. Powell would be replacing Harry W. Kelley, the flamboyant mayor who, after fifteen years in office, had come to personify Ocean City.

The new mayor is not the kind of man to be thrown off course by the intensive media attention that goes with his office. In fact, he is such a low-key, sensible, and generally unruffled man that the early attention has leveled off.

Mr. Powell was fifty-six at the time of his election, ten years younger than Mayor Kelley. He grew up on Dorchester Street, where his parents had a rooming house. Like the other children in those days, he used to stop by the Royalton Hotel, where Ethel Kelley, the former mayor's mother, fed him sticky buns and milk.

Coming along at a time when jobs were scarce, he worked as a carpenter, a painter, and a commercial fisherman. Then he went into real estate, working first for James B. Caine and then developing his own vacation-apartment rental business. He and his late wife, Blanche, had a daughter and two sons, all three still living in the beach area.

"I like being a part of things," Mr. Powell said at the time of his election as mayor. He had been a member of the Ocean City volunteer fire department for most of his life and was its chief for nine years. When he served as an Ocean City councilman for six years, his calm and reasonable approach to some of the most fiery issues more than a few times brought highly volatile meetings to a quieter simmer. He left the council to run for Worcester County Commissioner and held that office for ten years.

After Mayor Kelley died in February 1985, Mr. Powell was urged by a lot of the town's long-established business and civic leaders to file for the special election to replace him. There was a record 75-percent turnout for that election, and he ran well ahead of his nearest competitor in a four-way race. In the summer of 1990, Mayor Powell was completing his third two-year term in office and was ready to run for a fourth.

Mr. Powell is a product of the old Ocean City, but the issues he has had to cope with as mayor were not a part of anybody's thinking when he was growing up there.

Towering above all other issues has been the city's Beach Replenishment and Hurricane Protection Project. "It is the biggest issue for this town ever," he said as Phase II got underway in the summer of 1990.

The project had been studied for years by the U.S. Army Corps of Engineers but when first presented had been turned down by the city because of the high cost of the local share. The bulldozing and jetty building pursued and defended with fiery vigor by Mayor Kelley had been only stopgap measures.

The more costly jetties financed by the state and carefully engineered and constructed by stone setters, not only were taking up a lot of space on the beach but were not working, Mayor Powell contended. Some beaches where they had been built were actually losing sand. The jetty building was stopped before the planned project was completed.

To launch the massive long-range project proposed by the Army Corps of Engineers "will take big bucks," Mayor Powell said shortly after taking office, "and they will have to come from the city, county, state, and federal governments." Mayor Powell's terms in office have, as it happens, coincided with the years of Maryland Governor William Donald Schaefer, an Ocean City booster who has actively supported and attached his name to the Ocean City Beach Replenishment and Hurricane Protection Project.

On July 6, at the height of the 1990 vacation season, elected and would-be elected officials from city, county, state, and federal levels, along with invited guests and vacationers in beach garb who happened by, gathered under a tent on the beach at 89th Street to celebrate the official start of Phase II. It was a celebration complete with bumper stickers, T-shirts, and sun shades all presenting the slogan, "Dune it now!"

The project's logo is a simplified and colorful profile of a healthy beach rising from surf to dune crest and topped by a beach umbrella. Across it is written, "Rebuilding the Ocean City Beach—Phase II," and under that, "Governor William Donald Schaefer and the Citizens of Maryland."

Brochures were distributed to the crowd explaining why and how the program will be carried out. "The extensive development in Ocean City has disrupted the natural erosion/replenishment cycle," the brochure begins. "With over $2 billion of improvements in Ocean City, the natural migration of the island must be held back.

"Maryland enjoys a relatively narrow window to the Atlantic Ocean. It is very precious to us. Ocean City provides recreation and entertainment to millions of visitors each year, producing annually in excess of $85 million in revenues."

Inside, the brochure explains that Phase I of the project was completed from May through September of 1988. Sand from two borrow sites about two miles offshore was pumped to the beaches from dredges through 30-inch steel pipes on the ocean bottom. Bulldozers shaped the sand to the required slope, creating a beach 220 feet wide in front of the line of beachfront structures. The $12-million cost of Phase I was shared by the state of Maryland, Worcester County, and Ocean City.

Phase II, the start of which was being celebrated, continued into the early summer of 1991 and was paid for by the U.S. Army Corps of Engineers as well as the state, county, and city governments. In this phase, the beach continues to be replenished by dredging and pumping sand from offshore. Six-foot dunes were created from 27th Street north to 146th Street where they connect with the dune line in Delaware. The dunes are held in place by sand fences and plantings of dune grass. From 4th Street to 27th Street, a steel bulkhead now rises about 3 feet above the Boardwalk on the ocean side. It is encased in concrete with a concrete cap about 27 inches wide. To the casual eye, it looks like a continuous bench extending the length of the Boardwalk. There is access to the beach via forty-eight ramps and stairs with gates that can be closed during storms.

The Ocean City Beach Replenishment and Hurricane Protection Project is run from a special office in the Maryland Department of Natural Resources administered by a young woman named Nancy Howard.

Before the project could begin, the city had already met its biggest challenge: obtaining public easements along the oceanfront where private property rights extended across the beach. This was achieved by negotiation, with no cash payments involved except for the last property—the beach house on the north side of the Carousel, which had been a landmark since it was built by James B. Caine in 1968. On July 19, 1990, it disappeared so suddenly as to seem that it had never existed. Then under new ownership, the beach house had been appraised by the state, and a settlement had been reached in court to remove it and open the beach to public preservation and use.

Keeping the beach is a big and very costly project, and beach replenishment will be a continual necessity as far into the future as one can see. For, Ocean City's sandy beach, its great natural asset and the reason for the resort's existence, has turned out to be not so natural after all.

The Beach Replenishment and Hurricane Protection project will change the face of Ocean City as much as anything that has happened in the resort's past. It conjures in the mind's eye a double exposure of a child's sand castle and a multimillion-dollar high-rise or town-house complex.

A castle in the sand is at once the most changeless and changing phenomenon on the ocean beach. The building of sand castles is a timeless diversion. But the most elaborate construction, with towers, battlements, and moats, will be gone in the morning; an infinity of sand will have been lifted by the rising tide and carried somewhere else. Sand is suspended in every wave that topples and falls, and sand is washed from the beach as every wave recedes.

Among the exhibits in the engrossing Ocean City Life-Saving Station Museum at the end of the Boardwalk is one in which sand from beaches all over the world has been collected in similar containers for comparison. From the Pacific islands is the black sand created by the disintegration of volcanic rock. From such renowned addresses as Hyannis, Massachusetts, and Newport, Rhode Island, the sand is coarse and uninviting to bare feet. Along the glamorous French Riviera, the beach material is a not-so-glamorous small, flat stone called shingle. In Alaska the beaches are formed of cobbles rather than grains of sand. About the only sand in the exhibit comparable to that of Ocean City and the neighboring beaches of Assateague and Delaware, is the sand from Rio de Janeiro, Barbados, and St. Simons Island, Georgia.

Maryland's ocean beaches, once known only to the fisherman, the adventurer, the seeker of solitude, have never before been so accessible to so many people. Nowadays it is easier to find "the flash and flare" described by the teenager on the Boardwalk, than space to be alone.

The transformation of barren sand to teeming resort city has meant jobs, big moneymaking opportunities, and a tax base for a rural, isolated county that is the envy of most urban areas. But can the true value of a barrier island be measured in money? That is one of the many questions over which the natural order and the values of our society collide.

The 295 barrier islands strung along the Atlantic coast are, the environmentalist will argue, part of an intricate system beyond the control of developers, economists, governments, or the U.S. Army Corps of Engineers. If unencumbered by structures, the islands "give" with the sea, ever moving and changing and forming new contours. The natural movement and resilience of these islands is restricted when they are fastened down by heavy structures, roads, and parking lots. It is an intensive handicap, like loading a runner with weights. "A beach doesn't 'erode' unless there is a building on it. It only moves and changes," one of the scientists in this field has asserted. The millions of dollars being spent on beach-erosion control and flood-protection projects are therefore not actually being spent to save or protect the beach, but the buildings on it.

At the same time that some departments of government are studying the hazards of coastal development, the threats of beach erosion, sea-level rise, and global warming, others are building highways and bridges across bays and rivers to get more and more people to the ocean beaches. The dates of traditional holidays have been changed to create longer weekends, thereby bringing still more vacationers to beach resorts. A federal flood insurance program contributes to beach development by protecting builders from excessive loss in future storms. Most notably of all, millions of cubic yards of sand are being pumped onto depleted beaches at Ocean City and elsewhere up and down the East Coast to protect billions of dollars' worth of oceanfront development.

Ocean City is a city on the sand. Seen from the sea or from above, it is a frail and vulnerable city imperiled by wind, flood, and the follies of man.

From the beachfront looking out, it is a different story. As the sun rises with a vivid flare on an August morning at the height of the season, a hundred thousand people watch from the beach, from condominium balconies, and from departing fishing boats. In the glow of dawn they ride bicycles down the Boardwalk, stand alone at the ocean's edge, practice group meditation in a cluster on the sand, cast lines into the surf, or simply pause briefly on their way to somewhere to watch as the unbroken pathway of light widens across the sea to the far horizon.

Whatever the future holds, this is one of life's high moments—the start of a new day at the beach.

Sources

Much of the information in this book comes from notes and clippings collected by the author during the seventeen years (1969-1986) that she reported on the Eastern Shore for *The Sun.*

Earlier coverage of Ocean City by the Sunpapers comes from the newspaper's microfilm library in Baltimore.

Other material was discovered in vertical files, special collections, and oral-history tapes in the public library in Snow Hill and files in the Maryland Room in the Salisbury State University library. The files at both libraries contained clippings from publications past and present—*The Beachcomber, The Eastern Shore Times* of Berlin, the Salisbury *Daily Times,* the *Ocean News,* the *Ocean City Times*, the *Maryland Coast Press*, *The Democratic Messenger* of Snow Hill, *Eastern Shore Magazine*, the *Tidewater Times*, the *Maryland Conservationist*, *Maryland Magazine*, *Annapolitan*, *The News American*, *The Washington Post*, *The Sun*, and *The Evening Sun*.

BOOKS AND OTHER PUBLICATIONS

Assateague Island. Washington, D.C.: National Park Service, U.S. Department of the Interior, 1980.

Baker, Bobby (Robert Gene), with Larry L. King. *Wheeling and Dealing, Confessions of a Capitol Hill Operator.* New York: W. W. Norton & Co., 1978.

Barrier Islands and Beaches: Proceedings of the 1976 Barrier Islands Workshop, Annapolis, Maryland, May 17-18, 1976. The Conservation Foundation, 1976.

A Century of Seashore Hospitality. Ocean City, Md.: Ocean City Centennial Committee, 1975.

Corddry, George H. *Wicomico County History.* Salisbury, Md.: Wicomico Historical Society, 1981.

Dryden, Beryl and Bill. *The Tides of March, A Story of the Storm, March 6 and 7, 1962, in Ocean City, Maryland.* Berlin, Md.: Eastern Shore Times Press, 1962.

The Eastern Shore of Maryland, Wonderful Advantages Over the West. An 1879 farm catalog published by W. Halstean, real estate agent in Easton, Talbot County, Maryland.

Fehrer, Ilia. *Dynamics of Maryland Barrier Islands.* Printing made possible by Maryland's Coastal Resources Division, with financing by the League of Women Voters Educational Fund and the Office of Coastal Zone Management, U.S. Department of Commerce, 1980.

Haymon, John C. *Rails Along the Chesapeake.* Salisbury, Md.: Marvadel Publishers, 1979.

Hurley, George and Suzanne. *Ocean City, A Pictorial History.* Virginia Beach, Va.: The Donning Company, 1979.

Laws, Victor. *Maud and Other Family Legends.* New York: Carlton Press, Inc., 1990.

Legal Aspects of Sand Dunes in Maryland. A paper delivered by L. Hollingsworth Pittman at the annual meeting of the American Shore and Beach Preservation Association in June 1961.

The Maryland Wetlands. A study by William N. Hedeman, Jr., assistant general council for the United States Army Corps of Engineers, 1972.

Ocean City, Maryland. Season of 1892: A Prospectus of the Sinepuxent Beach Co. Reproduced by the William F. Chew & Co., and Precision Built Homes, Inc., no date.

Ocean City, Maryland: 1989 Business Directory. Ocean City, Md.: Ocean City Public Relations Office, Department of Tourism, 1989.

Truitt, Charles J. *Historic Salisbury Updated.* Salisbury, Md.: Historical Books, 1982.

Truitt, Reginald V. *Assateague . . . the Place Across.* Natural Resources Institute, College Park, Md.: University of Maryland, 1971.

Truitt, Reginald V. *High Winds . . . High Tides.* Natural Resources Institute, College Park, Md.: University of Maryland, 1968.

Truitt, Reginald V. and Dr. Millard G. LesCallette. *Worcester County, Maryland's Arcadia.* The Worcester County Historical Society Bi-Centennial Edition, 1977.

Who's Minding the Shore? A Citizen's Guide to Coastal Management. Prepared by the Natural Resources Defense Council, Inc., for the U.S. Department of Commerce, 1976.

Worcester County Maryland, Land of Opportunity. Reprint of the Worcester County section of a book entitled *Delaware and the Eastern Shores of Maryland and Virginia.* Wilmington, Del.: The State Publishing Company, 1926.

Wroton, William H., Jr. *Assateague.* Salisbury, Md.: Peninsula Press, 1970.

FIRST-HAND SOURCES

The author considered the key to this book to be personal interviews and loans of family pictures and papers. She owes much to the late Harriet Showell Bald, Kate Bunting, Judge Dale Cathell, Thelma Conner, the late Betty Gordy, Irma Jester, Florence Massey Black, Imogene Pierce, Roland E. Powell, Hilda Savage, John Dale Showell III, L. G. (Bill) Shreve, Raymond S. (Steve) Smethurst, Dan Trimper III, Dr. Frank Townsend, and the staffs of the Snow Hill branch of the Worcester Country Public Library and the Ocean City Life-Saving Station Museum.

Index

Jesus can heal anything

if you believe...

hat to bear [illegible]

God had been [illegible]

But sometimes [illegible]

by them [illegible]

remember because [illegible]

had to past day [illegible]

but He has not me there [illegible] to give me

strength to carry you through [illegible]

comfort me with His love and leave me [illegible] home.

a gift of encouragement

FOR

FROM

DATE

Beyond the Sorrow

There's Hope in the Promises of God

TAMMY TRENT

THOMAS NELSON
Since 1798

NASHVILLE MEXICO CITY RIO DE JANEIRO

Published in Nashville, Tennessee, by Thomas Nelson. Thomas Nelson is a registered trademark of HarperCollins Christian Publishing, Inc.

Thomas Nelson titles may be purchased in bulk for educational, business, fund-raising, or sales promotional use. For information, please e-mail SpecialMarkets@ThomasNelson.com.

Project Editor: Pat Matuszak

Project Manager: Kathy Baker

Designed by Koechel Peterson & Associates, Minneapolis, Minnesota

ISBN-13: 978-0-7180-3887-8

Printed in the United States of America

14 15 16 17 18 19 LSI 6 5 4 3 2 1

The **Lord** *is close to the brokenhearted,*

and he saves those whose spirits

have been crushed.

PSALM 34:18 NCV

The Lord Is Near to the Brokenhearted

This story is not just my life's story. All who risk loving, risk losing the one they love. Sometimes that loss comes through death of the one we love, other times love itself seems to have died when a relationship is broken. In every loss, we have to look to the very source of love, to Jesus Christ, for strength to keep pressing on. He has given us precious promises in His Word to bring the pieces of our lives back together. The Bible is like an eternal love letter that will give us hope through all of life's trials and unite our hearts with His.

I've just made it through the hardest weekend of the year for me—the anniversary of the day I lost my husband, Trent, in a diving accident. As a young married couple, we thought we'd have a long lifetime to grow old together. We had just begun to talk about starting a family when he was taken from me. If you could see me sitting here, you'd see a woman who's still very broken. I must admit, there are still days when all I want to do is close the window shades and curl up on the couch praying that I'll wake up from this unbelievable dream that my life has become. I've traveled through grief and sorrow, and God keeps calling me to a new place, to take a step—just one step at a time—that will take me **beyond the sorrow** *into His joy.*

His Invitation

One of the most important choices anyone can make in life is to keep living, no matter what circumstances surround you. It is never hopeless when you know the Lord, when you know who God really is—not some figure up on a throne, but someone who loves you and wants to have a personal relationship with you. Knowing we are not alone and that we will be comforted is what helps us make it through. God is still good when life is hard. And His invitation to choose life is always there for us.

. . . choose life,

that both you and your descendants may live;

and that you may love the LORD *your*

God, that you may obey His voice,

and that you may cling to Him,

for He is your life . . .

DEUTERONOMY 30:19, 20 NKJV

My Choice: To Say Yes!

I'd always been taught that God has a plan for my life. I truly believed that it was an adventurous plan, filled with life and love and a relationship with God. I didn't create my husband, God did. And He didn't create Trent to fulfill my plans, He created Trent to fulfill His plans. Ultimately, that means we are living out God's will, not our own, and at the end of our life's story He will be glorified.

"I have good plans for you," says the Lord. "I have good plans for you, not plans to hurt you. I will give you hope and a good future."

JEREMIAH 29:11 NCV

I had to live out that belief in God's plan when tragedy struck. God had been part of my life since I was a child, but sometimes it seemed like I was praying to someone who lived on a big throne in heaven, not sitting next to me on my couch. But His presence has become so real to me since I lost Trent. I had to just depend on Him in a close, personal way. And He has met me there. He has kept His promise to give me strength to carry on through the dark days, comfort me with His love, and lead me back home.

I was sent to help the faith of God's chosen people and to help them know the truth that shows people how to serve God. That faith and knowledge come from the hope for life forever, which God promised to us before time began. And God cannot lie.

TITUS 1:1, 2 NCV

Drawing Near

When I first lost my husband, it seemed impossible to even breathe. Shock, then sadness, and sometimes fear, literally took my breath away. But God's healing came into my life one day, one step, and even one breath at a time. Today, I am not only breathing again, I am dancing. Connie Neal wrote a book called *Dancing in the Arms of God* to describe how it felt to follow the Lord through life's difficulties. At first, I could not imagine ever dancing again. Ever being that happy. It was a struggle just to sit up and get out of bed. But I could feel the very presence of God reaching out to me. I could sense the prayers of my family and friends when I couldn't pray myself. There was hope in that for me.

Draw near to God
and He will draw near to you.

JAMES 4:8 NKJV

When you draw near to God in times of trouble, you learn who He really is. Then you learn:

- You can trust Him.
- He is not sitting in heaven on a throne, but walking with you here on earth.
- He wants a personal relationship with *you*.
- You can know the depth of His love for you.
- Your soul craves relationship with God.
- You can call on Him for help *first,* not after other sources have failed.

Dancing Like No One Is Watching

I love these thoughts I heard from my very good friend Luci Swindoll:

"Work like you don't need the money. Love like you've never been hurt. Dance like no one is watching, and live like it's heaven on earth."

Sometimes all we want is a safe path with no risks. But you can't dance if you don't risk standing up and trying to take a step forward. You can't live if you don't take any chances either. We need to say yes to life, even if we can't control the outcome of our life's story. Be brave. Choose to live and to embrace your life with joy.

"Then you will call my name.
You will come to me and pray to me,
and I will listen to you.
You will search for me.
And when you search for me with all your heart,
you will find me! I will let you find me,"
says the LORD.

JEREMIAH 29: 12–14 NCV

Faith is a risk, but not having faith is also a risk. We risk missing out on our lives becoming a part of the greatest love story of all time—the story of a God who loved us so much that He left heaven to be with us.

"God loved the world so much
that he gave his one and only Son
so that whoever believes in him
may not be lost,
but have eternal life.
God did not send his Son
into the world
to judge the world guilty,
but to save the world through him."

JOHN 3:16, 17 NCV

IS A RISK

Give and Take Rhythm

Maybe we want a quick push-button fix for every difficulty. Our modern world is like that: three steps to solve every problem from fitness to relationships. But Jesus never said life would be easy—He just promised that He wouldn't leave us alone. So in the midst of our problems, we are not alone even when we are the only ones in the room. We feel His presence and strength when we pray.

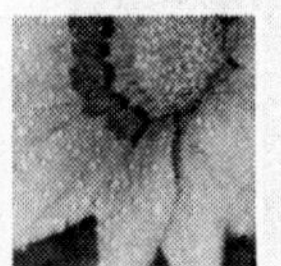

"If ye love me, keep my commandments.
And I will pray the Father,
and he shall give you another Comforter,
that he may abide with you for ever;
even the Spirit of truth;
whom the world cannot receive,
because it seeth him not,
neither knoweth him:
but ye know him;
for he dwelleth with you,
and shall be in you.
I will not leave you comfortless:
I will come to you."

JOHN 14:15–18 KJV

* *God also sends people to comfort us so we will know He has heard our call for help. We can ask for guidance to wisely discern which people have been sent by God to affirm us and speak strength into our lives. We need to invite those people into relationship and nurture those ties. I purposely gathered a circle of supportive friends around me just to hang out. I called them when I needed help, because I could trust that they meant what they said when they promised to be there for me. After they had been so faithful to help me, I wanted to give something back. I invited a core group of friends to come to my home for dinner regularly. I needed to be able to give back even in my own loss. There was strength in receiving help and strength in giving something back.*

"Give, and you will receive.
You will be given much.
Pressed down, shaken together,
and running over, it will spill into your lap.
The way you give to others
is the way God will give to you."

LUKE 6:38 NCV

A Surprise Partner

Sometimes God answers our prayers by sending people to rescue us who we haven't asked for help.

One day I was working in my yard trying to trim a branch off of a tree. It was a tree that Trent gave me for my birthday in April 2001, and I didn't want to ruin it; but I didn't have a strong enough saw to cut through the entire branch. I sat down there and cried. I missed my husband so much at that moment. He would have known what to do and how to take care of it for me.

"I hate this!" I yelled at God. "This is what my life is going to be like from now on, isn't it?" I felt so frustrated and so out of control.

Suddenly, a neighbor lady pulled up in her car and saw that I needed help.

"Tammy, you need a chainsaw? Wait a minute." I watched her pull into her driveway and could hardly keep from laughing as the little woman came out of her garage toting a full-size chainsaw.

"I just had this hanging on my wall," she explained. She knew how to use it, too! In minutes, we had taken care of the problem branch that I'd struggled with for an hour.

I hadn't asked her for help, but she had seen the need and freely given something that I'd never have thought to ask her for. Her soft-spoken personality just didn't shout, "I have a chainsaw!"

Sometimes people have hidden gifts. What is hanging on the wall in your garage? And could there be "chain-saw ladies" out there just waiting for the opportunity to share their unexpected gifts with you?

✱ *The Endless Circle*

Savor this day and hold close the ones you love. Life is a gift.

C.S. Lewis pointed out that the people we meet in this life are the ones we will fellowship with forever in heaven. Eternity begins here. Today. It has to do with the immortal beings you eat lunch with and sit next to on the bus.

Celebrate the lives of those you love. Support their hopes and dreams. It only takes one person who will come into your life and say "You are important. You are beautiful." Pray for God's best in your life. If your heart and intention is to glorify God, He will bring you to people who will help you celebrate your life and who will stand with you.

When I talk to teens about dating and relationships, I encourage them to look for another person with the same faith. We all need big examples in our lives, people who will gently push us towards the things of God and also challenge our walk with Him.

Dear friends, we should love each other, because love comes from God. Everyone who loves has become God's child and knows God. . . . He sent his one and only Son into the world so that we could have life through him. . . . if God loved us that much we also should love each other. No one has ever seen God, but if we love each other, God lives in us, and his love is made perfect in us.

1 JOHN 4:7, 9, 11, 12 NCV

Joining the Circle

I have received so many stories of God being faithful to His promises from others who have experienced loss. Their testimonies are amazing and remind me that believers form a circle of encouragement:

Soar Like Eagles

I had suddenly become a young widow, a single mom, and had moved to a new community. God's grace was sufficient as He planted us to make a difference in the lives of others who hurt. My life is blessed because of God's love to help work through the grief and to help others on this journey. Recently, I learned eagles don't fly around the storm; they fly through it, creating a vision of splendor when they arrive. We must go through the storm. God's love is sufficient to have a purpose as we endure the storms of life. We were meant to soar like the eagle.

~ Elaine Cook

Sunrise to Sunset

Just over a year ago I lost my youngest son to a tragic accident. He was 13 and the light and laughter of our lives. At first I was very angry at God for taking my son away from me. I felt that He had taken Garrett away, and I thought that I would never have joy or happiness in my life. Then things changed slowly and I realized that God had given me a way to be with my son again. By accepting Jesus Christ as my Lord and Savior, I will be reunited with Garrett as he had accepted Jesus as his Savior just one year before he died. I used to look at each passing day as another day without him. Now through my faith in God and His promise of eternal life, I thank Him for each sunrise and each sunset, because I know that it brings me one day closer to home with my God and Garrett.

LORI KELLY

Joining the Circle

Wise Instruction

When counseling people throughout his thirty-five years of ministry, my father was often asked, "Why am I having to go through this?" He would reply: "Would you rather God explain it to you or provide His grace and comfort during those tough times?" People would always answer something like this: "Good point, Pastor. It is not important that I fully understand why—just that I feel God's loving arms around me during this difficult time."

BETH MORTELL

Do not worry about anything,
but pray and ask God for everything you need,
always giving thanks. And God's peace,
which is so great we cannot understand it,
will keep your hearts and minds in Christ Jesus.

PHILIPPIANS 4:6, 7 NCV

"For I am persuaded
that neither death nor life,
nor angels nor principalities nor powers,
nor things present nor things to come,
nor height nor depth,
nor any other created thing,
shall be able to separate us
from the love of God
which is in Christ Jesus our Lord."

ROMANS 8:38-39 NKJV

ALL THE LORD'S WAYS ARE LOVING AND TRUE...
MY EYES ARE ALWAYS LOOKING
TO THE LORD FOR HELP.

PSALM 25:10, 15 NCV

You have not seen Christ,
but still you love him.
You cannot see him now,
but you believe in him.
So you are filled with a joy
that cannot be explained,
a joy full of glory.

1 PETER 1:8 NCV

Standing Tall

Without God I could have never made it when my world was turned upside down. My teenage son's life was football. On an October day, with only eight seconds left in the game, he was severely injured. His career, quality of life, and everything was gone! Today he lives in a wheelchair, paralyzed from the shoulders down. Yet his main focus is sharing his story and living God's plan. As he inspires others through his faith in God, his main goal is to stand tall beside his wheelchair. God's love is why I am able to live!

KEDDITH ANDREWS

The Spirit Himself bears witness with our spirit
that we are children of God, and if children,
then heirs—heirs of God and joint heirs with Christ,
if indeed we suffer with Him,
that we may also be glorified together.

ROMANS 8:16, 17 NKJV

For we walk by faith, not by sight . . .
We are confident . . .
we make it our aim . . .
to be well pleasing to Him.

2 CORINTHIANS 5:7–9 NKJV

For we know that if our earthly house, this tent, is destroyed, we have a building from God, a house not made with hands, eternal in the heavens.

2 CORINTHIANS 5:1 NKJV

We have small troubles for a while now,
but they are helping us gain an eternal glory
that is much greater than the troubles.
We set our eyes not on what we see
but on what we cannot see.
What we see will last only a short time,
but what we cannot see will last forever.

2 CORINTHIANS 4:17 NCV

Joining the Circle

Worship

Ten years ago I left a marriage that had devastated me emotionally, physically, spiritually, and financially. Things couldn't get any worse—until he committed suicide. I went from believing God would walk with me through the Valley of the Shadow of Death to knowing it for a fact, because He did so. Worship brought peace and hope. Through worship I could escape to His presence and experience His tender kindness in the midst of my pain.

Worship reminded me that He is deeper than my pain, bigger than any circumstance, and able to heal me. I could lose everything except eternal life with Jesus.

ANNI BARR

[Jesus said] "He who believes in Me,
as the Scripture has said,
out of his heart will flow rivers of living water"
JOHN 7:38 NKJV

Hope and Purpose

I just want people to know that God can take what's left of your life and give you a new purpose to continue on. When I heard these words from the doctor: "I'm sorry, there is nothing we can do," it cut to my heart with the force of an atomic bomb. My 11-year-old son, Dustin Tyler Brack, had lost control and hit a tree while snow skiing on our family vacation. In the blink of an eye nothing mattered to me—not a house, car, clothes, money... nothing!

Dustin wrote in his journal that he wanted "to minister to everyone," so I have committed my life to fulfilling his goal. When I get to heaven, I not only want to hear Jesus say, "Well done," but I want Dustin to run up to me and say, "Wow, Mom, you did an awesome job for me!" I thank God that He gave me this hope and purpose to keep going! He can do the same for you!

~ Darla Brack

Joining the Circle

A Gift of Love

It is in our greatest time of sorrow that our Heavenly Father is most near. My Savior was there when I was a pregnant teen living in a maternity home five hours away from my family and keeping my pregnancy a secret. Knowing from the beginning I needed to surrender my child up for adoption, I endured a very lonely time with the anticipation of a very difficult ending.

I delivered a beautiful, healthy baby boy. After three days together I walked down the hospital hall to hand him to the nurse. As I kissed his head and walked away I truly felt the "peace that passes all understanding" that can only come from the Holy Spirit.

After the sorrow, I have been blessed with a sweet husband and two precious children. God has allowed me after ten years to break free from the guilt and shame I had held for so long. It is through our greatest trials that His greatest strengths can be revealed to bring honor and glory to His name.

~ *Elizabeth Kilgore*

"PEACE I LEAVE WITH YOU,

MY PEACE I GIVE TO YOU;

NOT AS THE WORLD GIVES

DO I GIVE TO YOU.

LET NOT YOUR HEART BE TROUBLED,

NEITHER LET IT BE AFRAID."

JOHN 14:27 NKJV

Leaving Footprints

My husband, Trent, struggled to know what his purpose in life was. I sit on this side of heaven seeing that question fulfilled. The testimony of Trent's life still draws others to Christ when I share his story. I am able to minister to large groups of teens about our love story and how we surrendered our relationship to God. I talk to adults about how his dedication taught me to follow Christ. Trent's walk through this world is still marking a path for others to follow.

To live your life on earth in such a way that when you're gone it continues to impact others—even people whom you've never met—is the greatest purpose a believer can fulfill. Trent didn't think about that outcome as he humbly followed Jesus to the best of his ability—it was just a natural movement for him that ended up leaving a legacy here on earth.

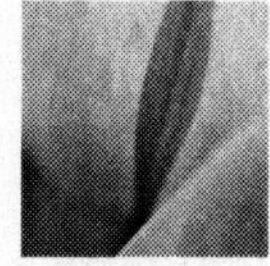

Beloved, now we are children of God;
and it has not yet been revealed
what we shall be,
but we know that when He is revealed,
we shall be like Him,
for we shall see Him as He is.
And everyone who has this hope in Him
purifies himself,
just as He is pure.

1 JOHN 3:2, 3 NKJV

WALK AS CHILDREN OF LIGHT
(FOR THE FRUIT OF THE SPIRIT IS IN ALL
GOODNESS, RIGHTEOUSNESS, AND TRUTH),
FINDING OUT WHAT IS ACCEPTABLE
TO THE LORD.

EPHESIANS 5:8, 9 NKJV

Trust with All Your Heart

One afternoon, I sat on a blanket reading some scripture verses and these simple thoughts came to mind again: "Tammy, choose life. Trust with all your heart and hold onto your Father in heaven."

This journey will never be easy. Maybe easier, but not easy. God's hand is still a mystery to me, and I probably would still trade in everything to have Trent back. Especially when I'm all alone and just want to grow old with the one I love. I wish I'd been able to tell him everything his life meant to me. I wish I had one more chance to tell him that I love him, that he changed my life, that he was the smartest man I ever knew. Just one more time to do something special for him and to see him smile.

My heart still belongs to Trent, and I keep my wedding ring on tight to honor him and all that I experienced through him. It's amazing how I can feel so complete inside living with a hole in my heart.

*Many waters
cannot
quench love.*

SONG OF SOLOMON 8:7 NKJV

Pace Yourself

All in all, I'm doing well and I can see the future clearly. It's hopeful, so I keep running this race. With my running shoes tied tightly, a bottle of water in my hand, and my sunglasses on, I pace myself. But there is a race ahead of me for the rest of my life.

DO YOU NOT KNOW THAT THOSE
WHO RUN IN A RACE ALL RUN,
BUT ONE RECEIVES THE PRIZE?
RUN IN SUCH A WAY THAT YOU MAY OBTAIN IT.
AND EVERYONE THAT COMPETES FOR THE PRIZE
IS TEMPERATE IN ALL THINGS.
NOW THEY DO IT TO OBTAIN A PERISHABLE CROWN;
BUT WE FOR AN IMPERISHABLE CROWN.
THEREFORE I RUN THUS: NOT WITH UNCERTAINLY.
THUS I FIGHT: NOT AS ONE THAT BEATS THE AIR.
BUT I DISCIPLINE MY BODY,
AND BRING IT INTO SUBJECTION, LEST,
WHEN I HAVE PREACHED TO OTHERS,
I MYSELF SHOULD BECOME DISQUALIFIED.

I CORINTHIANS 9:24–27 NKJV

Physical running and exercising have been great therapy for me. I began to run and work out at a local YMCA as soon as I got settled back at home. I needed something to do during the quiet evenings when all the busyness of the day was over and the sun had set. If I sat alone in my house too long, I'd start to think about everything that had happened and create "what if" scenarios. My problems grew into mountains in my lonely thoughts, and I knew I couldn't let myself sink too far. I had to protect myself from sinking into grief past the point of no return.

Going to the gym every night created an atmosphere for me that I needed. Light and noise, without having to speak a word of my pain. Just me and God "working it out." And every once in a while "by chance" someone would come into the sauna and start talking about something I needed to hear at that very moment. It always made me laugh to know God would chase me down even in a sauna.

Let us run with patience the race that is set before us,
looking unto Jesus the author and finisher of our faith;
who for the joy that was set before him endured the cross,
despising the shame, and is set down
at the right hand of the throne of God.

HEBREWS 12:1 KJV

All Around You

Familiar scripture verses had surrounded my life for years, but in the difficult times each one took on a new meaning. Scripture immediately was a lifeline holding out hope. They wrapped me in comfort as I was desperately trying to figure out what went wrong and answer all the whys and find where God was in all of it. My relationship with His words changed to the extent that I understand them more and have applied them to my life more than ever before. I couldn't help but grow in the Lord as He put my life back together. Even though I don't care for the new plan, some days I even hate it, I do believe that I am walking in God's will for my life. I probably would change it in a heartbeat, but I also know I'm walking in my destiny now. I trust Him with my future. This is and was God's plan all along.

BUT HE KNOWS THE WAY THAT I TAKE;
WHEN HE HAS TESTED ME,
I SHALL COME FORTH AS GOLD.

JOB 23:10 NKJV *

. . . It is painful, but later,
after we have learned from it,
we have peace . . .

* HEBREWS 12:11 NCV

Looking Over Your Shoulder

I think I will always feel regrets. I don't feel regrets so much from teenage spats or splits, because I think those things just happen as we're maturing and trying to discover who we are as individuals, but I regret hurts in our marriage. Things I did. Things I said. Things I didn't say. Things I should have done. Trent was always my example, and I took that for granted. I sometimes find myself saying out loud before I go to bed, "I love you, Trent, and I'm so sorry I ever hurt you. Please forgive me. I wish you were here!"

If I didn't understand that God forgives, I couldn't let go of my regrets. I couldn't forgive myself. When I realize that all people are broken and with sin, but God fully forgives us, then I can forgive myself for all those shortcomings. I know that my husband understood that and would be the first to agree with God's perspective and forgive. We have to break the chain of unforgiveness by receiving God's promise of mercy.

If we say we have no sin,
we are fooling ourselves, and the truth is not in us.
But if we confess our sins, he will forgive our sins,
because we can trust God to do what is right.
He will cleanse us from all the wrongs we have done.

1 JOHN 1:8, 9 NCV

ALL HAVE SINNED AND ARE NOT
GOOD ENOUGH FOR GOD'S GLORY,
AND ALL NEED TO BE MADE RIGHT WITH GOD
BY HIS GRACE, WHICH IS A FREE GIFT.
THEY NEED TO BE MADE FREE FROM SIN
THROUGH JESUS CHRIST.
GOD GAVE HIM AS A WAY TO FORGIVE SIN
THROUGH FAITH IN THE BLOOD OF JESUS' DEATH.

ROMANS 3:23-24 NCV

Take a Breath

My greatest healing came in taking a year off to allow the time to heal and to learn to rely on the Lord for everything. Not my music. Not my career. But God alone. I just simply let Him put my life back together again. I didn't know if I'd ever want to sing or write again. Honestly, I didn't want to. It took some time, but after a year, I walked back up on a platform and slowly began to sing and dance again. Yes, there has been great comfort and healing in that for me. There is joy in that for me again.

It's a new ministry now, and one I think my husband would be so proud of.

People who have heard my story have told me that they are inspired to keep following the Lord through their own struggles. They see a woman who seems to have every excuse to be depressed or to fall into bitterness, but there I am still singing and even laughing. I'm encouraging them as they see the faithful choices I've made after losing someone so close to me. They say, "There is someone who has gone before me into joy." And that testimony renews their strength. I want that peace to surround my life and draw others to Him.

". . . HE HAS SENT ME
TO HEAL THE BROKENHEARTED,
TO PROCLAIM LIBERTY
TO THE CAPTIVES . . ."
ISAIAH 61:1 NKJV

Steps of Healing

There is a lot of healing still going on in my life. I think I'll probably be healing the rest of my life from this. And even though I'm physically not married to Trent, he is still one of the biggest parts of my life. His example. His witness. His life. It is all a part of my deeper testimony now. My beloved is still in this with me, and I love that.

"GOD IS LOVE.
WHOEVER LIVES IN LOVE
LIVES IN GOD,
AND GOD IN HIM."
1 JOHN 4:16 NKJV

God's Word never fails to bring comfort. Many people have sent in testimonies like this one:

> There have been times in life when I felt I couldn't take another breath or face another day. The sorrow I felt was great; circumstances were hard. In these moments God's Word became hope for a better life. The Bible was His voice when I wasn't sure He cared. Life can be hard; we know it will be. When it is, we can hold on to His promises; they are certain. He never fails.
>
> He is near to the broken-hearted and He helps in times of trouble. He gives beauty for our ashes and joy for all the mourning.
>
> ~ *Deborah Bailey*

I am happy over your promises
as if I had found great treasure…
Those who love your teachings will find true peace,
and nothing will defeat them.

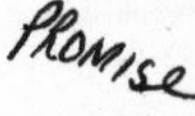

PSALM 119:162, 165 NCV

PS ·119:162-165

Sonshine

It's been raining for two days straight, but I somehow manage to find the warmth of the sun pushing through the clouds. It's still the very thing that leads me on…the sun…the Son!

God once said, "Let the light shine out of the darkness!"
This is the same God who made his light
shine in our hearts by letting us know
the glory of God that is in the face of Christ.
We have this treasure from God,
but we are like clay jars that hold the treasure.
This shows that the great power is from God,
not from us.
We have troubles all around us,
but we are not defeated.
We do not know what to do,
but we do not give up the hope of living.
We are persecuted,
but God does not leave us.
We are hurt sometimes,
but we are not destroyed.

2 CORINTHIANS 4:7–9 NCV

"These people who live in darkness
will see a great light.
They live in a place
covered with the shadows of death,
but a light will shine on them."

MATTHEW 4:16 NCV

HERE IS THE MESSAGE WE HAVE HEARD
FROM CHRIST AND NOW ANNOUNCE TO YOU:
GOD IS LIGHT AND IN HIM
THERE IS NO DARKNESS AT ALL.

1 JOHN 1:5 NCV

"You are the light that gives light to the world.
A city that is built on a hill cannot be hidden.
And people don't hide a light under a bowl.
They put it on a lampstand so the light shines
for all the people in the house. In the same way,
you should be a light for other people.
Live so that they will see the good things you do
and will praise your Father in heaven."

MATTHEW 5:14, 15 NCV

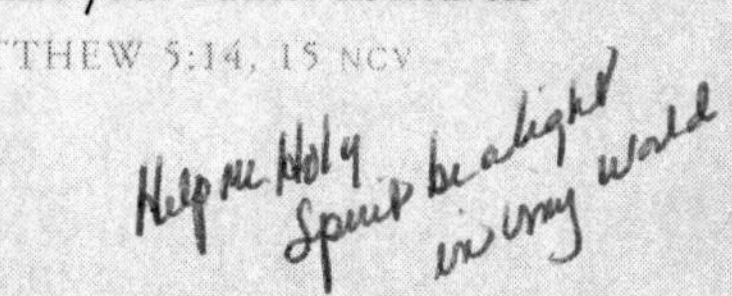

Easter Memories

During the church service a wave of memories flooded my mind as I remembered walking in and out of that very sanctuary with my husband many, many times before. It was our home church while growing up and growing into our marriage. I fought back the tears as I felt my lips whispering softly, "Where are you, Trent? I wish you were still here with me. I miss you so much and I hate being without you." Oh yes, there is still healing in my life as the clock spins around and around, but the longing and the memories and the deep love haven't faded even for one moment in my life. So I was glad to be there, in church on Easter Sunday celebrating the Resurrection of Jesus and Trent's new life.

Jesus said to him,
"I am the way, the truth, and the life.
No one comes to the Father except through Me.
If you had known Me, you would have known My Father also;
and from now on you know Him and have seen Him."

JOHN 14:6, 7 NKJV

"Let not your heart be troubled;
you believe in God, believe also in Me.
In My Father's house are many mansions;
if it were not so, I would have told you.
I go to prepare a place for you.
And if I go and prepare a place for you,
I will come again
and receive you to Myself;
that where I am,
there you may be also."

JOHN 14:1–3 NKJV

A Door to Forever

One Easter Sunday, I walked through the woods and began to walk up the pathway to Trent's grave. (It's so hard for me to say that word.) I sat down and stared off into the woods for probably five minutes until I couldn't hold back the tears anymore. I just cried and cried. And then I got up and started circling Trent's grave over and over again. Through my cries all I could say was, "Can you just get up, Trent! Can you just get up now!" Oh how I wished that could be reality. But I knew it wasn't, and I think that's why I couldn't stop crying. I finally pulled myself together. I thanked Jesus for the cross. I can't bring Trent back, but I will see him again. I will.

That is a promise because of that cross. Thank You, Jesus, for dying for Trent and me. Eternal life is so precious and truly a gift to all of us. What hope that brings! Even in the pains of life… there is hope. And with that thought, I got back into the car and headed down the road again.

It will never be easy for me. Never! But I was glad I went there on such a special day, Easter Sunday. I felt loved in that moment. In that place. How glorious it truly was. I can't help but feel a little closer to heaven each time I'm there. The presence of the Lord is always so strong… even in my pain…even in my tears. I am not alone.

"Jesus wept."

JOHN 11:35 NKJV

Cling to God

All our lives Trent and I had looked to God for guidance, for wisdom, for comfort. And so when I understood that my husband was gone from this world, even though my heart was breaking and I couldn't understand how God would allow such a thing to happen, I knew I didn't want to run away from Him. Desperate to cling to the only thing I knew was true, I found myself crying out to Him, "There are a million questions, and I don't understand any of this." As my body ached with sadness and confusion, I just kept asking God to remind me that He was real. And He did. Somehow, even though I didn't think I could ever endure such loss emotionally or physically, God let me know He was and is there. He is not a belief or a concept—He is my true Friend.

Weeping may endure for a night,
but joy comes in the morning.

PSALM 30:5 NKJV

To You I will cry, O LORD my Rock:
Do not be silent to me...
Blessed be the LORD because He has heard...
The LORD is my strength and my shield;
My heart trusted in Him, and I am helped;
Therefore my heart greatly rejoices,
and with my song I will praise Him...
Save Your people...
Shepherd them also,
And bear them up forever.

PSALM 28:1, 6, 7, 9 NKJV

He Understands Our Tears

What a beautiful fall day—the sky is blue and it's about 72 degrees outside. I'm sitting by the pool taking it all in. I have jeans and a sweater on, but at least my bare feet are getting a tan.

I take a deep breath as I listen to the gentle sounds of water rippling in the pool while the wind blows the trees in the woods behind me. I hear the birds playing and the leaves falling. It's so peaceful here. My heart is peaceful even through the tears that still fall.

YOU NUMBER MY WANDERINGS;

PUT MY TEARS INTO YOUR BOTTLE;

ARE THEY NOT IN YOUR BOOK?

PSALM 56:8 NKJV

put my tears into Your bottle

The Seasons of Memories

Fall is one of the hardest seasons for me. It will always remind me of leaving home with Trent to go to Jamaica in the late summertime and then coming back home without him in mid-October when autumn had arrived. So much had happened in my life during the season of change. The very smell of fall reminds me of the very first time I walked back into our home alone. How scared I was. How alone I felt. How confused I was. How my heart was shattered and broken. Despite all the hardships, I also remember how it felt good to be home. There was a feeling of peace in our home that was beyond understanding.

A special moment that I will always remember happened when I pushed the button to start our computer. I waited for the screen to light up, and then I caught my breath when I saw a little square appear in the lower left–hand corner. It looked like a sticky note stuck there on the screen. It said, "Tammy is who I dream of. Can't wait to see you."

I sat there, stunned, by the message Trent had left for me to find. I was amazed how he continued to comfort me, even from heaven.

Keep on loving each other.

HEBREWS 13:1 NCV

We're In This Together

Even though it's still so hard for me, I'm reminded today of God's love for me. His healing touch. The way He provides. How understanding He is. How He's honestly taken care of me. Now, that doesn't mean I'm all healed and on the other side. Quite the contrary. I think I'll be healing the rest of my life, and most days I still feel like I'm only halfway there. But I'm moving forward and trusting in the Lord, even though I don't always understand. He's right there with me.

Those who sat in darkness and in the shadow of death,
Bound in affliction and irons . . .
They fell down, and there was none to help.
Then they cried out to the LORD *in their trouble,*
And He saved them out of their distresses.
He brought them out of the darkness
and the shadow of death,
And broke their chains in pieces.

PSALM 107:10, 12–14 NKJV

Promise

Why am I so sad?

Why am I so upset?

I should put my hope in God,

And keep praising him,

my Savior and my God.

PSALM 42:11 NCV

He Feels Our Pain

I had a vision not that long ago. I was driving home from a friend's house, and I couldn't stop crying. I looked over at the passenger's side and could almost see Jesus. He reached out for my hand, said nothing, and with the sweetest loving look on His face, He just cried with me. I remember that vision whenever I can't stop crying. What comfort to know He hurts when we hurt.

SINCE WE HAVE A GREAT HIGH PRIEST,
JESUS THE SON OF GOD,
WHO HAS GONE INTO HEAVEN,
LET US HOLD ON TO THE FAITH WE HAVE.
FOR OUR HIGH PRIEST IS ABLE
TO UNDERSTAND OUR WEAKNESSES.
WHEN HE LIVED ON EARTH
HE WAS TEMPTED IN EVERY WAY THAT WE ARE,
BUT HE DID NOT SIN.
LET US FEEL VERY SURE
THAT WE CAN COME BEFORE GOD'S THRONE
WHERE THERE IS GRACE.
THERE WE CAN RECEIVE MERCY
AND GRACE TO HELP US
WHEN WE NEED IT.

HEBREWS 4:14–16 NCV

That Long Walk

The walk along the half-mile trail to where Trent is buried will always be filled with the most painful steps I will ever have to take. The deepest sorrow and grief came over me one of those times, and I felt as if I couldn't take another step. This is where my friends' prayers reached me and gave me strength outside of my own, because somehow I took another step and another until making it through the woods to the top of that hill. It was a beautiful afternoon as I watched just one butterfly playing around me. I sat in the chair, put on my headphones, and listened to my song "Father God" repeatedly as I held my Bible in my arms. With tears falling from my eyes, I felt the peace of God and slowly fell asleep right there. I could have stayed there all day.

Isn't it funny? I don't like going there, but once I get there I have a hard time leaving. After about three hours, I sat up, placed my *Breathing* CD on the ground next to Trent (as if to leave one for him) and kissed the memorial cross that stands before him.

I look to the hills, but where does my help come from?
My help comes from the LORD, *who made heaven and earth.*
He will not let you be defeated.
He who guards you never sleeps....
The LORD *is the shade that protects you from the sun.*
The sun cannot hurt you during the day,
and the moon cannot hurt you at night.
The LORD *will protect you from all dangers;*
he will guard your life.
The LORD *will guard you as you come and go,*
both now and forever.

PSALM 121 NCV

God's Treasure-Hunter

The walk back to my car from Trent's gravesite gets easier with time, and God continually reminds me that He is with me. Once I spotted a yellow snake under a fallen tree. You might not think that would be an encouraging sign, but it was for me because Trent loved snakes. He even had a fifteen-foot python that he would take to children's schools for show-and-tell. And his favorite color was yellow. Because Trent was colorblind, that was the one color he could see clearly. I got a smile on my face at that moment. I hate snakes (and this one was staring at me) but it was another reminder from God that I am not alone. He's always thinking about me.

If you don't stop and look, you'll miss God's reminders. But if you seek, you will find that all your treasures are being stored up in heaven. Here, we're all just passing through. I got to experience one of my heavenly treasures early. His name is Trent Lenderink.

"DON'T STORE TREASURES FOR YOURSELVES HERE ON EARTH WHERE MOTHS AND RUST WILL DESTROY THEM AND THIEVES CAN BREAK IN AND STEAL THEM. BUT STORE YOUR TREASURES IN HEAVEN WHERE THEY CANNOT BE DESTROYED BY MOTHS OR RUST AND WHERE THIEVES CANNOT BREAK IN AND STEAL THEM. YOUR HEART WILL BE WHERE YOUR TREASURE IS."

MATTHEW 6:21 NCV

"The kingdom of heaven
is like a treasure hidden in a field.
One day a man found the treasure
and then he hid it in the field again.
He was so happy that he went
and sold everything he owned to buy that field.
Also, the kingdom of heaven is like a man
looking for fine pearls.
When he found a very valuable pearl,
he went and sold everything he had
and bought it."

MATTHEW 13:44, 45 NCV

Familiar Steps

If you really believe with your whole heart that God is in control of your life, then you'll trust Him with it no matter what. We all imagine what life might be like if circumstances were different—but we live in the reality of the life that has been given us.

A woman sent me an email of how she was praying for me because God had shown her that I sometimes pictured my husband coming back through the door into our home. That was true. I did. Seeing Trent come through the door was just such a familiar sight. I sometimes look at that door and can still see him opening it.

But what do I do with that? At first I just fell to the ground and cried out to God. I had to mourn the loss of that moment. I sit here on this couch now, three years later, looking at that door. Somehow, God is enough. I'm choosing joy. One day at a time with the Lord, every day.

I think we all can picture someone coming in the door who could change our circumstances. But the reality is that Trent isn't coming home. The situation isn't going to change. This is my life now. But although I can't change this, I can change the outcome with the help of God. This is my part of the story. I get to write the next chapter by what I do with this life I have now. The choices I make become the words to the next chapters.

Look Around

Look for God. Look for Him in your circumstance. He is there. If you challenge yourself to look for Him, you will find Him near.

At the beginning of your loss, the situation is all about you: your loss, your situation, your feelings. You need time to process that. Then you look beyond the sorrow and cry out, "Where are You, Jesus?" That is when you realize that you are not alone. Then you are able to say with certainty that God is enough.

I think you first have to be allowed to process those inner feelings that are more about you. If people or circumstances push you to skip over that seemingly selfish part, you will have to deal with it later. You'll have to backtrack and work through that stage. You can't ignore what has happened to you as an individual. Your life has changed, and it doesn't seem like anything good can come of that. I was allowed to go through that process of mourning, and I think that's why, years later, I can stand here and say God is healing me and that I've come through to the other side of sorrow.

Individual Styles

Someone sent me a poem that says grief is as individual as a fingerprint. We all have our own ways of dealing with this visitor—our constant companion after a loss. But we learn so much about ourselves, about our lives, from it. Like a mirror we see ourselves in its reflection, and we see that we are capable of strength, love, goodness, and humility. We see the love of our family and friends and the love of God being poured into our lives. We realize that we are vessels to both give and receive blessing. Before our sorrow, we may have been blessed to give. After, we learn the blessing of receiving.

My best friend, Pam Thum, and her husband, Steve, gave me this letter a year after my loss:

Dear Tammy,

We're celebrating a covenant with you that goes way beyond this world. It wraps around the farthest star, bounces off the top of the universe, and kisses the heart of a boy in the next world. I believe it started one day but never stops for eternity! A big hug and kiss from us to you in celebrating love…the forever kind.

Steve & Pam

Leading Others Through Their Sorrow

You can give precious gifts to people you care about when they are grieving. Most of them involve just saying "That's okay, I'm here for you" without further comment!

1. Allow them time to grieve. Give them permission to pause. Grief pulls the rug out from under us, and we need to sit a minute to get our bearings before we try to stand.

2. Give them permission to confess. We deal with disappointment in every part of our being, including our fleshly nature. Sometimes we need to confess that we are "unspiritual" in our reaction to grief. I had friends who were patient and non–judging when I cried out, "I hate this!"

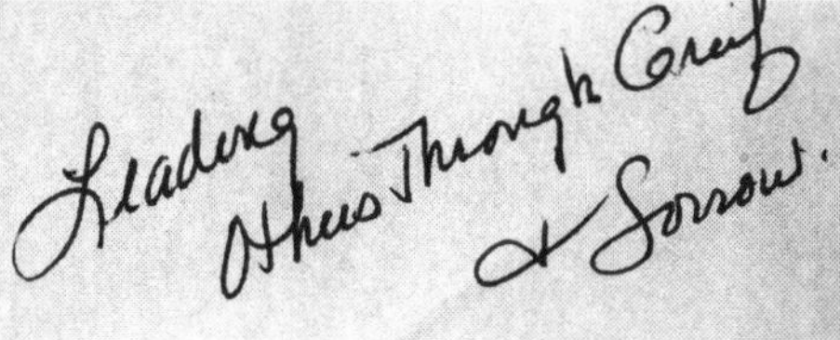

3. Give them permission to be angry. God can take our anger. He knows we might be angry with Him, even when He is trying to heal us. He waits patiently, like a rock in the storm of our emotion, for us to turn and receive His help.

4. Give them permission to move on when they are ready. Sometimes a person who is coming out on the other side of grief almost feels apologetic for moving beyond sorrow into a new life. Let them know this is okay.

5. Help them give the future, as well as the past, to Jesus. "What ifs" apply to both the past and the future. Share support from prayer, scripture, and personal experience about trusting God.

6. Celebrate with them as positive emotions return. Laugh. Be silly together. Remind them that you care about them just as much in the lighthearted times as in sorrow.

Share the Joy

Being happy in others' triumph helps us learn to find happiness in ourselves. I was so thrilled to read this testimony that a reader sent. She didn't give up!

About two years ago, my boyfriend of over four years broke off our relationship. As anyone can imagine, I was crushed and heartbroken. This was the man who I was supposed to marry. We had the ring picked out and was it ever beautiful! After the breakup, I became hurt and was very angry at God. I kept asking, "Why is God doing this to me?"

About eight months later, I hit rock bottom. I turned away from my family and God. I was so angry with Him. After all, He was ruining my plans for my life. Once I hit rock bottom, I realized I couldn't do this anymore on my own. I had to turn back to God and ask Him for help. I do know God was there all along. He was just standing back waiting for me to turn back around to Him. He brought me back out of my depression and helped me to realize that there was hope that life would go on, even though I thought my life couldn't get any worse. My advice to any girl who is going through a breakup or divorce: turn to God as soon as you can. It's not worth the heartache and pain that you put yourself through without the help of your Heavenly Father showing you that there is light. Although it may be dim at first, it will get brighter over time.

JULIE WILLIAMS

In the Arms of Family

I am blessed to spend time with my family. My favorite place to be. In the arms of my family. Always love. Always joy. Always adventure. Always there.

My mom shared these thoughts about my loss in my book *Learning to Breathe Again:*

> When I think back on that experience, as difficult as it was, I'm amazed by how God sends His grace in the most painful and frightening situations. In the hours following Tammy's call with the news that Trent was missing, peace filled my mind as I thought of the healing that had occurred just weeks earlier between Tammy's dad and me. Trent's passion for life and love was responsible.... Walls came down that night, and we laughed and enjoyed our time together.... I felt a great warmth, understanding then that forgiveness is the best medicine in the world.... the Holy Spirit reminded me of Jesus' promise to Tammy—to all of us: "I will never leave you or forsake you." And, "I will send you a comforter."

... He Himself has said, "I will never leave you
nor forsake you."
So we may boldly say:
"The Lord *is my helper; I will not fear."*
HEBREWS 13:5, 6 NKJV

He Will Carry You

God's Word was my strength immediately after I lost my husband and continues to be my source of comfort today. One of the Psalms that helped me in the first days of my sorrow was Psalm 30. I opened my Bible and immediately my eye fell on the fifth verse. This is how I read that passage:

Although you may mourn throughout the night and sorrow will endure throughout the night—probably throughout many nights, Tammy—My joy will always come in the morning. My joy will always meet you in the morning. When you feel like you can't breathe, when you feel like you can't walk, when you can't see, when you can't get through the day…I'm still there carrying you. When you can't breathe one more time, then just rest your head on the pillow, and I'll be right there beside you. When you wake up the next morning, I'll be right there beside you. My joy will cover you. And joy will be the very thing that will bring you back to life again, because without it, you'll never survive this grief. Just trust Me, Tammy. Trust Me.

Let It Go

WORDS & MUSIC BY TAMMY TRENT

No matter where you go
Or where you're from,
He watches over you from above.
He looks inside your heart
And sees your face.
Whenever there is pain,
He brings His grace.
So, let it go and be free.
Let it go and you'll see.
Jesus can heal anything
If you believe.
Let it go.
No matter how you feel,
You're not alone.
He's standing by your side
To lead you home.
With all that you've been through,
You must press on.
I know that He would want you
To be strong.

[JESUS SAID,] "COME TO ME,
ALL YOU WHO LABOR AND ARE HEAVY LADEN,
AND I WILL GIVE YOU REST.
TAKE MY YOKE UPON YOU AND LEARN FROM ME,
FOR I AM GENTLE AND LOWLY IN HEART,
AND YOU WILL FIND REST FOR YOUR SOULS.
FOR MY YOKE IS EASY
AND MY BURDEN IS LIGHT."

MATTHEW 11:28–30 NKJV

Uplifting Notes

Sometimes the Lord shows me His encouragement through the words of others. Close friends, or sometimes even strangers, send notes of encouragement just when I need them most. Here is one from my close friend Pete Orta that is such a beautiful word-picture of what he saw happening in my life:

Dear Tammy,

You are like an iron glove with a glass fist inside. Life has come at you head on, and you are standing strong. Even if your legs give out on you sometimes, your spirit keeps running. You have the softest insides, because your outside has had to be so tough. It has protected your heart and your dreams. Now life has been able to touch your heart, and it hurts even more than most people's. Hurt has walked in and it won't leave like you want it to. But I sit back and watch your spirit inside get a little stronger and the outside get a little softer. You will be able to explain life by not being able to explain life. You will be able to understand life because you are not able to understand life. Knowledge in life is experience; it's not being able to explain everything. It's like a blind person will only stumble in a room where they have never been. You have had to walk through a cold dark room, and the knowledge of that will set people free. There's not an answer in words; there's only knowledge in your experience. And with that experience you will change the world!

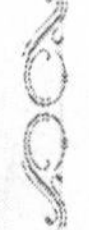

There is a future in your life. I'm just sorry you were not able to choose it.

Love,
Pete

Uplifting Notes

Dear Tammy,

My husband, age 27, passed away in November. The Lord showed me that I needed to allow Him to come in and fill this endless gap. As I did, the pain was intensified because this sorrowful room was illuminated. I then received this phrase:

To feel + to deal = to HEAL.

As I allowed Him to enter this painful place, it did illuminate the vastness of its size, but I would continue to not resist the pain. He would reveal issues and memories that hurt, but I accepted them, dealt with it, and gave it back to Him as He brought healing to my heart.

CARI STEWART

Dear Tammy,

I, too, fell madly in love with my teenage sweetheart! We married while still in high school. At 44, he died in an accident. No chance to say "Goodbye", "I'm sorry", "I love you"...the usual things you wish you could say just one last time.

So many regrets, so many questions: "Why? Why now, after struggling to get by, raise a family...?" This was supposed to be "our time"—time to be together, grow old together...but now he was gone. I felt my heart would burst; many times I wished it would. You see, over the years, Jesus had knocked at my heart's door, but I wouldn't let Him in. Then, when nothing could ease the ache or fill the void in my heart, He knocked again. My Savior forgave me. He lifted me up and gave me such peace and joy. He showed me that I could still live...laugh...love again, and that as a child of God, I am worthy to be loved! I remarried seven years ago. Mike's love for Christ carries over into every aspect of his life and our marriage. When I look at him, I see Jesus and I have to say, "Thank you, Lord! I wouldn't change a thing!"

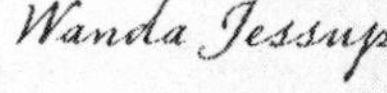

Gifted

People say how I've inspired them, but honestly, I'm inspired by their love and prayers and support for me. Especially when I'm a girl they don't even know. In some letters people just open up their hearts to me as if we have been friends for years. Love is an amazing gift.

Dear Tammy,

It's hard opening doors inside yourself to places you vowed never to go. Never revisiting the pain because it reminds you that life is not perfect. Never recalling the loneliness because it reminds you that you are not self-sufficient. Yet when I revisit those places of trial, I can see how the hand of God was there even though I could not see it. The times in my life where I felt the weakest, the times when I thought I could not run this race of life one more mile, those were the times God made me strong.

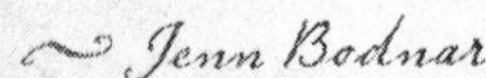

Dear Tammy,

When I was 22 and single, I found out that I was pregnant. I thought my world was coming to an end. But my mom told me something that completely changed me. She told me I had to let the Lord give me joy in the situation. That one sentence completely changed how I felt about my situation. When I allowed the Lord to give me joy I found that things were not as bad as I thought they were. I realized that God loved me no matter what and it didn't matter what other people thought or said about me.

That was nearly fourteen years ago, and now I have a son who wants to be a youth pastor when he grows up. So, no matter what things look like, let God give you joy and you really will make it through no matter how bad things seem. God Bless!

AMORETTE HELM

Patterns of Promise

From generation to generation, God has revealed Himself as a personal God who wants an intimate relationship with each one of us. He wants us to know Him, talk to Him, and trust Him.

God promises to help us in difficult times. "Do not be afraid or discouraged, for the LORD is the one who goes before you. He will be with you; He will neither fail you nor forsake you" (DEUTERONOMY 31:8 NLT). When pain and suffering strike and doubts flood your mind, put your confidence in the living God. He will never let you down.

We'll never be able to find an explanation for all circumstances in life, but we must remember that God is in control. The Bible says that God's thoughts are not our thoughts and His ways are not our ways (ISAIAH 55:8). God is sovereign and nothing in our life escapes Him. "God has made everything beautiful for its own time. He has planted eternity in the human heart, but even so, people cannot see the whole scope of God's work from beginning to end" (ECCLESIASTES 3:11 NLT).

Instead of asking God "why" about the pain, ask "what next" and "how."

STEVE RUSSO

Father & Daughter Dance

I always wondered why I was different. Growing up I knew my friends had something I did not. It bothered me some, but for the most part I never asked any questions. Then one day while sitting with my mom, those difficult words escaped my mouth: "Why do I not have a dad?"

My mother explained that upon conceiving me out of wedlock, my father did not want anyone to know I was his child and instantly left my mother's life. From that moment, the most heartbreaking revelation became planted in my mind: "I was not wanted!" I've struggled many times with that thought, but God's love and grace have always given me a hope that draws me closer to Him. God has encouraged me that although I have never known an earthly father, He is my one true Father! In His own words God reminds me of that each time I read Psalm 68:5, "[God is] a father to the fatherless."

—

Leigh Ellen Eades

He is a father to orphans,
and he defends widows.
God gives the lonely a home.
He leads prisoners out with joy...
Praise the Lord, God our Savior,
who helps us every day.
Our God is a God who saves us;
the LORD *God saves us from death...*
God, people have seen your victory march;
God my King marched into the holy place.
The singers are in front
and the instruments are behind.
In the middle are the girls with the tambourines.
Praise God in the meeting place.

PSALM 68:5, 6, 19, 20, 24–26 NCV

Hidden Treasure

At the age of 47, I was lying in bed in the hospital prepared for a lumpectomy. I had taken my Bible with me and was reading it when my eyes fell on the passage "Man shall take a weapon to you and it shall do you no harm." I closed my Bible, was totally confident that there was no cancer. I was going to be fine. My surgeon came in that evening before surgery, asked if I was okay and if my husband would be there with me the next morning during surgery. I replied that I told him to go to work, as we needed the money for our expenses and we were both confident God had spoken. I shared the passage from the Bible with the surgeon who replied that he was a Christian, also.

No cancer was found during the surgery. Later, I searched the Bible over trying to find that comforting passage again, but was unsuccessful. One day, I saw a preacher on TV offering an engraved coin that you carry in your pocket. The passage of Scripture imprinted on it was Isaiah 54:17, "Man shall take a weapon to you and it shall do you no harm." I sent for two of them! To this day my husband and I carry those coins as a reminder of the grace and love of God and how He gave me confidence at a very troubling time.

MAXINE LEATHLEY

Whatever It Takes, Lord

My story of hope and grace does not compare to Tammy losing her sweetheart, but for moms who have an unsaved child I give you this: God loves him or her more than you do. I was at the point of breaking down until God reminded me that, as it is with everything else in this life, I never owned my son. I was only borrowing Bobby from the Lord as Samuel's mother did when he was growing up. I found hope in knowing that God's grace is sufficient and He has a plan for Bobby that I could never fulfill. His love is greater than anything I could ever conceive.

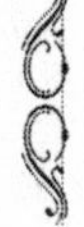

I laid on my face before the Lord one night and said, "Thy will be done in his life." I asked God to release me of any guilt I felt, to give me the strength to watch Bobby's trials, and to allow me to help another mom one day. As I sat in a courtroom to hear my son be given ten months in a federal prison, the words "Thy will be done" rose inside of me, and a peace washed over me that can only come from God. Though there was pain, the peace was strong. So I say: rest in God's peace and continue to walk in the anointing He has placed on your life that the world may see His grace.

Kimberly H. Byrum

Grace Full

My life's passion is to rest in God's hope. The hope I have comes from a deep assurance that God promises to transform ashes into beauty. I have dwarfism, and sometimes it feels hopeless to overcome the stereotypes others have of me. Etched in our minds and hearts are statements we have been labeled with.

The One with all authority to label or condemn does not do so. With Christ, every label was nailed to the cross. We now live in God's promises of a new identity. What hope! Slough off limiting labels and begin to view yourself the way Christ does.

JEN MONTZINGO

...give them beauty for ashes,
The oil of joy for mourning,
The garment of praise for the spirit of heaviness;
that they may be called trees of righteousness,
the planting of the LORD, that He may be glorified....
Instead of your shame you shall have double honor,
and instead of confusion they shall rejoice in their portion.
Therefore in their land they shall possess double;
Everlasting joy shall be theirs....
"All who see them shall acknowledge them,
That they are the posterity whom the LORD has blessed."

ISAIAH 61:3, 7, 9 NKJV

Dance of Healing

At our family Christmas celebration five years ago, my sister and I had a huge fight that caused us not to speak to each other for more than a year. The rift between us was so insurmountable that my sister did not come to my wedding when I got married in January of the next year. At the time of our fight, I had just returned to a close walk with the Lord. My sister was in a bad marriage and was not walking with God. However, five years later my sister is remarried to an awesome godly man, I am married to an awesome godly man, and our relationship, with Christ at the center, could not be better.

A year ago my sister moved from Oklahoma to Florida and I was devastated for her to be so far away. However, both of us were trusting God's direction for her life. Even when there seems to be no hope in a situation, Christ can bring healing of hearts and healing of lives.

M. VOLREL

God has chosen you and made you his holy people.
He loves you. So always do these things:
Show mercy to others, be kind,
humble, gentle, and patient.
Get along with each other, and forgive each other.
If someone does wrong to you,
forgive that person because the Lord forgave you.
Do all these things;
but most important, love each other.
Love is what holds you all together in perfect unity.
Let the peace that Christ gives control your thinking,
because you are all called together
in one body to have peace.
Always be thankful.
Let the teaching of Christ live in you richly.

COLOSSIANS 3:12–16 NCV

Hold On

The only pain worse than the abuse one receives at the hand of another, is the pain that's self-induced, that comes from low self-worth, lack of focus, ambition, and fear. The enemy likes nothing more than for us to be so consumed with what we've done that we forget Whose we are. At your lowest times—times when you feel that there's no turning back from the mistakes you have made—hold on to the fact that with every breath, therein lies a new opportunity to grow, to change, to discover God's purpose for your life. Trust me, it's bigger than anything you've already done—good or bad.

SHELLIE R. WARREN

I ask the Father in his great glory
to give you the power to be strong inwardly
through his Spirit. I pray that Christ will live
in your hearts by faith and that your life
will be strong in love and be built on love.
And I pray that you and all God's holy people
will have the power to understand
the greatness of Christ's love—
how wide and how long and how deep
that love is. Christ's love is greater
than anyone can ever know, but I pray
that you will be able to know that love.
Then you can be filled with the fullness of God.
With God's power working in us,
God can do much, much more than
anything we can ask or imagine.

EPHESIANS 3:16–20 NCV

Warrior's Dance

My story of hope is one of survival. My childhood memories are of seeing my parents suffer with diseases. My mother was diagnosed with cancer when I was 12, and she was not expected to live five years. At the same time, my father was dealing with rheumatoid arthritis. For eleven years he had one surgery a year.

I was fearful of my parents abandoning me by death. As a teenager, I sank into depression and thought of suicide daily, though I attended church often.

My dad died when I was 19. He thought he was going to faint, started to fall, and I caught him. We both fell to the floor, and he died right there. I watched his life disappear. My mother passed away seven years later, the

day after I returned from my honeymoon. It wasn't until my child reached three years old that I sank into depression over losing my parents.

A friend gave me a book called *This Present Darkness* by Frank Peretti that truly opened my eyes to spiritual warfare. I discovered how to fight for my life, my heart, my emotions, and my mind through prayer. Satan longs to use our past to hold us down through self-pity, guilt, loneliness, and feelings of abandonment.

Even though losing my parents hurt me deeply, it's given me a platform to talk to youth about respecting and loving their parents. When you tell a story of brokenness and can paint a picture of reality to our youth, they listen. I now have fully embraced hope that I will see my parents again, face-to-face. It's taught me to really live each day to the fullest, love my kids more, and have compassion for the weary.

~ *Lisa Bevill*

Testing

It has been said, "Out of the test, the testimony comes." I say, "out of our mess, our ministry was birthed." In the past couple of years, our ministry and family suffered many attacks and difficult circumstances that threatened to derail our very existence. My faith was not only tested, but it seemed broken beyond repair as I witnessed the enemy's attempts to destroy my beautiful daughters. We experienced betrayal, rejection, abuse, sickness, and despair. But the foundation of faith was strong. What the enemy meant for harm, God has turned into a harmony of powerful testimonies. Jeremiah 29:11 has been our hope, "I know the plans I have for you says the LORD, plans to prosper you, to give you hope and a future." Our motto is: Faith is stepping out on nothing and feeling it become something.

JENNIFER J PASQUALE

He who dwells in the secret place
of the Most High
Shall abide under the shadow of the Almighty.
I will say of the L*ORD,*
"He is my refuge and my fortress,
My God, in Him I will trust."
Surely He shall deliver you from
the snare of the fowler
And from the perilous pestilence.
He shall cover you with His feathers,
And under His wings you shall take refuge;
His truth shall be your shield and buckler.
You shall not be afraid of the terror by night . . .
For he shall give His angels charge over you
To keep you in all your ways.

PSALM 91:1–5, 11 NKJV

Arms of the Savior

I choose joy! Inner joy. My beloved husband of twenty-five years passed away five months ago, suddenly, without warning. That inner joy I speak of is the steady assurance of God's presence in my life. He knows my future and I am in His hands. There are and will be very hard times. I know I will not "get over it," but with God's grace I will "get through it."

Oh, I still hurt, cry, grieve, and wonder why my beloved was taken so early. But I also have an inner peace and joy that reigns in my life. An assurance that Bart is in the strong and capable arms of our Savior, and so am I... here on earth for a little while longer.

COLETTE MEREDITH

I will praise You with my whole heart;
...And praise Your name
For Your loving kindness and Your truth;
For You have magnified Your word
above all Your name.
In the day when I cried out, You answered me,
And made me bold with strength in my soul....
Though I walk in the midst of trouble,
You will revive me;
...And Your right hand will save me.
The LORD will perfect that which concerns me;
Your mercy, O LORD, endures forever;
Do not forsake the works of Your hands.

PSALM 138:1–3, 7, 8 NKJV

Night of Tears

A phone call from a police officer late at night and my seemingly idyllic life blew up in my face. My seventeen-year marriage to my pastor husband was over. In that one moment everything changed. I found myself alone in the city of Houston, Texas, after moving here only six months before. I had no family here and had two little girls, ages 12 and 9, depending on me. It was time for me to depend on the promise that God had made, "I will never leave you or forsake you." And He never has. My favorite prayer throughout the process of getting on with this new life was: "God, don't let a bitter woman raise my children, even if the bitter woman is me!" He has answered that prayer!

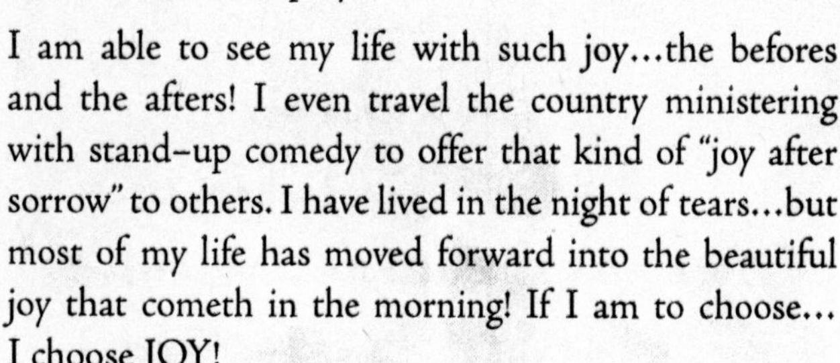

I am able to see my life with such joy...the befores and the afters! I even travel the country ministering with stand-up comedy to offer that kind of "joy after sorrow" to others. I have lived in the night of tears...but most of my life has moved forward into the beautiful joy that cometh in the morning! If I am to choose... I choose JOY!

SUSAN O'DONNELL

". . . THE LORD, IS MY STRENGTH AND SONG;
HE ALSO HAS BECOME MY SALVATION."
THEREFORE WITH JOY YOU WILL DRAW WATER
FROM THE WELLS OF SALVATION.
AND IN THAT DAY YOU WILL SAY:
"PRAISE THE LORD, CALL UPON HIS NAME;
DECLARE HIS DEEDS AMONG THE PEOPLES,
. . . SING TO THE LORD,
FOR HE HAS DONE EXCELLENT THINGS."

ISAIAH 12:2–5 NKJV

Timing Things

I can recall visiting my grandmother at her home near the ocean. I was privately going through some rough times. Somehow she knew. As we both sat on the bench facing the Atlantic Ocean, she turned to me and said, "Troubles are like the waves of the ocean: they will come, but they have to go." It brought back to me the scripture in Ecclesiastes that speaks of times for everything. She was right; my times of trouble come and go, but the sun still shines and the beach still stands...and so do I.

THOM ROBERTS

To everything there is a season,
A time for every purpose under heaven:
A time to be born,
And a time to die;
A time to plant,
And a time to pluck what is planted;
A time to kill,
And a time to heal,
A time to break down,
And a time to build up,
A time to weep,
And a time to laugh;
A time to mourn,
And a time to dance;
...He has made everything beautiful in its time.

ECCLESIASTES 3:1–4, 11 NKJV

Standing Close

People often ask me what they can do for friends who are experiencing loss. I responded to a pastor this way: I think the biggest role you can play is being there if and when they need you. Just you. Not even your words necessarily, but your love and prayers. Standing in the gap for them when they cannot stand alone… when they don't know what to pray. In the days to come, find people to bring meals…to send cards…to mow the grass…to clean the house…to run errands. People in sorrow may not ask for help, but they will love knowing they are not facing this loss alone. Give them space if they need it… time…few words are better because there are no fitting words in these moments. We know Jesus is our comforter, but allow others to find that for themselves, too. Stay close in case they need you to pick them up emotionally or spiritually.

You can be God's love letter to those who need Him.

YOU YOURSELVES ARE OUR LETTER,

WRITTEN ON OUR HEARTS,

KNOWN AND READ BY EVERYONE.

YOU SHOW THAT YOU ARE A LETTER FROM CHRIST...

NOT WRITTEN WITH INK

BUT WITH THE SPIRIT OF THE LIVING GOD.

IT IS NOT WRITTEN ON STONE TABLETS

BUT ON HUMAN HEARTS.

2 CORINTHIANS 3:2–4 NCV

Taking Steps

One bit of wisdom that I learned from my experience of loss was that I needed to take care of myself. I actually had to look at myself from the outside and remember to do things for my mental and spiritual health. It's true that there are ways to be an encouragement to yourself! Here are some ideas that helped me:

- Play music that encourages you. A song can contain a message that we "get" more than a sermon. Have ready a selection of CDs that inspire you or make you dance. Play them in your home and car. Jog or exercise to music. Sing your prayers.
- Exercise regularly. Everyone has their own idea of what "good exercise" is, but we can all do something to maintain our health and encourage a healthy outlook. Walk, stretch, dance in front of the mirror, go on a bike ride, swim laps, or work in the yard.

- Post scripture promises and encouraging words and notes from friends around your home, car, and workplace. I hung a decorative sign over my office door that reads: "Breathe!" A sign in my kitchen says, "Believe!" I still have the "sticky" note that Trent left on our computer that says "Can't Wait to See You!"
- Plan a trip. Give yourself something to look forward to. Go back to places that were special to you as a child, and visit friends and family who will support your growth on this journey.
- Get a massage when you can. For the first year after I lost Trent, every Tuesday at 10 p.m., I was given a massage at my home by a sweet Christian girl named Rondolyn Florence, who felt she was supposed to give to me. There is healing in touch. There is healing in releasing what's deep inside. A massage can be a safe and peaceful place to let go and let God.

Goals

I set realistic goals for each day. I may have an impossible list of things that need taking care of, but I prioritize things that are most important and possible to get done in one day. For the leftover things—there's always tomorrow!

In setting goals for myself and my growth beyond the sorrow, I realize I will never be perfect. But there needs to be progress. Small triumphs, like getting my closet organized, show me that I'm moving forward. Letting go a little bit at a time brings healing.

I journal my needs, as well as God's answers to prayer. Looking back over prayer requests that have been answered helps me realize I am progressing. Re–reading my hopes and goals often helps me keep focused on the future.

Use creative techniques along with journaling. I once drew a cross, cut it out, and then wrote out my frustrations, anger, and pain on it. Then I stood over a trash can and ripped it up and threw it away. "I'm letting go! It is finished!" I shouted, remembering Jesus' sacrifice on the cross.

Find a Bible devotional that you can understand. Don't give up. Keep looking for one that works for you to use every day. Fight for your spiritual life!

Reach Out

Hold up your testimony for other people's sake. I have lost count of how many times people have told me, "I was ready to give up because my trials were so hard, but when I heard your story, I said 'If Tammy can go through all that, I can make it through my troubles.'"

We have all suffered in this world to some degree. Those of us who have experienced deep loss need the comfort of others who have gone before us. Somehow that makes the fight a little easier. We all have a place where our testimony is a light in the darkness to those who need to hear a word of encouragement or see a person who is standing strong in the face of difficulty. Even if they are not in need of your advice today, people will remember your story when they face trials in the future.

Remember that young people are watching. You are a mentor and one who holds up a standard against the darkness of this world in which they live. How can your testimony change the world around you for God? Your home? Your school? Your workplace? It only takes a small candle to light up a whole room that is in darkness. You don't have to have a great singing voice or eloquent speech to say a few encouraging words that will open up someone's heart to healing. Sometimes no words are necessary—a smile or a gentle hand on someone's shoulder is all that is needed to turn their day around, or better yet, turn around their life!

Memories

Surround yourself with memories. Cherish the old ones and remember to create new ones. I have our wedding portrait on the wall surrounded by three ceramic crosses with the words *believe, hope,* and *faith* engraved on them. I have photos of us together all around the house just as they've always been. I don't want to forget the hope that I have in Christ that we will be together again in heaven. I don't want to forget the wonderful memories we shared. Trent was my best friend and still is my inspiration. We have a "forever" relationship. I continue to build new forever relationships with my family and friends, and someday I will be able to share them with him.

We are all travelers in the wilderness of this world,

and the best we can find in our travels is an honest friend.

ROBERT LOUIS STEVENSON

I THANK MY GOD
EVERY TIME I REMEMBER YOU. . . .
I HAVE YOU IN MY HEART.

PHILIPPIANS 1:3, 7 NCV

New Life

When I first lost Trent, I felt like the whole world was moving on and that I was floating outside of it, just trying to find my place. After a while, it seemed like I gently fell back to the earth, and when my feet touched the hard ground, I met Jesus there—waiting for me. After floods of tears, I trusted God with my emotions. I had no doubt He cared, and through His love I discovered who I really was. I looked at myself as if from the outside, and I saw a little girl whose life was just beginning again. When our picture-perfect lives come crashing down, the truth of God's love and promise will carry us through.

Seasons change. Seasons of life move along. Each new one draws us out of the old one. I'm coming to life again. My confession of faith is like a battle. I raise a clenched fist and declare, "Yes!"

Yes, I will fight the lies of the enemy—defeat, depression. Yes, Lord, I will be a survivor. My battle cry is "Yes!"

People who hear me echo back "Yes!" from their lives. They join me in the battle cry, and at that moment there is no misunderstanding. We choose life, love, and our Lord.

Keep Dancing!

When I'm out ministering, I move from the battle of acceptance into dance. Into worship. There is strength in that. Totally free, totally fearless. I dance like no one is watching, and I dance like everyone is watching. Because this is also my confession. I hope people go home from a Tammy Trent event and dance in their own ways. Move the chairs and the furniture! Push everything away! Make room! Give yourself space! Give yourself permission to laugh and have fun even in your circumstances. Break free. It's time to move beyond the sorrow through the hope of God's promises. His promises never fail. Never! And they will bring you back to life again.

God's invitation is compelling: "This is about us and your healing. You need Me. Here I am. I'm not going anywhere. Shut the door. Let's spend time together. Just us."

The dance is one of the few ways that two will ever learn to move as one. Trust Him with your steps. He's a great leader. Don't be afraid to follow.

"THE LORD YOUR GOD IN YOUR MIDST,
THE MIGHTY ONE, WILL SAVE;
HE WILL REJOICE OVER YOU WITH GLADNESS,
HE WILL QUIET YOU WITH HIS LOVE,
HE WILL REJOICE OVER YOU WITH SINGING."

ZEPHANIAH 3:17 NKJV

PRECIOUS PROMISES FROM GOD'S WORD

When you feel you are in this all alone,
God's promise is: HEBREWS 13:5

*. . . He [Jesus] Himself has said,
"I will never leave you nor forsake you."* NKJV

When you don't know what to do next,
God's promise is: PROVERBS 3:5, 6

*Trust in the LORD with all your heart, And lean not on
your own understanding; In all your ways acknowledge Him,
And He shall direct your paths.* NKJV

When you don't think you can do the things
you need to do, God's promise is: PHILIPPIANS 4:13

I can do all things through Christ who strengthens me. NKJV

When you are out of strength to go on,
God's promise is: MATTHEW 11:28–30

*"Come to Me, all you who labor and are heavy laden, and
I will give you rest. Take My yoke upon you and learn from Me,
for I am gentle and lowly in heart, and you will find rest for your souls.
For My yoke is easy and My burden is light."* NKJV

When you feel that life is impossible,
God's promise is: LUKE 18:27

*[Jesus] said, "The things which are impossible
with men are possible with God."* NKJV

When you are afraid,
God's promise is: 2 TIMOTHY 1:7

God has not given us a spirit of fear,
but of power and of love and of a sound mind. NKJV

When you need to feel loved,
God's promise is: JOHN 13:34

"A new commandment I give to you,
that you love one another;
as I have loved you, that you also love one another." NKJV

When you don't think you have enough faith,
God's promise is: ROMANS 12:3

...God has dealt to each one a measure of faith. NKJV

When you feel overwhelmed,
God's promise is: PHILIPPIANS 4:19

And my God shall supply all your need
according to His riches in glory by Christ Jesus. NKJV

When you don't think you have the wisdom,
God's promise is: 1 CORINTHIANS 1:30

Because of God you are in Christ Jesus,
who has become for us wisdom from God. NCV

Tammy Trent

Tammy's story is one of despair and unexpected grace. In September 2001 she and her husband, Trent (from whom her stage name comes), spent a few days in Jamaica—part mission trip, part vacation. On September 10, Trent went free diving and never returned. The search began. As Tammy waited through the night and into the next morning for news of her husband, she watched the news as two planes plowed into the Twin Towers in New York—and later that day she had to identify the body of her husband. Tammy's story of God's grace in the midst of such pain, fear, and loss touches everyone she ministers to. It is one thing to call the Lord "Shepherd'—it is another to be carried by Him when you can no longer stand. Tammy is constantly amazed by our Lord's commitment to us in the worst moments of our lives.

You'll find Tammy with a full touring schedule, including dates with Women of Faith (www.womenoffaith.com). She also has written the book *Learning to Breathe Again: Choosing Life and Finding Hope After a Shattering Loss.*

For more information about Tammy, her music, and her message, please visit www.tammytrent.com.